JAPAN'S ASIAN DIPLOMACY

The LTCB International Library Trust

The LTCB (Long-Term Credit Bank of Japan) International Library Trust, established in July 2000, is the successor to the LTCB International Library Foundation. It carries on the mission that the foundation's founders articulated as follows:

> The world is moving steadily toward a borderless economy and deepening international interdependence. Amid economic globalization, Japan is developing ever-closer ties with nations worldwide through trade, through investment, and through manufacturing and other localized business operations.
>
> Japan's global activity is drawing attention to its political, economic, and social systems and to the concepts and values that underlie those systems. But the supply of translations of Japanese books about those and other Japan-related subjects has not kept pace with demand.
>
> The shortage of foreign-language translations of Japanese books about Japanese subjects is attributable largely to the high cost of translating and publishing. To address that issue, the LTCB International Library Foundation funds the translation and the distribution of selected Japanese works about Japan's politics, economy, society, and culture.

International House of Japan, Inc., manages the publishing activities of the LTCB International Library Trust, and Sumitomo Mitsui Trust Bank, Ltd., manages the trust's financial assets.

JAPAN'S ASIAN DIPLOMACY

A Legacy of Two Millennia

OGURA KAZUO

translated by David Noble

 LTCB International Library Trust / International House of Japan

Transliteration of Foreign Words

The Hepburn system of romanization is used for Japanese terms, including the names of persons and places. Except in familiar place names, long vowels are indicated by macrons. An apostrophe is used to distinguish syllable-final *n* from *n* at the beginning of a syllable. The spelling of non-Japanese words that have been incorporated into Japanese reflects the way these words are pronounced by Japanese speakers.

Chinese words are romanized using the pinyin system.

The romanization of Korean words follows the Revised Romanization of Korean.

The local custom of placing the family name first has been followed for the names of Japanese, Chinese, and Korean persons.

This book originally appeared in Japanese as *Nihon no Ajia gaikō: Nisen'nen no keifu* (Tokyo: Fujiwara Shoten, 2013). International House of Japan retains the English-language translation rights under contract with Ogura Kazuo and through the courtesy of Fujiwara Shoten.

First English edition published May 2015 by International House of Japan
11-16, Roppongi 5-chōme, Minato-ku, Tokyo 106-0032, Japan
Tel: +81-3-3470-9271   Fax: +81-3-3470-9368
E-mail: ihj@i-house.or.jp
URL: http://www.i-house.or.jp

Printed in Japan
ISBN 978-4-924971-39-4

Contents

CHAPTER TWO

The Interaction of Domestic and Foreign Policy

PART II

FOREIGN RELATIONS OF JAPAN, CHINA, AND KOREA IN HISTORICAL PERSPECTIVE

CHAPTER THREE

The History of *Seikanron* Thought

CHAPTER FOUR

Two Millennia of Sino-Japanese History: Five Wars and Their Antecedents

Preface to the English Edition

Most books and articles on Japanese diplomacy start with the "opening" of Japan in the middle of the nineteenth century. It is as if Japan's international relations began with the Meiji Restoration and with exchanges with Europe and the United States.

Japan's longtime traditional relations with Korea and China have, consequently, been left out of the history of Japanese diplomacy.

There is another gap to be filled. This is related to the angle of analysis of Japanese diplomacy in modern times. Japan's relations with Korea or China after the Meiji Restoration have tended to be observed and analyzed in the context of Japan's relations with the "West" and not in the dimension of the interplay of East Asian countries' foreign policies.

However, in the coming years when, for Japan, the economic and political weight of China, India, and other nations of Asia is likely to increase, it may be inevitable that Japan's diplomacy toward other Asian nations will have, if not more affinity, at least somewhat more relevance to Japan's diplomacy practiced before the advent of European civilization in Asia. It is also important that the interplay of foreign policies of East Asian countries themselves should receive more of the spotlight in the analysis of Japanese diplomacy.

It is with this perspective in mind that this book focuses on Japan's relations with China and Korea over the past fifteen hundred years or so.

Ogura Kazuo
February 2015

Preface to the Japanese Edition

A history of friendly relations is easy to write, but delving into the antecedents of conflict is quite difficult.

For example, a surprising number of people are apt to say that the two-thousand-year history of relations between Japan and China is fundamentally one of friendship, and the Sino-Japanese conflicts of the twentieth century are no more than a brief page in a much longer story.

But this is mistaken.

There have been at least five periods of warfare between Japan and China, not counting the Japanese intervention in the Boxer Rebellion of 1900. And with the exception of the Song dynasty, Japan has fought against every major dynasty or government in China (and if one factors in the defeated Song generals and their troops who participated in the attempted Mongol invasions of Japan under the Yuan dynasty, then some would say even the Song should not be excluded).

With regard to relations with Korea, there are those who like to emphasize the historical background to the peaceful ties that have been established between Japan and the Republic of Korea, beginning with the Korean embassies to Tokugawa Japan. But is this really true? It would not seem to be the case.

Throughout Japanese history—from the Yamato court and the Heian nobility on down through the Kamakura shogunate, the era of Hideyoshi, and the early Meiji-period debates over punitive action against Korea—there was always agitation for intervention, conquest, and control of the Korean peninsula.

At present, Japan's relations with both China and South Korea are tense, exacerbated by disputes over territory. And with regard to North Korea, an essentially punitive foreign policy stance continues.

This state of tension in East Asia demands of Japan a vision for the future of its Asian diplomacy. In considering what such a vision should be, it seems necessary to extend the temporal axis of our investigation to see what lessons might be learned from diplomatic efforts as early as those of Himiko or Prince Shōtoku. This is because I am convinced we have to construct a new Asian diplomacy, based on recognition of the fact that Japanese diplomacy toward Asia in modern times has essentially operated as a dependent variable of the diplomacy of the Western nations. In other words, do we not need to examine how Japan related to Asia in the period before it plunged into a "modernity" that imposed upon Japanese diplomacy the challenge of how to cope with an international society centered on the West?

If we survey the history of Japan's Asian diplomacy along such an extended temporal axis, the first thing that becomes apparent is that Japanese foreign policy has tended to be strongly influenced by domestic considerations and deficient in long-range strategic thinking. Thus, we must first of all address the question of the ways in which this entanglement of foreign and domestic policy has cast its shadow over Japan's diplomacy in Asia.

At the same time, we must pay attention to the fact that perceptions of nationhood and national territory have also shaped the context of international conflict and friction in East Asia. Disputes over Takeshima/Dokdo and the Senkaku/Diaoyu islands appear at first glance to be territorial issues in the legal sense but, in fact, beneath the surface lie deeper questions of historical and national perception involving the issue of national territory and sovereignty.

When invested by a nation with a specific ideological content— for example, the desire to oppose or overcome Japan—such territorial issues can easily be connected with issues of "spirit" or ideology. Conversely, in strategic diplomacy, one must fundamentally think of the nation not merely in terms of its geographic territory, but as an ideological space embodying a certain national spirit.

It is for this reason that I commence this book by discussing the relationship between the ideals of Japanese diplomacy and the realities of its foreign policy in Asia.

Ogura Kazuo
December 2012

List of Tables

PART I

FUNDAMENTALS OF JAPAN'S ASIAN DIPLOMACY

CHAPTER ONE

The Ethos of Japan's Asian Diplomacy

1. THE FRAMEWORK OF JAPANESE DIPLOMATIC THOUGHT

It has become something of a cliché to observe that diplomacy is the pursuit of national interest, but if we consider the goal of a nation's foreign policy to be the expansion of its international influence, then a range of intellectual and moral issues naturally becomes involved. In matters of national security as well, the popular consciousness and the question of what values and principles are to be defended has an influence even more powerful than factors such as defense capabilities, economic power, or technological capacity.

So it is only natural that in studying Japan's diplomacy toward Asia we should consider the philosophy, values, and ideals underlying it. Unfortunately, it would seem that previous studies of the relationship between Japanese thought and Asian diplomacy have focused almost exclusively on two phenomena: (1) the aggressive ideology embodied in the concept of the wartime Greater East Asian Co-Prosperity Sphere and similar ideas; or (2) Pan-Asianism as an ideology of resistance to Western colonialism (or, in recent years, to official policies prioritizing Japan's bilateral relationship with the United States).

Yet if we look back over the history of Japan's foreign affairs and national security policies, it soon becomes clear that the heart of the matter lies in a different dimension—or at least requires investigation

3

from a different angle. In other words, our perspective should address the question of how the nation of Japan perceives itself vis-à-vis Asia (and the world at large) and how it should develop its future foreign policy toward Asia.

We tend to see the nation of Japan as a geographical entity, or as an economic sphere, or as an ethnic and cultural unit. But just as the United States owes more of its identity as a nation to a specific shared ideology and ethos than to the geographic entity formed by its fifty states, there should be a similar concept of a Japanese identity. We must acknowledge that the ideology, recurrent in Japanese history, of Japan as the so-called "divine land" (*shinkoku*) transcended the simple notion that the physical territory of Japan had been especially blessed by the gods, arriving at the idea that "Japan" was a land established on the basis of a particular ethos.

Japan as the "divine land"

A classic articulation of the concept of the Japanese nation as a spiritual entity, and a defense of that concept as the basis for national security and foreign policy, is *Risshō ankoku ron* (A Treatise on Pacifying the State by Establishing Orthodoxy) by the Buddhist monk Nichiren (1222–82). Written in 1260 and presented to Hōjō Tokiyori, de facto head of the Kamakura shogunate, this text attributed responsibility for a recent series of natural disasters to the spread of the Nenbutsu (*Jōdo*) sect popularized by the priest Hōnen,[1] and called for promulgation of an official order prohibiting the sect, arguing that the establishment of the "Correct Law" (*shōbō*) would lead to the peace and security of the land of Japan. What is noteworthy about this text from the perspective of foreign policy is Nichiren's insistence that unless the "Correct Law" is promulgated throughout the land, Japan will invite foreign invasion and domestic disorder. Japan as a nation is conceived as a spiritual entity whose foundation must be religious orthodoxy.

Some years after Nichiren's text was written, an official communication from the Mongol Empire[2] demanding the opening of relations reached Japan, and at this point Nichiren's writings took on considerable diplomatic and political significance. Worship of the gods and buddhas came to be thought of as an important aspect of national defense, and the Kamakura shogunate called on Buddhist temples throughout the country to pray for the fate of the nation. Thus, Nichiren's thought led to the emergence of an ideology of the defense of Japan as a sacred land.

There was a psychological mechanism at work in Nichiren which perceived a need for internal unity for reasons of foreign policy or national security and at the same time viewed domestic oppositional forces as equivalent to external enemies. The intense politicization we see in sectarian disputes also demonstrates the intimate connection between foreign policy and ideology. Taking this a step further, it also suggests that the regime in power at the time, in addition to wielding power and military might, could also be seen as an agent imbued with a particular ideological authority. Viewed from this perspective—whatever Nichiren's original intent in writing it—*Risshō ankoku ron* is clearly a work of political ideology addressing both foreign and domestic policy.

For Nichiren, the secular world is one in which the law or dharma (*hō*, the Buddhist teachings) must be made manifest. And because of this, institutions such as society and the state or nation take on a quasi-religious character. Examined politically, the ideology of the divine land may be seen as a way of envisioning the nation as an entity comprised of shared principles or ideals. Insofar as Japan is seen as a divine land, internal struggles and conflict should be avoided, and national security and spiritual unity may be understood as belonging to the same dimension. (A concrete example of the notion that domestic conflict should be avoided in the divine land may be seen in the efforts to resolve a dispute over water rights between the Iwashimizu Hachiman Shrine and the Kasuga Shrine in 1236).[3]

This political function of the divine land ideology can also be glimpsed in the Japan of the 1930s. As the nation increasingly placed itself on a wartime footing, the implementation of the internal security laws and efforts to encourage or to force the populations of Japan's colonies to worship at Shintō shrines proceeded apace as Japan attempted to define itself as a unitary spiritual realm.

Ideology and Japanese foreign relations

The reflection of a particular principle or ideology in foreign policy and the linking of this to domestic policies is of course not something limited to the manner of Japan's response to the Mongol threat in the thirteenth century. The official letter that Toyotomi Hideyoshi, late sixteenth-century military ruler of Japan, presented to the members of the Korean mission to Japan in 1590[4] contains a passage claiming that at the time of his own conception, his mother dreamed that the "wheel of the sun" had entered her womb, and that a diviner had predicted that the glory of her son's name would resound throughout the world. The letter goes on to declare his intention to realize that prophecy by spreading his fame throughout the three countries of Japan, Korea, and China.

This document is a direct expression of Hideyoshi's self-deification; but connected with this ambition to invade Korea and China is something close to a deification of Japan itself, as the country over which he rules. Or, to put it another way, his ideals of domestic rule and justifications for external expansion are bound up with his vision of himself as a child of the sun and with the sacralization of Japan. A similar tendency may be seen in Meiji-period (1868–1912) efforts to deify the emperor — a process whose logic can be located in the need both to unify the nation and to resist the threat of Western colonialism.

It is necessary to understand this background when we consider contemporary Japanese relations with China and the Korean peninsula. The extraordinary sensitivity of the Chinese regarding official visits to Yasukuni Shrine by Japanese government leaders is not simply an issue of responsibility for World War II and the powerful national sentiments surrounding that issue. It also has to do with the historical background to these shrine visits: the conception of Japan as a "divine land" and deification of the Japanese emperor that served as the ideology and rationale for Japanese policy and diplomacy until the end of World War II. That South Korea has made such an issue of "compulsory" shrine worship during the colonial era (1910–1945) is not merely as a demand for contrition with regard to Japan's colonial domination; it also calls into question the entire ideology that sustained Japan during that period.

6

Moreover, the relatively long period following World War II during which Japan had no formal relations with China and Korea (diplomatic relations with China were restored in 1972; with South Korea in 1965) was not solely attributable to the impact of war and colonial domination. It was also because the ideological confrontation between liberal democracy and communism exerted a major influence on Japan's Asian diplomacy. That process tends to be described in shorthand as an East-West conflict, but in fact Japan as a nation was understood to be a member of the liberal and democratic camp, and its defense to be bound up with the defense of liberal and democratic values. It is undeniable that this state of affairs long impeded the restoration of diplomatic relations with Communist China and increased the complexity of Japan's relationship with the Korean peninsula.

Himiko and shamanism

Broadly examined, in the nearly two millennia of Japan's relations with Asia, Japan has shared with the other East Asian countries a variety of value systems—among them Daoism, Buddhism, and Confucianism—that have possessed political and strategic significance.

The earliest example of this is from the reign of Himiko, a female ruler of a third-century Japanese chiefdom called Yamatai-koku. Himiko, motivated by strategic considerations and domestic political goals, concluded an alliance with Wei-dynasty China based on a certain "commonality of values."

This was reflected in the exchange of official gifts between Himiko's envoys and the Wei court, but also in an unusual custom, the selection of a "mourning keeper" (jisai) by the Yamatai envoys to accompany them on their sea voyage to China. This custom is described in our primary source for this period, the "Gishi wajin den" (as it is known in Japanese), a section of the Wei zhi, an official history of the Wei dynasty containing accounts of contacts with the "Wa people" (the Japanese) in the second and third centuries:

When they go across the sea to visit China, they always select a man who does not comb his hair, does not rid himself of fleas, lets his

7

clothing get dirty as it will, does not eat meat, and does not lie with women. This man behaves like a mourner and is known as the "mourning keeper." When the voyage meets with good fortune, they all lavish upon him slaves and other valuables. In case there is disease or mishap, they kill him, saying he was not scrupulous in observing the taboos.[5]

This might be interpreted in anthropological terms as a form of ritual or magic to ensure the safety of sea travel, or perhaps a manifestation of belief in oceanic deities.[6] Yet we might also speculate that the custom of the "mourning keeper" had, in addition to this ritualistic aspect, an element of diplomatic and political significance.

Although she was served by a large entourage of shrine maidens (*miko*), Himiko was said to communicate her will through a single male retainer.[7] Viewed in this light, it is quite possible that Himiko was attempting to convey the spirit of *kidō* ("the way of demons"; a form of shamanism)—and something of her own shamanic power and authority—to the Chinese in the personage of the "mourning keeper." The Daoist patriarch Zhang Lu is believed to have been active at that time in China, and supernatural beings known as "demon gods" (*guishen*) were venerated throughout northeastern China and the Korean peninsula.[8]

Thus, the description of the "mourning keeper" in the *Wei zhi* and the fact that there were related shamanistic and Daoist customs and practices in China during that era suggest that Himiko may have been signaling to the Chinese that her country of Yamatai and the court of Wei in northern China were bound by a common ideology and system of values (as well as hinting at the source of her own power and authority). This is also suggested by the official gifts dispatched to Himiko by the Chinese court. In 238, Himiko sent an envoy named Nashonmi to the Wei. Here is a list of goods presented by him to the Chinese, and those he received in return:

Gifts presented by the Japanese

Male slaves	4	
Female slaves	6	
Mottled linen	2	bolts, each 4.7 meters in length

Gifts presented by the Chinese

Red brocade with dragon patterns	5	bolts
Red silk carpets	10	
Madder-dyed cloth	50	bolts
Indigo-dyed cloth	50	bolts
Dark blue patterned silk	3	bolts
Finely patterned carpets	5	
White silk	50	bolts
Gold	8	taels
Swords	2	
Bronze mirrors	100	
Pearls	50	catties
Red pigments	50	catties

What should be noted here is that the Chinese gifts (in addition to being considerably more elegant than those presented by the Japanese) seem to have been specifically selected with reference to Himiko's shamanic rituals or magical practices. The carpets, bronze mirrors, pearls, and red pigment stand out in this regard. This could be interpreted as a sign that the Chinese recognized Himiko's shamanic powers and wished to indicate that they shared this mode of thought.

In this way, Himiko managed to forge a kind of alliance between Yamatai-koku and the Wei, in a political context in which Yamatai was on the verge of war with another Japanese state called Kuna, while in China the Wei dynasty itself was challenged by the kingdoms of Wu and Shu—an alliance that we might say was broadened and deepened by the possession of a common, or at least similar, system of values.

Shared values and internal politics
As the case of Himiko suggests, when strategic relations between states are bolstered by a sense of shared values, these values often have more than diplomatic significance; they may also have implications for the maintenance and strengthening of the domestic political order in both countries.

9

The missions sent by Prince Shōtoku (574–622) of Japan to the Sui-dynasty Chinese court were strongly colored by this. In the official letter borne by the Japanese envoy, Ono no Imoko, to the Sui court in 607, there is a passage which reads, "[We] hear that the Bodhisattva Prince west of the sea has revived the Buddha dharma," emphasizing the Buddhist faith shared by the Yamato and Sui courts. That one of the principal purposes of the Japanese mission to the Sui was the importation of the Buddhist teachings is evident not only from the text of the official letter, but also because the envoy Ono no Imoko was accompanied by several dozen Buddhist monks. It is also clear that the domestic political situation in Japan at the time was creating a demand for a transition from belief in individual clan gods to Buddhism as a unified national religion supporting an emperor-centered state system.

When shared values are stressed in this way, the significance often transcends the diplomatic sphere to embrace such domestic political considerations. This is also apparent in the enthusiasm with which the fifth Tokugawa shogun, Tsunayoshi (1646–1709), received the Korean mission sent in 1682 to offer congratulations on his accession to the title of shogun. Tsunayoshi's reception of the Korean mission was indirectly linked to the strengthening of the ideological underpinnings of his regime. Tsunayoshi's government was one that valued philosophy and scholarship, and was seeking to supplant the martial values of the early shogunate with the establishment of civil political authority. One means of accomplishing this was the establishment of an official academy, the Shōheikō, for the encouragement of Confucian studies (specifically Song Neo-Confucianism). For a regime laboring to turn Confucianism into a state-sponsored ideology, relations with Korea, whose political system was already centered on the Confucian teachings, took on significance as an expression of shared political values.

Viewed in this way, there was great significance to be found in the fact that in the foreign relations conducted through the medium of the Korean envoys of the Tokugawa period, Yi-dynasty Korea and the Tokugawa shogunate were able to mutually affirm that a shared Confucian ideology was situated at the core of their respective governance. If we understand this, then the reason why both sides were so sensitive to

Table 1-1. Korean Missions to Tokugawa Japan

Year	Korean Year	Japanese Year	Shogun	Chief envoy	Purpose
1607	Seonjo 40	Keichō 12	Hidetada	Yeo Yugil	Repatriation of prisoners; demand for formal apology; restoration of diplomatic relations
1617	Gwanghaegun 9	Genna 3	Hidetada	O Yungyeom	Repatriation of prisoners; demand for formal apology; congratulations on unification of Japan by Tokugawa
1624	Injo 2	Kan'ei 1	Iemitsu	Jeong Rip	Demand for formal apology; congratulations on accession of Shogun Iemitsu
1636	Injo 4	Kan'ei 13	Iemitsu	Im Gwang	Celebrating peace
1643	Injo 21	Kan'ei 20	Iemitsu	Yun Sunji	Celebrating birth of Ietsuna. From this time forward officially titled as "embassies" (Jap. *tsūshinshi*; Kor. *t'ongsinsa*)
1655	Hyojong 6	Meireki 1	Ietsuna	Jo Hyeong	Congratulations on accession of Shogun Ietsuna
1682	Sukjong 8	Tenna 2	Tsunayoshi	Yun Jiwan	Congratulations on accession of Shogun Tsunayoshi
1711	Sukjong 37	Shōtoku 1	Ienobu	Jo Taeeok	Congratulations on accession of Shogun Ienobu
1719	Sukjong 45	Kyōhō 4	Yoshimune	Hong Chijung	Congratulations on accession of Shogun Yoshimune.
1748	Yeongjo 24	Kan'en 1	Ieshige	Hong Gyehui	Congratulations on accession of Shogun Ieshige
1763–64	Yeongjo 40	Meiwa 1	Ieharu	Jo Eom	Congratulations on accession of Shogun Ieharu
1811	Sunjo 11	Bunka 8	Ienari	Kim Igyo	Congratulations on accession of Shogun Ienari (embassy received at Tsushima rather than Edo)

Source: Kwon Inseop, *Chōsen to Nihon no kankeishi* (Akashi Shoten, 2000), table on p. 218, with minor revisions by the author.

issues of protocol concerning the reception of the missions, and occasionally clashed over such issues, becomes naturally evident. In short, it was because affirming that they shared the ideology of Confucianism, and the protocol so deeply grounded in it, was a matter of great importance to both sides.

A shared concept of modernization

Historically speaking, the next issue to be considered is whether or not Japan has shared common ideas and ideals with other Asian nations in the modern era that commenced for Japan with the Meiji Restoration of 1868. Perhaps the ideal most prominently articulated during the Meiji (1868–1912) and Taishō (1912–25) periods in Japan was the modernization of society. Did Japan attempt to share this ideal and ideology with the rest of Asia?

Seen from an international perspective, Japanese modernization has possessed two distinct aspects: on the one hand, the Westernization that Japan undertook in the struggle to achieve recognition of its rightful place in international society; on the other, Japan's quest to defend itself from Western colonialism. The intersection of these two aspects engendered another issue: the rejection of the Sinocentric worldview that had informed the existing international order of East Asia.

China strove to enter the modern world while keeping the old Chinese world order intact; the Korean royal court and the governments serving it also hesitated to shed the tradition of Confucian thought. But Japan had committed itself to spreading the logic and ideals of modernization throughout East Asia, and was unable to find in these regimes partners who would share a common vision of Asian modernization. The result was that Japan's modernization hastened the collapse of Imperial China and led to the Japanese annexation of the Korean peninsula. The effects of this continue to cast shadows to this day. This is one reason why China and South Korea, even after their successes in setting their respective economic development firmly on track, still (or perhaps even more than before) tend to make a diplomatic and foreign policy issue out of the past history of their relations with Japan.

Why? Because at present, in order for these countries to be able to genuinely share with Japan the logic and ideology of modernism and economic growth, they must objectively reevaluate the role that Japan played in the modernization of China and Korea. However, in order to acknowledge the role played by Japan, a reassessment of the role played by individuals who cooperated with Japan is unavoidable. And this raises issues concerning the legitimacy of the post–World War II regimes of both China and South Korea.

One reason that issues of the past and of historical understanding continue to so readily develop into political problems in relations between Japan and China and Korea (setting aside nationalistic sentiments for the moment) is that for a long time the ideology of modernization was something that had not been truly shared in Japan's bilateral relations with these two countries (this becomes particularly evident in comparison with Japan's relations with Taiwan).

Contemporary Japan as an ideological entity

How does Japan understand itself as an ideological entity in the context of its Asian diplomacy?

In considering this question, we must first look at the values prioritized in its relationship with the United States, which Japan currently emphasizes as its partner in foreign relations on the basis of shared values.

If we compare the language used in major joint communiqués and press releases by Japan and the United States over the course of the last fifty years, we find (as shown in table 1-2) that beginning in the late 1980s the concept of the Japan-US "partnership" began to be stressed, and parallel to this, a celebration of "shared values."

This hints at a certain change taking place in the Japan-US alliance from the late 1980s onward. For a considerable period of time the alliance had been one of bilateral cooperation for defense, founded on the maintenance and strengthening of a relationship of mutual trust. However, with the passage of time this gradually evolved into a framework in which Japan and the United States could cooperate as partners to maintain and bolster certain shared values in the global context.

Table 1-2: Changing definitions of Japan-US relations in joint communiqués and press releases

Date	Communiqué issued by	Definition of relationship	Principles mentioned
22 June 1957	Prime Minister Kishi President Eisenhower	A close relationship…based on mutual interests and trust	Equal sovereignty, mutual interests and cooperation
13 January 1965	Prime Minister Satō President Johnson	An alliance… based on common beliefs and goals	
1 August 1973	Prime Minister Tanaka President Nixon	Relations of friendship and cooperation based on shared political values and a sense of mutual reliance	Recognition of the valuable role being played in maintaining world peace and prosperity; cooperation for common goals
6 August 1975	Prime Minister Miki President Ford	A mature, reciprocal, mutually supportive relationship	Constructive and creative cooperation
8 May 1981	Prime Minister Suzuki President Reagan	Alliance	Solidarity, friendship, and mutual trust
2 January 1985	Prime Minister Nakasone (press release after talks with President Reagan)	Irreplaceable Japan-US relationship	Trust, responsibility, friendship
1 September 1989	Prime Minister Kaifu (press release after talks with President George H.W. Bush)	Partnership on a global scale	Sharing the fundamental values of liberty and democracy

Date	Communiqué issued by	Definition of relationship	Principles mentioned
8 January 1992	Prime Minister Miyazawa President George H.W. Bush	Global partnership	Political and economic freedom, democracy, rule of law and respect for human rights
17 April 1996	Prime Minister Hashimoto President Clinton	The most successful bilateral relationship in history	Shared values, i.e., the maintenance of liberty, pursuit of democracy, and respect for human rights
19 March 2001	Prime Minister Mori President George W. Bush	The cornerstone of peace and security in the Asia-Pacific region	Friendship, mutual trust, and shared democratic values
30 June 2001	Prime Minister Koizumi President George W. Bush	A partnership for security and prosperity	Shared values, mutual trust and friendship
29 June 2006	Prime Minister Koizumi President George W. Bush	The most mature bilateral relationship in history	Response to a common threat, promotion of universal values

In other words, this underscored the fact that the Japan-US alliance, formed to deal with the military tensions created in Asia as a result of the East-West conflict engendered by the Cold War, had been transformed into a cooperative security framework of global proportions. The stress on shared values signified that the goal of the alliance was not so much to counter a particular country or bloc, but to internationally (and domestically) maintain and strengthen a specific international order and the philosophy and values supporting it.

Shared values in the Asian diplomacy of contemporary Japan

Following this historical analysis of the content and significance of shared values in the Japan-US alliance, how should we consider this issue of shared values (or lack thereof) in Japan's contemporary Asian diplomacy? More specifically, to what extent has Japanese diplomacy applied such ideals as democracy and liberty in its diplomatic approach to Asia?

The establishment of diplomatic relations with the Republic of China and the Republic of Korea can be seen as the inevitable consequence of the East-West conflict and Japan's strategic relationship with the United States, so to see this as a reflection of the value system of Japanese foreign policy would seem to require a fair amount of hindsight. A diplomacy grounded in liberal democratic value was more clearly reflected in the nature of the support given to democratic forces in Korea during the regime of Park Jeonghui. During the Park era, when Japanese government officials prioritized their relationship with his military regime out of strategic considerations, support for the democratic opposition was left to Japan's own opposition parties and other political activists. In other words, at the official level, shared values took a back seat to strategic interests.

However, when Park was assassinated in October 1979 and Cheon Duhwan took power in a military coup, the Japanese government under Prime Minister Suzuki Zenkō deferred summit conferences with the Korean leader for the two years of his unelected regime. This was a form of Japanese diplomatic sanction in response to Cheon's antidemocratic actions, including the violent suppression of the student movement during the Gwangju Uprising.

Similarly, in the wake of the Tiananmen Incident in 1989, Japan joined the Western nations in implementing sanctions against China, and for some time suspended high-level political contacts between the two countries. This, too, could be described as a diplomatic measure implemented in response to the Chinese government's adoption of behavior that amounted to a blatant rejection of Japanese values. Yet at the same time, the Japanese government warned that "there is also the fear that if China is indiscriminately isolated from international society, this will only serve to weaken more moderate domestic political forces," and adopted a more flexible position than some of the Western nations on humanitarian aid and cultural exchange. In this, we see strong evidence of the Japanese sense that the common values of liberal democracy cannot simply be forced upon the Asian nations from outside.

We might go further, and say that implicit in this stance are certain contemporary Japanese ideas about the role of ideology in foreign affairs. When a certain system of values is articulated in conjunction with foreign policy, this essentially signifies that a country or society sees itself as a place where those values can and should be realized. America's strong espousal of the values of liberty and democracy in foreign policy is grounded in a sense of these values as being the founding ideals of the United States, while the European Union's emphasis on human rights and equality in international politics arises from the EU's conviction that these are core European values. In either case, the country or society becomes a kind of classroom for the inculcation of such values—a quasi-religious or philosophical realm.

Here we should note that in the case of the Chinese Communist Party, the nation and society of China were seen as a realm in which the philosophy of communism was to be realized. To confront a country shaped so centrally by its ideology with the challenge of sharing a different set of values is in itself a form of ideological combat, and postwar Japan has tended to hesitate to introduce such conflict into its diplomacy (particularly in Asia). This is not only because Japan has a past history of trampling upon human rights and democracy in Asia with its own aggression and colonial domination; it is also because contemporary Japan (despite its espousal of democracy and freedom) has not necessarily made these particular values and ideals fundamental to its existence as a nation. Yet there is an even more subtle factor at work here—the Japanese perception of how values themselves should be dealt with in the realm of international politics.

Japan's modernization since the Meiji period has not been simply a Westernization of Japanese technology, knowledge, and patterns of daily life. The process itself required that this Westernization be undertaken in a "voluntary" and organic way in order for it to gain social acceptance—because the more it appeared to be something being compelled by external forces, the greater the danger that it would meet with unexpected opposition from within the nation. Viewed in this way, Japan's diplomatic position on Asian democratization might be said to include an attempt on Japan's part to tacitly share the fruits of its own bitter experience of modernization with the other nations of Asia.

2. ASIAN ANTICOLONIALISM AND JAPAN

In considering Japan's sharing of values with the other nations and peoples of East Asia, in addition to the traditional values systems and religious thought represented by Daoism, Buddhism, and Confucianism, we must also consider the extent to which in modern times Japan has shared political beliefs with these nations, an ideology of opposition to Western colonialism.

The Vietnamese anti-French resistance movement and Japan

The dilemma of Japanese foreign policy in the late nineteenth and twentieth centuries was that it must situate itself between two poles: one being the effort to secure its national interests and enhance its international status through cooperation with the Western powers; the other being support for resistance movements in the other Asian countries that were being reduced to colonial or semi-colonial status. How, in practice, did Japan's leadership respond to this dilemma?

In short, the Japanese government took care not to trespass upon the interests of Qing-dynasty China or of the Western powers, while at the same time it turned a blind eye to the support of anticolonial movements by private-sector Japanese political activists. A typical example of this was the way in which the Japanese government dealt with movements for reform or revolution in Vietnam.

At the beginning of the twentieth century a movement known as Đông Du ("Go East") arose in Vietnam, which encouraged young Vietnamese to travel to Japan to study, in the hope that they would return to lead the resistance against the French. The Tokyo Shinbu Gakkō, a government-sponsored military academy for foreign students, initially admitted four Vietnamese students, but then refused to accept any more. As a result, several hundred Vietnamese students enrolled in private Japanese schools.[9] This happened to coincide precisely with a period in which France and Japan were establishing a new level of diplomatic and economic cooperation, with mutual agreements to honor and protect French rights and interests in Indochina and the stability of the regions of South China proximate to the Japanese colony of Taiwan, and thus important to Japanese interests.

One noteworthy aspect of this process is the influence that alarm over the "Yellow Peril"[10]—a growing sentiment in Europe at the time— had on the establishment of the Franco-Japanese entente. In other words, France was seeking to contain the Japanese "threat" symbolized by the "Yellow Peril" within the framework of the entente, while Japan was seeking to use the same agreement to defend its rights and interests in Taiwan and seek acceptance by the Western powers. This meant adopting the role of a passive bystander with regard to the revolutionary activities of Asian intellectuals.

Not only that: beginning in 1908 the Japanese government adopted policies tightening its surveillance over the activities of foreign students in the country,[11] presumably out of concern that Vietnamese activists, Chinese revolutionaries, and members of the Korean independence movement might be establishing relations of solidarity with one another and with Japanese socialist organizations.

In the end, the Japanese government's policy of containment with regard to Asian independence movements was nothing more than an effort to secure Japan's own colonial possessions through cooperation with the imperialist powers, and an implicit acknowledgment and support for their colonial domination of Asia. Moreover, this policy was not merely a matter of foreign relations; it simultaneously had domestic political implications.[12]

We might say that the growing "Yellow Peril" scare among the Western powers encouraged the Japanese government to attach even greater importance to the security of its own colonial possessions and its cooperation with the Western powers to that end. Moreover, as the possibility increased that anticolonial activists might forge alliances with Japanese sympathizers, foreign policy considerations were augmented by domestic political concerns, and the result was a gradual distortion of the framework of Japanese foreign policy in Asia.

The Philippine independence movement and Japan

The official Japanese response to the independence movement in the Philippines resembled its handling of the Vietnamese anticolonial movement against the French.

In April 1899, the Chinese revolutionary Sun Yat-sen, who had strong ties to a number of Japanese political activists, attempted to serve as a go-between for efforts to procure arms for Emilio Aguinaldo, leader of the Philippines movement to gain independence first from Spain and then from the United States.[13] The weapons were never delivered, in part because the transport ship sank, and Aguinaldo's insurgency failed, but the Japanese military is believed to have been indirectly involved in the efforts to arm Aguinaldo.[14] On the other hand, those responsible for Japanese foreign policy were opposed to supporting Aguinaldo out of consideration for the US response—an indication that already, at the end of the nineteenth century, there were significant differences between civilian diplomats and the Japanese military in their conception of Japan's Asian policies.

In this regard, statements at the time by Foreign Minister Aoki Shūzō and Army Chief of Staff Kawakami Sōroku are highly indicative of the two positions. Aoki expressed the opinion that Japan should not sell arms to Aguinaldo, since the United States had explicitly requested that it refrain from doing so. Kawakami, on the other hand, argued that even though the cause of Philippine independence was probably

hopeless at the time, Japan should support the independence movement because it would create positive sentiment toward Japan among
the people of the Philippines that might endure for fifty or even a hundred years. In other words, while the foreign ministry was emphasizing
a diplomacy of cooperation with the great powers, the army was stressing what would today be called "public diplomacy" and the winning of
the "hearts and minds" of local people.[15]

Conversely, this would also seem to suggest how easy it can be to
link the manipulation of popular opinion through "public diplomacy"
with the possible exercise of military force (or the possibility of elimi-
nation of an existing regime by military force). In this way, long before
World War II, the Japanese military attempted to utilize revolutionary
forces in Asia while the foreign ministry worked to restrain such efforts
from the perspective of international cooperation. What lay behind
these differences in approach were fundamentally different ways of
thinking about the desirability of preserving the status quo of the existing international order versus working to transform it.

In any case, in foreign policy related to anticolonial and antigovernment
movements, it is important for Japan to consider not only its relations with
the government of that country or with other nations, but also not to forget
the long-term impact on Japanese relations with the people of the region.
A diplomatic episode that occurred during a 1995 visit to Vietnam by
Prime Minister Murayama Tomiichi indicates the importance of such
a perspective. In informal discussions prior to the formal talks between
Murayama's delegation and Vietnamese government leaders, Prime
Minister Võ Vân Kiệt expressed deep gratitude for the support that
members of the Japan Socialist Party and other Japanese people of good
conscience had provided to Vietnam during the difficult period of the
war of resistance against the United States.[16] These words of the prime
minister of Vietnam to Murayama, who was head of the Japan Socialist
Party (JSP) and prime minister of a coalition cabinet supported by both
the JSP and the Liberal Democratic Party, were quite significant.

A similar situation could be seen after the establishment of Kim
Daejung's government in South Korea in 1998. Kim's government
relaxed long-standing restrictions on the importation of Japanese

popular culture into Korea, and it is likely that this decision was influenced by the sympathy and support shown by many Japanese intellectual and cultural figures for the democratization movement led by Kim during the years of the Park regime.[17]

Antiestablishment movements and anti-Japanese movements

Anticolonialism transcended beliefs and ideologies to connect with a variety of antiestablishment or antigovernment movements. Precisely because such forces can easily be associated with alterations in the existing international order, it is usually quite difficult, in terms of foreign policy strategy, to engineer cooperation between antiestablishment forces in a particular country and foreign governments.

However, when the government of a country harbors anti-Japanese tendencies or tacitly supports anti-Japanese movements among its people, it might become possible for Japan to utilize antiestablishment or insurgent movements to act as a constraint on that country's government leadership. A historical example of this can be seen in the case of Sun Yat-sen (Sun Wen).

Between 1908 and 1910, the Qing Dynasty, in an attempt to defend itself from the imminent threat of revolution, called on foreign governments to crack down on Chinese revolutionaries operating internationally. It was in this context that the *Tatsu Maru* incident occurred, in which the arrest by Qing authorities of the captain of a Japanese freighter carrying arms to Chinese revolutionaries led to a deterioration of Japan's relations with the Qing and also inspired anti-Japanese agitation in China, including a boycott of Japanese goods.

Uchida Ryōhei, a Japanese activist with close ties to Sun Yat-sen — and who was also in close communication with the Japanese foreign ministry — contacted Sun with a request for his cooperation in restraining the anti-Japanese movement. Sun's response was to claim that the anti-Japanese boycott was being financially supported by Qing officials in Canton, and to counteract this he would need funds himself.[18] In any event, we can consider this to be a case in which Japan was attempting to use antiestablishment forces in an effort to counteract anti-Japanese activity.

We may summarize the political significance of these historical experiences as follows. In today's world, when Japan provides some form of support for democratic movements against authoritarian governments, one is apt to think that Japan is doing this to show that it is acting in concert with the conscience of an "international society" centered in the Western nations; but insofar as such movements for democratization may also have the effect of restraining anti-Japanese sentiment at the popular level, we might say that Japan's support for such movements possesses a certain diplomatic significance of an entirely different order. The problem, however, is that for historical reasons official Japanese support (even if indirect) for dissident activists invites conflict with the country's government and runs a significant risk of encouraging an alliance between the government and anti-Japanese activists at the popular level—a risk that might be said to work as a significant constraint on the range of foreign policy options open to Japan.

3. THE "ASIAN MONROE DOCTRINE"

In considering Asian efforts to conceive of a genuinely "Asian" international diplomacy, we cannot ignore a mode of thought that has been called the "Asian Monroe Doctrine."

In Asia, resistance to Western colonialism led to the idea that Asian affairs should be left to Asia to determine—a type of Asian Monroe Doctrine—and the notion that Japan should bear primary responsibility for leading Asia in achieving this became a central pillar of Japanese diplomacy in the period from the end of the nineteenth century to World War II.

This concept first took concrete form in Japanese diplomacy in the process leading up to Japan's annexation of Korea. The text of the Japan-Korea Protocol of 1904, signed soon after the outbreak of the Russo-Japanese War, and the words and actions of Itō Hirobumi, dispatched as special envoy to Korea a few days after the protocol was signed, suggested Japan's sense of its own responsibility or mission in Asia, as well as a concomitant sense that halting Russia's advance into Asia was a major issue to be faced in achieving what was termed "an enduring peace in the Far East" (*Tōyō kōkyū no heiwa*).

Article I of the protocol called upon the government of Korea to "place full confidence in the Imperial Government of Japan" for the purpose of "firmly establishing peace in the Far East." Article III stated that Japan would "definitively guarantee the independence and territorial integrity of the Korean Empire."[19] In light of the fact that it would be Japan itself that would rob Korea of its independence only a few years later, it would be more reasonable to interpret these statements as indicative of an intent to rid Asia of Western forces and a sense that it was Japan's responsibility to do so. Moreover, the personal letter from Emperor Meiji that Itō Hirobumi carried with him to the king of Korea stated that Japan had declared war on Russia in 1904 "out of genuine concern for an enduring peace in the Far East."

But this idea of an Asian Monroe Doctrine was not something Japan was pursuing unilaterally. The truly global imperial power of the period, Great Britain, actually encouraged Japan to assume this responsibility in Asia, thus laying the foundation for the Anglo-Japanese Alliance of the early twentieth century. The first agreement cementing the alliance, signed in 1902, recognized Japan's special interests in Korea and that it would be "admissible" for Japan "to take such measures as may be indispensable in order to safeguard those interests if threatened either by the action of any other Power, or by disturbances arising in China or Korea. . . ."[20] A revision of the agreement, supplanting it in 1905, removed all qualifiers and spoke of "Japan possessing paramount political, military and economic interests in Korea," with Britain recognizing "the right of Japan to take such measures of guidance, control, and protection as she may deem proper and necessary to safeguard and advance those interests."[21] What is problematic here is the way of thinking underlying these agreements.

At the beginning of the negotiations for the first agreement forming the alliance, Hayashi Tadasu, Japanese ambassador to Great Britain, wrote to the British foreign minister that "the Koreans are incapable of governing themselves, and thus . . . the question that arises here is: who shall govern that country?"[22] A similar way of thinking pervaded Britain at the time. For example, George Curzon, British viceroy of India in the late nineteenth and early twentieth century, once remarked, "Only

24

a fool would encourage the independence of Korea for the sake of its people; it would be tantamount to signing their death-warrant."[23] The significance of this is clear. Japanese intervention in Korea was seen as justified not only from the perspective of preventing incursions by third countries (with Russia foremost in mind), but also out of distrust for Korean domestic administration and a belief that Japan had a responsibility to reform it.

It is not necessarily accurate to describe these developments solely as a manifestation of the Asian Monroe Doctrine, but the idea of leaving Asia to the Asians—i.e., Japan—was one that emerged as early as the period of the Russo-Japanese War. The fact that this received the blessing of Great Britain may be said to have been a major factor in determining the subsequent direction of Japan's Asian diplomacy.

The Twenty-One Demands and Japan's outlook on Asia

The Asian Monroe Doctrine was connected with a certain "sense of responsibility" toward Asia, in the background of which lay a peculiar cohabitation of resistance to Western colonial domination and collaboration with it (in the hope of defending Japan's own independence and national interests).

This apparently contradictory cohabitation arose from Japan's determination that the flag of modernization that it had raised should fly not over Japan alone but all of Asia. Yet modernization could not be accomplished without a certain amount of contact—and cooperation—with the West. This is also clear from the history of the reform and open-door policies initiated by Deng Xiaoping in China.

In an era in which Western colonialism had been established throughout the world, the path open to Japan to both cooperate with that system, and at the same time to maintain its own independence, was to simultaneously serve as the advance guard of Asian modernization and as a defender of the fundamental order supporting colonialism in Asia. This stance arose partly out of Japan's own bitter experience in its attempts during the Meiji period to negotiate an end to the unequal treaties it had signed with the Western powers toward the end of the Tokugawa shogunate.

On 3 March 1881 (Meiji 14), the chief secretary of the Japanese legation in Britain called on an undersecretary of the British Foreign Office to discuss the subject of treaty revision. The legation secretary said, in effect, that in its existing treaties with Japan the British enjoyed all possible rights and privileges, but had won them through threats and coercion. Because of this, Britain should agree to limit some of these rights in future without any additional concessions by the Japanese. The British undersecretary's response was clear:

> I cannot accept your statement. Almost all of our treaties with the Far Eastern nations are the same. If in fact it was the case that Japan had its rights taken from it by coercion, then one would think there should have been no reason to remain silent about it until the present. . . .
>
> Great Britain is involved in all of these matters in the Far Eastern nations, as it is in China and Siam—so why should Japan alone be different?[24]

Why shouldn't Japan accept what China and Siam (Thailand) had accepted?—this question held the utmost significance. The implication was that because, from the European point of view, China and Siam did not possess "civilized" systems of law, they must continue to concede to the Europeans special rights and privileges—and that because Japan was also a Far Eastern nation, it was to be viewed and treated similarly. This episode signified why modernization would become a kind of credo for the Japanese. The idea that not only Japan but all nations of Asia should embrace modernization and construct new institutional frameworks to adapt to it became one of the pillars of Japan's Asian diplomacy—transcending the mere pursuit of national interest to become something of an article of faith.

This attitude is clearly manifested in the negotiations surrounding the Twenty-One Demands. These negotiations, conducted from January to May 1915, concerned a broad range of Japanese "demands" and "wishes" concerning China, from the disposition of the former German concessions in Shandong Province and the extension of Japanese rights and privileges in Manchuria to rights over mining operations in China proper and the dispatch of Japanese "advisors" to the Chinese central government. The negotiations were characterized by the extremely one-sided and threatening attitude adopted by the Japanese delegation, and the extent to which the demands involved interference in the internal affairs of the Chinese government.

The overbearing attitude of the Japanese was concretely displayed in the mechanics of the negotiations. Without any preliminaries, preambles, or working sessions with their Chinese counterparts, the Japanese delegation peremptorily presented their list of demands directly to the highest official in the Chinese government, Yuan Shikai.[25] It is obvious that this strategy was meant to take advantage of the weakness of Yuan's government and immediately effect top-down political machinations (while at the same time giving Yuan himself confidential assurances of the utmost Japanese support in securing his position). The Japanese also refused to negotiate on individual items in their long and complex list of demands; they stubbornly insisted that the talks must address the list as a whole. Moreover, in the course of the negotiations, the Japanese threatened to go over the head of the Chinese delegation to deal directly with Yuan Shikai, and to reject the Chinese counterproposal on the pretext that the attitude of the Chinese was indecisive.[26]

Not only was the Japanese negotiating stance threatening; it also involved repeated verbal insults to the Chinese. Japan's own diplomatic records contain episodes such as the following, regarding the words and behavior of the Japanese minister to China, Hioki Eki, who was responsible for the negotiations on the Japanese side:

> [Hioki] treated them to his broadest sneer, saying that the Chinese response was altogether too self-serving.[27]

> [Hioki] reproached them for their insincere attitude. . . . accusing them of sophistry and word games.[28]

What is noteworthy about the Japanese attitude in these negotiations is its connection with the so-called Tripartite Intervention at the end of the Sino-Japanese War of 1894–95 and to the concept of an Asian Monroe Doctrine. For example, in approving Japan's entry into World War I, Prime Minister Ōkuma Shigenobu expressed the opinion that ridding China of German forces would serve as a revenge for Germany's role in the Tripartite Intervention.[29] This suggests that he and many other Japanese embraced a sense that Japan was morally justified in undoing the work of the Tripartite Intervention, in which Germany had joined Russia and France (after behind-the-scenes maneuvering by the Chinese) in pressuring Japan to return the Liaodong Peninsula to China after Japan had seized it in the Sino-Japanese War. This moral sense was also related to the broadening support within the Japanese government at the time for the concept of the Asian Monroe Doctrine. Around the time of the outbreak of World War I, sentiment had been growing in Japan that the stability of China was something that the Chinese were unlikely to achieve on their own, and that Japan should assume some form of responsibility for ensuring that stability; it was also at this time that the Asian Monroe Doctrine of Asia being ruled by and for the Asians began to be vigorously preached.[30] With the spread of such ways of thinking, Japanese diplomacy toward China began to take on a moralistic tone—and consequently grew increasingly unilateral and rigid.

4. JAPANESE DIPLOMACY IN THE SHADOW OF THE "YELLOW PERIL"

Dealing with Yellow Peril ideology

In reviewing the history of Japan's diplomacy in Asia, one might at first think that the Japanese response to the issue of race was of little relevance. Race and racism might be a theme of Japan's relations with the Western nations—anti-Japanese immigration laws in the United States, or the spread of Yellow Peril ideology in Europe, for example—but it would seem safe to say that it was not a dominant theme of Japan's relations with other Asian nations.

Yet it would be difficult to deny that a sense of racial or ethnic identity was part of Japan's sense of solidarity with Asia—and if this is the case, then we must assume that the question of how Japan has dealt with the rest of Asia is connected in a fundamental way with how Japan has responded to issues of race and ethnicity. In other words, from the perspective of Japan's diplomacy in Asia, we must ask whether or not Japan has conducted its foreign policy for the sake of Asia as a whole, and with a sense of belonging to some common Asian or oriental ethnic or racial group. From this point of view, one of the first questions that arises is how did Japan, as an Asian nation, deal with the rise of Yellow Peril ideology in Europe?

The concrete impact of that Yellow Peril ideology on the history of Japanese foreign policy can be said to have begun with the Tripartite Intervention in 1895. If we scrutinize the changes that took place in the international situation following the Tripartite Intervention and for a number of years thereafter, it is clear that the spread of Yellow Peril ideology in Europe did not serve as an impetus for encouraging Asian solidarity, but instead served to increase the fragmentation of Asia. The process was one that might be viewed either as tragedy or farce. It commenced with the First Sino-Japanese War.

Immediately after the Treaty of Shimonoseki was signed in 1895, ending the war between Japan and China, Kaiser Wilhelm II of Germany, influenced by Yellow Peril talk among his immediate entourage, professed to have had a vision in which war clouds in the Far East were the prelude to an apocalyptic struggle between the white and yellow races, and between Christianity and Buddhism.

One of the principal figures responsible for preaching the Yellow Peril to Kaiser Wilhelm II was Max von Brandt, former German minister in Beijing, whom Wilhelm had summoned from retirement in the countryside and was presently resident in Berlin. Von Brandt made much of the threat posed by the Yellow Peril, bidding the Kaiser to recall the Mongol and Tartar invasions of medieval Europe, and arguing for the necessity of all of Europe to set aside particular interests and band together for common action. He went on to warn that Japan's industrial organization would one day make it a fearsome competitor for European industry, and asserted that since Russia was the strongest bulwark against the Asiatic races, Germany should support Russian proposals to build a Manchurian railway.

Two distinct types of Yellow Peril thinking are evident here. The first is straightforward Yellow Peril rhetoric: warning that the rise of Japan may threaten Europe. But there is another element at work, too, which is a line of thought suggesting that China should be weakened by stripping it of its rights and privileges in its own territory of Manchuria and establishing a Russian sphere of influence and profit there. Behind this lay a contempt for the Chinese as a "yellow race" and a sense that the incursion of Western colonialism into their territories was virtually inevitable. As we shall see, Yellow Peril ideology was characterized by this duality: on the one hand, there was Western alarm at the rising power of the "yellow race" (here primarily signifying Japan); while on the other there was Western condescension toward its weakness (in this case directed principally at China).

What enabled these two contradictory aspects of Yellow Peril thinking to be fused into a single theory of international strategy was the idea that Japan (the rising threat) might instruct and mold China (heretofore seen as weak and worthy of contempt), and that if these two nations formed an alliance in Asia, then a truly formidable Yellow Peril would come into being.[31] Adolf Marschall von Bieberstein, German foreign secretary at the time of the Tripartite Intervention, informed Count von Hatzfeldt, German minister to England, in a telegram that Germany could be said to have a dual purpose in relation to the issue of the disposition of Chinese territory and the Tripartite Intervention — the first aspect of which was "to prevent an alliance of the yellow race under Japanese leadership."[32]

This type of Yellow Peril thinking was a major factor inducing Germany to take the initiative in the Tripartite Intervention; moreover, the Germans skillfully conveyed these ideas to Russia, where they became a major influence on the actions of Tsar Nicholas II. This can be seen in a letter from Kaiser Wilhelm II to Tsar Nicholas II praising Russia's decision to join the Tripartite Intervention:

For that is clearly the great task of the future for Russia to cultivate the Asian continent and defend the Europe from the inroads of the Great Yellow race.[33]

Three aspects of the Yellow Peril

The kaiser's words to the tsar embodied three distinct (but intimately related) aspects of Yellow Peril thinking in Europe at the end of the nineteenth century.

The first was concern over the "threat" to European civilization, and especially the European colonial system in Asia, posed by "the yellow race," particularly the challenge of Japan. A second aspect was the idea that the European nations had a mission to bring the light of modern European civilization to Asia—and that the peoples of Asia should not be permitted to stand in the way of the accomplishment of that mission. Then there was a third aspect, albeit closely interwoven with the first two. And that was to see resistance on the part of Asia as resistance to imperialism itself—and thus, in the German and Russian empires, to see it in the same light as popular domestic rebellion, and to see its repression as connected to the domestic security of the empire.

These three aspects of the Yellow Peril—alarm over the resistance of Asia (the yellow race) to the Europeans, the European sense of a mission to civilize Asia, and the maintenance of imperial rule in Europe itself—appear in their most classic form in an infamous picture sent by Kaiser Wilhelm II to Tsar Nicholas II, accompanied by a letter from Wilhelm describing the image as follows:

> The development of the Far East, especially its danger to Europe and our Christian Faith is a matter which has been greatly on my mind ever since we made our first move together in Spring. At last my thoughts developed into a certain form and this I sketched on paper. I worked it out with an Artist—a first-class draughtsman— and after it was finished had it engraved for public use. It shows the Powers of Europe represented by their respective Genii called together by the Arch-Angel Michael,—sent from Heaven,—to *unite* in resisting the inroad of Buddhism, heathenism, and barbarism for

the Defence of the Cross. Stress is especially laid on the *united* resistance of *all* European Powers, which is just as necessary also against our common internal foes, anarchism, republicanism, nihilism. I venture to send you an engraving begging you to accept it as a token of my warm and sincere friendship to you and Russia.[34]

"Peoples of Europe, guard your dearest goods": Engraving by Hermann Knackfuss

Of these three aspects of the Yellow Peril concept, the first was a major factor in the background of the Tripartite Intervention, while the second—Europe's mission civilisatrice in Asia—served as the pretext or legitimation for the Russian advance into Manchuria as well as being a major factor behind the Russian rapprochement with Qing China following the Sino-Japanese War.

The Sino-Russian rapprochement and its significance
Russia believed that its advance into the Far East was necessary to bring civilization to Asia; as a concrete step toward that goal it reached an agreement in 1896 with China to establish the Chinese Eastern

Railway (a private-sector company) to construct a rail line across Manchuria. They also agreed to dispatch Russian troops to guard the railroad and its right-of-way, and form an offensive and defensive alliance in preparation for a Japanese attack.[35]

Thus the Sino-Russian agreement might be said to have been concluded by Russia with the aim (or pretext) of civilizing Asia by European hands. But we might also see another aspect of the Yellow Peril concept at work here, and another goal: that of alienating Qing China and Japan from one another and encouraging conflict between them in an effort to divide the "yellow race" against itself. Another way of looking at this would be to say that, at the end of the nineteenth and beginning of the twentieth century, Japan was regarded (at least in Germany and Russia) as a challenger to European domination of the Far East, while China was seen as an ideal—and semi-compliant— area for the expansion of European influence. So we cannot dismiss the Yellow Peril ideology as merely rooted in racial prejudice and an emotional antipathy of the "white" toward the "yellow" race; we should carefully note that it possessed a strongly strategic aspect and functioned as a variety of political propaganda.

The Yellow Peril and the Anglo-Japanese Alliance

Since, as we have seen from a variety of different perspectives, Yellow Peril thought in Europe actually had Japan as its principal object, the Japanese were confronted with the serious issue of how to both resist and to cope with it. The experience of the Tripartite Intervention etched into Japanese consciousness the extent of European alarm over the emergence of Japan on the international scene. And the Anglo-Japanese Alliance was one response to this situation.

It would be difficult to see Yellow Peril ideology in its strictest sense as one of the principal motivations leading the Japanese to sign the original treaty establishing the alliance in 1902. From the Japanese side the conclusion of the alliance with Britain was driven more by alarm over Russian advances into Manchuria in the wake of the Boxer Rebellion of 1900, as well as the increasing penetration of Russian influence into Korea. Yet at the same time it is impossible to deny that one of the motives underlying the alliance was for newly rising Japan not to have to take on a "league" of European nations opposing it (in other words, to prevent a situation in which the Western powers ganged up on Japan).

So in this sense the Anglo-Japanese Alliance was a Japanese strategic move to counter the sort of European alarm over Japan that was manifested in the Yellow Peril ideology. If anything, however, the influence of Yellow Peril thought on the first Anglo-Japanese agreement (1902) was to be seen more on the British side than on the Japanese. Briefly stated (and mirroring Japanese intentions), the British saw the alliance as a means to contain the rising power of Japan.

For example, in a book written in 1895 while the Sino-Japanese War was still in progress, Henry Norman, active as a member of the House of Commons, advocated for a British alliance with Japan after describing the situation in Asia in the following terms:

> The question then recurs, what does Japan want?
>
> This brings us back to the aforesaid undercurrent of national sentiment in Japan which would express itself, if it spoke at all, in the declaration, "Asia for the Asiatics." In other words, I am able to say from positive knowledge that the Government of Japan has conceived a parallel to the Monroe Doctrine for the Far East, with herself at its centre.[36]

Fear that Japan might one day lead the other peoples of Asia in opposition to Western colonial domination began to be voiced in Britain as well around the time of the first Anglo-Japanese Alliance; the alliance was seen as a strategy for dealing with this concern by drawing Japan into the camp of the Western colonial powers (or at least this was one motivation for the alliance).

Moreover, as tensions increased between Japan and Russia, this idea (i.e., restraining Japan by means of an alliance) became even more prevalent in Britain. This is suggested by the fact that in April 1904, Edward VII of Britain assured the Russian ambassador that the Anglo-Japanese Alliance was, if anything, intended as a constraint upon Japan.[37] Even if we make allowances for the likelihood that the king's words were in part intended to mollify the Russians and avoid a head-on confrontation between Britain and Russia, it is also undeniable that Great Britain, with the stability of its colonial dominion over India as a central pillar of its foreign policy, also feared that the rise of Japan in Asia might stimulate the movement for Indian independence, and thus was beginning to feel an increasing need to contain Japan. This can be seen in the British proposal, during the negotiations for the second Anglo-Japanese Alliance in 1905, that the scope of the alliance be expanded to include the Indian subcontinent.[38]

We might say that Japan's acquiescence in this manner of thinking on the part of the British was precisely what made the Anglo-Japanese Alliance possible. To put it another way, by making itself an ally of a "white" nation, Japan strove to leave Asia and the "yellow race" behind.

The historical significance of Yellow Peril ideology

We should note that this Japanese response to the Yellow Peril ideology, while in part an acknowledgment of Japan's own weakness and an attempt to augment its power through a strategic alliance, at the same time possessed a defensive and accommodationist aspect concerned with forestalling the concern of other nations over the rising national power of Japan.

In this sense, while Yellow Peril ideology aroused Japanese antipathy and resistance, it also served as a catalyst for Japan's assimilation into the Western colonialist system.[39] Thus, and precisely for this reason, while the Yellow Peril rhetoric may have pushed the Japanese emotionally in the direction of "Asia," in terms of foreign policy it actually had the effect of severing Japan from "Asia."

The Russo-Japanese War and Japan's farewell to Asia

As we have seen, the Anglo-Japanese Alliance was a major turning point and catalyst for Japan's parting of the ways with Asia; but an event that had an even greater impact on Japanese relations with the Asian continent was the Russo-Japanese War of 1904–05. Here as well, Yellow Peril ideology influenced Japan's diplomatic strategy in both overt and less obvious ways.

As war with Russia loomed, the Japanese government seriously considered two different diplomatic approaches to China in the event of an outbreak of hostilities. The first would be to request China to take joint military action with Japan against the Russians; the second would be to request China to maintain strict neutrality. In the end, Japan asked China to remain neutral. The principal reasoning behind this decision was fear that if Japan brought China directly into a war with Russia this would fan antiforeign sentiment in China and might increase China's internal instability. But there was an additional reason—concern that cooperation between Japan and Qing China would be perceived as a league of the "yellow race" and further incite Yellow Peril fears in Europe.[40] This concern on the part of Japan would become a major factor in stifling the idea of an alliance with China.

Moreover, while this might appear at first glance to be a matter of strategy or tactics, behind such considerations lay a more instinctive Japanese reaction to a deeper element of Yellow Peril ideology—one rooted not so much in racism as in a conception of Asia as being "uncivilized" or "barbarous." The depiction of Japan in Anatole France's novel, *The White Stone*, conceived as a roundtable discussion among European intellectuals, suggests that the essence of Yellow Peril ideology was based less on racial considerations than on historical European prejudices against Asia as barbaric and backward—prejudices supported by sentiment, also historical in nature, that sought to rationalize European colonial domination. One of the characters in the novel makes the following remarks concerning the Russo-Japanese War:

Japan, which in 1894 had beaten the Chinese on land and on sea, and had taken a part, in 1901, in the pacifying action of the Powers, saw with concentrated fury the advance of the voracious and slow-footed she-bear. And, while the huge brute indolently stretched out its muzzle towards the Japanese beehive, the yellow bees, arming their wings and stings together, riddled it with burning punctures.

"It is a colonial war," was the expression used by a high-placed Russian official to my friend Georges Bourdon. Now, the fundamental principle of every colonial war is that the European should be more powerful than the peoples whom he is fighting ; this is as clear as noonday. It is understood that in these kinds of wars the European is to attack with artillery, while the Asiatic or African is of course to defend himself with arrows, clubs, assegais and tomahawks.

The Japanese have departed from these rules.[41]

In short, with the Russo-Japanese War, Japan had taken a major step away from "barbaric Asia."

The League of Nations and the failed Japanese proposal

The fundamental response of Japan to the Yellow Peril ideology was to overcome it by positioning Japan as a member of Western society. In this sense, Japanese foreign policy, beginning with the Anglo-Japanese Alliance, possessed aspects of secession from or betrayal of Asia. The issue of race involved issues of Japanese identity and of the behavior appropriate to Japan as part of the "yellow race." Japan's handling of its proposal to insert a racial equality clause into the League of Nations Covenant in 1919 must be seen not merely as an issue of its diplomatic stance toward the League itself, but also as an aspect of Japanese foreign policy towards Asia.

At the Versailles Peace Conference, Japan proposed adding the following clause as an amendment to Article 21 of the League of Nations Covenant dealing with freedom of religion:

> The equality of the nations being a basic principle of the League of Nations, the High Contracting Parties agree that concerning the treatment and rights to be accorded to aliens in their territories, they will not discriminate, either in law or in fact, against any person or persons on account of his or their race or nationality.

It soon became clear that this draft was unacceptable to the United States, the nation of immigrants, and after private discussions with the Americans, Japan altered its proposal to read more as a goal to be striven for, with equal and just treatment to be accorded "as soon as possible."[42] Yet neither Australia nor Britain, as leader of the Commonwealth, were supportive of the proposal, and so Japan made further concessions, merely proposing that equal and just treatment of alien nationals be endorsed in principle. When even this was unable to gain acceptance by the United States and Australia, Japan proposed insertion of it into the preamble of the Covenant as "the endorsement of the principle of equality of nations and just treatment of their nationals." But even this proposal was rejected (in the final session of the League of Nations Commission charged with drafting the covenant) due to the opposition of Britain and the United States.

The Japanese government considered resubmitting its proposal to the plenary session of the League, but feared that it would not gain sufficient support to pass it in the face of such strong opposition from the United States and Britain, and judged that such failure would damage the standing of Japan within the League.[43] The Japanese delegation thus made a clear declaration of their government's position at the plenary session, but refrained from submitting their proposal to a vote.

The reason Japan did not pursue a hard-line approach on this issue to the very end was no doubt because the Japanese government and negotiators were well aware that the issue of racial equality was deeply bound up with that of immigration and had major domestic political implications for all of the nations involved.

Even more fundamentally, the motivation for the Japanese proposal was less an abstract moral opposition to racial discrimination than it was a more practical concern that Japan not be subjected to disadvantageous treatment within the League of Nations itself on account of race. The statement by British representative Robert Cecil—that in view of the fact that Japan was already a member of the Five Great Powers, its treatment should not be an issue insofar as the League was concerned[44]—intuited the most salient of Japanese concerns. To put it another way, Japan's efforts to insert the racial equality clause were primarily directed at achieving practical goals for Japan itself—not to serve as the moral representative of the peoples of Asia.

Even so, the rejection of the Japanese proposal shook Japan's faith in the League of Nations, as Makino Nobuaki, the Japanese plenipotentiary, eloquently stated in the following terms:

I think it only reasonable that the principle of equality of nations and the just treatment of their nationals should be laid down as a fundamental basis of future relations in this world organisation. If this reasonable and just claim is now denied, it will, in the eyes of those peoples with reason to be keenly interested, have the significance of a reflection on their quality and status. Their faith in the justice and righteousness, which are to be the guiding spirit of the Covenant, may be shaken. . . .[45]

The Japanese invasion of Manchuria in 1931 was condemned by the League of Nations. But Japan's dismissal of this condemnation, its exit from the League, and its pursuit of a strategy of aggression in Asia might all be said to have been aided and abetted by the League's own rejection of the racial equality clause proposed by Japan.

5. QUESTIONING THE CONCEPT OF PAN-ASIANISM

When considering the relationship of philosophy and values to Japan's Asian diplomacy, what comes immediately to mind in the contemporary world is the issue of so-called "Asian values." The East Asian Community proposed by Malaysia's Prime Minister Mahathir Mohamad, and Prime Minister Lee Kuan Yew's advocacy for the concept of an Asian democracy in contrast to Western European-style democracy, for a time gave rise to widespread debate over the question of what constituted "Asian values." In this debate, advocacy of Asian values was seen as resistance to the global spread of Western European values in unaltered form, and the political intent behind this advocacy was frequently a subject of primary concern. In other words, the emphasis on Asian values itself, regardless of content, was argued to be a reaction against the universalization of Western European values.

Certainly, viewed in historical terms, when Asian values were being stressed it was not a positive effort to encourage the sharing of those more widely in the world beyond Asia, but rather a logic of reaction against the West in general and America in particular. In short, it was a reactive, defensive response against the influx of European and American thought. However, we must note that the nucleus of this reactive response was neither ethnic nationalism nor a specific religion (such as Islam), but the concept of "Asia." Here resistance, and the defense of the identity of a nation or people, was conceived not as an individual nation's problem but as a common issue or theme for all of the nations and peoples of Asia.

Why this concept should suddenly arise is not entirely obvious. At first glance, it might seem to stem from having experienced a shared fate—the enduring common experience of the Asian countries (with the exception of Japan and a few others) as victims of European and American colonialism. Yet this would seem an insufficient explanation. To seek the source of one's own ideas and values in "Asia" meant that a certain political will to unite Asia was also at work, and thus a positive or active element rather than a merely reactive or passive one.

Toyotomi Hideyoshi's "Asian Values"

In discussing the problem of "Asian values" from this perspective, it is instructive to examine the thought of the sixteenth-century warlord Toyotomi Hideyoshi. By the early 1580s, Hideyoshi had subdued Shikoku and Kyushu and was well on his way to unifying the entire country of Japan—but in so doing, his own concept of "Japan" and what it meant to him began to expand.

In 1586, Hideyoshi sent a fourteen-point memorandum of instructions to Mōri Terumoto, one of his generals, in which he alluded to crossing the seas to Korea,[46] and the same year gave an audience to the Jesuit Vice-Provincial in Japan, Gaspar Coelho, in which he spoke of the "conquest" (*seibatsu*) of Korea and China.[47] This suggests that he saw the invasion of the Korean peninsula as a logical extension of his unification of Japan (and also felt similarly about the Ryukyu Islands).[48]

One question that arises is why Hideyoshi sought to expand the logic of his domestic hegemony not just to the Ryukyus and Korea, but even to Ming China. With Korea and the Ryukyus, there was at least some historical pretext for treating them as tributaries or dependencies of the Japanese domains of Tsushima or Satsuma, but this was of course absent in the case of China—so what was it that spurred Hideyoshi to the ambition of conquering the Ming?

This should be seen in the context of the advance of Western colonialism into East Asia. It is significant that the first stirrings of Hideyoshi's efforts at foreign conquest and his initial expression of such intentions happen to coincide with his contacts with Spanish and Portuguese missionaries. In particular, the deliberate revelation of his ambition to conquer China to Coelho can be read as an application of the logic of the expansion of the European colonial empires into Asia to the case of Japan and China.[49] And we should not forget that Hideyoshi's ambitions to invade continental Asia were also connected with a rejection of Christianity. If we examine the content of Hideyoshi's response in July 1591 to a letter from the Portuguese viceroy of India,[50] we find him protesting the use of Christianity to lead the Japanese people into "witchcraft," while at the same time arguing that the Shintoism, Confucianism, and Buddhism (*Shin-Ju-Butsu*) practiced across the entirety of Asia were all originally and essentially the same.[51]

Hideoyoshi's unification of Japan was accompanied by a clarification and expansion of the consciousness of Japan as a nation, and this process gradually incorporated the formation of the concepts we speak of when we refer both to geographical Asia as well as to Asia as a community of values.

Hesitation and resistance to Pan-Asianism

Pan-Asianism, the main ideological pillar of opposition to Western colonial domination, had various limitations and met with hesitation and resistance within Asia itself.

One example of this less than enthusiastic reaction from within Asia was manifested in the responses of Korea immediately prior to and during the Russo-Japanese War. For Korea, a certain degree of cooperation with the Western powers seemed likely to serve as a constraint on the established power of Qing China and the rising power of Japan. As symbolized by an incident in which the Korean king temporarily took refuge at the Russian legation in Seoul, during this period Western colonialist pressure on Asia, principally by Russia, tended to be seen by Korea as a useful counterweight to the rise of Japan rather than as something to be fended off through its own modernization and solidarity with the other Asian nations.[52]

A similar attitude may be observed in Qing China in the wake of the Sino-Japanese War of 1894–95. As previously noted, in 1896 the Qing government gave Russia rights to build the Chinese Eastern Railway and to station troops along the railway corridor, and at the same time formed an offensive-defensive alliance with the Russians with Japan as its object. Thus, even before Japan commenced any full-scale aggression on the Asian continent, both China and Korea displayed resistance and wariness when Japan attempted to raise the banner of Asian solidarity.

An additional factor is that, until the early twentieth century, anti-Western movements in China and Korea, like the Boxer Rebellion of 1900, were generally xenophobic in nature, taking a different form from the Pan-Asianism envisioned by the Japanese. In fact, a rapidly modernizing Japan was more likely to become the object of this xenophobic reaction than it was to become an ally. Precisely because of this, Japan was cautious about forming any kind of anti-Western alliance with the Qing. In fact, in the cabinet resolution establishing the fundamental orientation for diplomatic policy for Japan to take toward China once war with Russia became inevitable, the following thoughts were expressed:

> As the result of the Boxer Rebellion [the Chinese people] have come to harbor a considerable amount of resentment against foreigners in general. Once hostilities commenced with Russia, the blood lust and excitement would likely result in indiscriminate attacks on foreigners, and elements discontented with the Qing court and the present political system might seize upon this opportunity to foment internal disorder, and the situation might eventually spiral out of control.[53]

Here, Japan is making a clear distinction between anti-Westernism as Asian resistance to Western imperialism and anti-Westernism as generalized xenophobia.

Moreover, Japan was itself cautious about the idea of a league of Asian nations. This was (as previously noted) connected with the issue of the Yellow Peril. In the same cabinet document just cited, we find this passage:

> We have heard considerably less of white fear of the "yellow race" running rampant—in other words, the so-called Yellow Peril hysteria—in recent times, but such sentiments still lie dormant in the hearts of Europeans, ready to be aroused at the slightest provocation, and there is concern that these unfounded beliefs will unite them [against us]. Because of this, if Japan and China should join in a war against Russia, this could become the impetus for a resurgence of the Yellow Peril hysteria, creating considerable concern that this might result in other nations such as Germany and France involving themselves in the conflict.[54]

Pan-Asianism was thus shouldered aside by the Yellow Peril ideology and its anti-Asianism.

The Negative Concept of Asia

Pan-Asianism, the ideology seeking to unite Asia, was beset by many limitations and obstacles, both from resistance and hesitation within Asia and from factors external to it. Among the most profound of these obstacles was the perception that Asian thought and traditions were outmoded or uncivilized—that they had what might be termed negative value. The idea was widespread in Europe that the West represented modern civilization and Asia was uncivilized or barbaric, but this also began to influence the self-perception of the peoples of Asia.

Ironically, this phenomenon was manifested globally in its most vivid form at the time of the Russo-Japanese War. At the popular level there was a tendency to see the Russo-Japanese War as a race war, but from an Asian perspective it was not so significant that the Russians were "white" and the Japanese "colored." For in this context (despite the Russian tsar's use of Yellow Peril rhetoric and racial propaganda), Europeans saw "Asia" less as a racial category than in terms of its relationship to modernity: i.e., as a backward and uncivilized region of the world. To put it another way, rapidly modernizing Japan was no longer Asian—instead, significantly, there was a growing perception that "barbaric" Russia was the more "Asiatic" of the two.

A declaration issued by members of the Polish national assembly in Warsaw in March 1904 makes this point abundantly clear:

> The use of terminology such as a war between the white and yellow races or between European civilization and Asiatic barbarism perplexes us, because we know that Russia itself is barbaric and Asiatic. We know what lengths the courageous and industrious Japanese have gone to for the cause of civilization in the Far East; while at the same time, we have witnessed daily what Russia has done to eradicate European civilization in our land. Japan is not fighting against a champion of Europe—Nay! It fights against a race of Asiatic barbarians that is attempting to destroy the fruits of centuries of civilization and progress in Poland and Finland![55]

Yet was Japan truly the leader of Asian modernization, charged with the mission of transforming "Asia" from an uncivilized to a civilized realm? Was the "Asia" that Japan represented actually modern and civilized rather than backward?

If so, then the Pan-Asianism Japan stood for was one driven by the logic of modernization. But in that case, in what sense was there anything particularly "Asian" about it? Confronted with this question, it would seem that Japan almost unconsciously began to come to the conclusion that Asian things possessed a kind of negative value, opposed to the logic of modernization.

Asian modernization and Pan-Asianism

Based on what we have seen so far, it is clearly a mistake to interpret Pan-Asianism simply as a variety of anti-Westernism. Whether in pre-World War II Japan or in the discourse on Asia presented by the leaders of the Southeast Asian nations in the 1980s and 1990s, this tide of thought was expressed and advocated in countries that had already achieved a considerable degree of modernization. This suggests that advocacy of Pan-Asianism was associated with a form of self-redefinition. In other words, the progress of modernization had brought with it a certain Europeanization of manners, customs, and ways of thinking—but this in turn inspired efforts at self-redefinition, based on a realization that perhaps modernization did not necessarily entail wholesale Westernization.

This also meant that Pan-Asianism or advocacy for "Asian values" did not necessarily require a defensive effort to preserve traditional values, customs, or mores. The effort to redefine a changing self was itself predicated upon change, and the desire to arrive at new definitions. In other words, "Asia" did not have to be limited to the Asia of the past or present—it could also signify a future Asia, yet to be built. The nucleus of Pan-Asianism could reside, not in the defense of an existing Asia, but in the creation of values for an Asia yet to come.

CHAPTER TWO

The Interaction of Domestic and Foreign Policy

1. JAPAN'S DESIRE TO BE RECOGNIZED BY ASIA

I t is often said that foreign policy is an extension of domestic politics, but the real significance of this statement is not as deeply appreciated as one might think.

In Japan's case, the linkage between foreign policy and domestic politics could theoretically exist even in Japan's relations with the United States or Europe or Russia; and indeed, as in the case of Japan's security arrangements with America and the issue of Okinawa, it is obvious how easily the connection to domestic politics is made.

On the other hand, because of the geographic and cultural proximity in relations between Japan and other East Asian countries, we observe that the domestic political motivations of each country merge with one another to shape foreign policy strategy. In the past, the Park Jeonghui (Park Chung-hee) regime and the Liberal Democratic Party government in Japan were criticized for their "collusion" with one another—a term frequently employed to describe Japan's relations with other nations and a characteristic of Japan's Asian diplomacy. In other words, the Japanese government and the governments of other East Asian countries have tended to attempt to use one another, motivated more by domestic political reasons than diplomatic considerations or the specific issues at hand.

At various times in premodern history, such political utilization of another country for domestic political ends took the form of a particular Japanese regime seeking formal recognition by China in order to enhance its own domestic legitimacy. For example, an important motive behind the mission sent in the third century by Himiko to Wei-dynasty China was that her emerging state of Yamatai-koku was still little more than a coalition of clans, and she wished to more firmly establish monarchical rule (and her own authority) by donning the mantle of power borrowed from China.

Again, in 600, when through a vassal the Sui emperor queried an embassy sent to China by Prince Shōtoku concerning the manners and customs of the Japanese, it is said that the Japanese envoy responded that "the sovereign of Japan regards heaven as his elder brother and the sun as his younger brother."[1] The style of this explanation supports the idea that the mission was sent to inform China of the political regime of Japan and gain recognition for it.

When, in the famous official letter borne by Ono no Imoko to the Sui court in 607, the Japanese described their sovereign as "the Son of Heaven in the land of the rising sun" it would seem that a similar motive was at work. This letter has long been interpreted as an attempt to assert Japan's equality with China, sparking endless debate. But the crucial political motivation behind it was probably less an assertion of equality than it was the desire of the Japanese regime centered on Prince Shōtoku to be formally recognized by the newly risen Sui dynasty in China.

The same could be said, more or less, of the subsequent Japanese embassies to the Tang dynasty. But with the advent of the Nara court in Japan in the early eighth century a serious effort to remake Japanese institutions on the Tang model was underway, and what was sought was not merely recognition but to demonstrate to the Tang Chinese how thoroughly Japan had adopted their customs and to induce them to accord Japan a suitable status in return. This was displayed most typically and symbolically in the person of the 702 envoy to the Tang, Awata no Mahito, who dressed exactly as a Chinese civil official, could read literary Chinese, and apparently received the acclaim of the people of the Tang court.[2] And as time went by, the Japanese grew ever more sensitive to how their envoys to the Tang court were received.[3]

For a considerable time thereafter, a major motivation for Japan's contact with China was to give an account of the state of affairs in Japan and stress its commonality with Chinese culture. We can observe this tendency even in relations with Song-dynasty China, when the Japanese missions became almost entirely the province of Buddhist clerics rather than official government envoys, exemplified by the Japanese monk Chōnen's audience with the Song emperor Taizong. Chōnen, who arrived in Song China in 983, informed Taizong that Japan's imperial house had reigned in an unbroken lineage for many generations; this is said to have impressed Taizong, who found this in contrast to the frequent dynastic changes in China. This anecdote suggests the fervor with which Chōnen described Japan's political system and its current situation, an attitude colored by concern with the kind of "recognition diplomacy" described earlier.

This recognition diplomacy may be observed with the appearance of each new regime in Japanese history. At the beginning of the Tokugawa period, Ieyasu approached the Ming dynasty through the Shimazu family, lords of Satsuma domain, and other vassal daimyo, with a proposal to revive the tally trade (kangō bōeki).[4] These developments suggest that Ieyasu wanted to induce the Ming to recognize the legitimacy of his new regime, a point also implied by the fact that in the diplomatic correspondence Ieyasu uses terminology suggesting that Japan was itself receiving tribute from other countries.[5]

However, the most typical attempt to utilize the political authority of China to consolidate a personal political position was probably that of Ashikaga Yoshimitsu, the third Ashikaga shogun. In the early fifteenth century, as shown in table 2–1, Yoshimitsu dispatched a series of missions to Ming China bearing official letters of state. The impetus for this was clearly an effort by Yoshimitsu to don the mantle of Ming authority in order to establish the legitimacy of his own regime. And in fact, Yoshimitsu dressed in Chinese clothing when he gave audience to Ming envoys.[6]

Table 2-1: Envoys Between Japan and Ming China

Date	Sender	Envoy	Letter of state	Gifts
August 1401	Yoshimitsu Koitsumi	Soa	yes	yes
February 1402	Jianwen emperor (Hui emperor)	Tianlun Daoyi Yian Yiru	yes	Ming calendar
March 1403	Yoshimitsu	Kenchū Keimitsu	yes (two letters to Jiawen and Yongle emperors)	yes
May 1404	Yongle emperor	Zhao Juren	yes	gold seal, etc.
November 1404	Yoshimitsu	Myōshitsu Bonryō; handover of captured "leaders" of wakō pirates	yes	
May 1405	Yongle	Yu Shiji	yes	yes
November 1405	Yoshimitsu	Minamoto no Michikata	yes	yes
June 1406	Yongle	Pan Ci, Wang Jin	yes	official seals, etc.
June 1406	Yoshimitsu	Kenchū Keimitsu	uncertain	yes
May 1407	Yoshimitsu	Kenchū Keimitsu	uncertain	yes
May 1408	Yoshimitsu	Kenchū Keimitsu	uncertain	yes

Source: Based on information in Sakuma Shigeo, *Nichi-Min kankei shi no kenkyū* (Yoshikawa Kōbunkan, 1992) and other sources.

A perception of the benefits of trade did spur Yoshimitsu's enthusiasm for relations with the Ming court, but, more significantly, he had a specific political motive in this unstable era immediately following the end of the half-century-long conflict over which of the rival Japanese imperial lineages, Southern or Northern, was the legitimate dynasty. Yoshimitsu hoped to elevate himself to a position equal to that of the emperor and have that position recognized by the Ming court; in return, he would position Japan as a tributary state of the Ming empire. This intent is graphically illustrated by Yoshimitsu's famous letter to the Yongle emperor, in which he styled himself "your subject, Minamoto, Sovereign of Japan).[7] The use of "Minamoto" comes from there being two powerful Ashikaga clans, one of Minamoto descent and the other of Fujiwara descent; Yoshimitsu's line was Minamoto.

This sort of attempt by regimes to use one another can also be glimpsed — ironically, and in somewhat different form — in the case of Toyotomi Hideyoshi in the late sixteenth century. Hideyoshi had what might be described as a fantasy of invading Korea, then moving onward to seize the Ming capital of Beijing and install the Japanese emperor there, with the ten provinces surrounding it to be made the private domain of the imperial house.[8] Yet if we examine the details of Hideyoshi's actions, we may also interpret them as an effort to lend gravitas to his own regime by gilding it with the authority of the Ming. This is symbolized by Hideyoshi choosing to give audience to emissaries of the Ming court dressed in Chinese court costume in a room in which Ming paintings hung upon the walls.

It is also interesting to note that such an attitude and orientation were displayed in the course of Japanese history not only toward the great power of China, but in relations with the kingdom of Korea. For example, beginning around the sixteenth century, the daimyo of the Japanese domain of Tsushima is said to have annually sent a representative to Korea, who wore a Korean costume and bore a certificate of official rank bestowed upon Tsushima by the Korean court.[9] One might discount this as the behavior of a minor regional daimyo, but it almost certainly was done with the tacit knowledge of the central government. Moreover, the fact that Ieyasu chose to use Tsushima in his attempts to restore relations with Korea is of profound significance. Ieyasu's diplomacy toward Korea might be interpreted as an effort to secure international recognition for the hereditary status of the title of shogun and confirmation of its passage from Ieyasu to his designated heir Hidetada (given the timing of it, as well as the intent of drawing a clear line between the new Tokugawa regime and the still-existing remnants of the Toyotomi family and their supporters, who had engineered the invasions of Korea).

As we have seen, the Korean embassies of the Tokugawa period tended to be intimately associated with recognition of the regime. The Korean embassy of 1643 fits this scenario. The 1643 embassy was somewhat unusual in that it took the form of a mission of congratulation on the birth of an heir to shogun Iemitsu, but we may surmise that this was involved with the desire of the shogunate to secure international recognition for Iemitsu's status (especially since there had been persistent and bitter conflict with his younger brother Tadanaga over the shogunal succession).[10]

Nor is this issue of recognition of succession and changes in regime merely ancient history. For example, how much recognition to accord to the system of hereditary succession in North Korea is an issue that continues to trouble Japan and South Korea, irrespective of other issues regarding North Korea's stance on foreign relations. The South Korean administration of Lee Myungbak was confronted with the problem of what sort of representative to send to ceremonies sponsored by Kim Jong-un, since this would signify the degree of recognition that it was extending to the North Korean government. And in the 1980s, the Suzuki Zenkō cabinet was pointedly unenthusiastic about an official visit to South Korea by the prime minister, since this would signal complete recognition (and tacit support) by Japan for the regime of Cheon Duhwan, regarded as having suppressed the democratization movement. Even such a refusal to participate in recognition diplomacy underlines its significance.

In relations with China as well, the strategy or tactic of enlisting the authority of China for domestic political ends can be frequently observed, even today, if one looks closely. For example, some years ago when Prime Minister Abe Shinzō visited China, Japanese journalists made much of the meaning that, at the state banquet given for him by the Chinese, he was served not the top-ranking delicacy (bird's-nest soup), but a soup of sea cucumber, perceived as inferior. This was linked to ongoing criticism by certain journalists regarding what was labeled as Abe's political inexperience and lack of qualifications for his office. In short, at least as far as these journalists were concerned, one purpose of the prime minister's visit to China this time was an attempt to polish his foreign-policy résumé.

Moreover, Prime Minister Koizumi Jun'ichirō's official visits to Yasukuni Shrine, and his stubborn adherence to his position in the ensuing conflict with China, had the paradoxical effect of expanding his popularity among the Japanese people — a slightly different twist on utilizing relations with China to achieve domestic political ends.

"Recognition diplomacy" in the contemporary world

The longstanding tradition of Japanese diplomacy that desired recognition and understanding from the other countries of Asia was, in premodern times, primarily a desire to be treated as an equal and trustworthy neighbor by China and the states of the Korean peninsula. But in modern times a different nuance was added to this — a nuance which, over time, came to occupy even greater importance. And that was for Japan to be acknowledged as an important standard-bearer of the international order centered on the advanced nations of the West.

In other words, it became a major pillar of modern Japanese foreign policy to induce the countries and peoples of Asia to understand and appreciate Japan's status and position within the broader international society. In the period before World War II, when most of the Asian countries had been reduced to colonial or semi-colonial status, this led Japan to play the role of Asian representative of the Western ethos and the international order the Western powers had created. The result was that while on the one hand Japan might be seen as a model of modernity from which the other Asian nations might learn, it was also viewed with suspicion for having separated itself from the rest of Asia.

The following anecdote written by a member of a Korean embassy to early Meiji Japan who attended a reception at the posh Rokumeikan

(Deer Cry Pavilion)—a state-owned guest house for entertaining foreign dignitaries—gives full expression to the antipathy felt by those
associated with the Korean government toward Japan as a representative of Western-style modernization.

> The Japanese women all wore Western dress. I am told that this
> has been the style since the Restoration. When one sees how this
> "civilization" of the women surpasses or at least equals that of the
> men, one assumes that prior to their becoming "civilized" they must
> have been devoid of decency. There was one particularly amusing
> incident. A lovely young lady of not much more than twenty years
> of age approached me through the wave of humanity surrounding
> us, grasped my hand, and began speaking to me about something.
> When I queried the interpreter I discovered she was none other than
> the wife of the army minister, and was told that she had simply been
> thanking me for attending the banquet. An innocent scholar such
> as myself, who had of course never so much as held the hand of a
> prostitute or serving wench, could not help but be nonplussed by
> this unexpected turn of events. The interpreter said to me, "This is
> just a custom we have in my country for welcoming honored guests.
> Please do not take it amiss." Hearing this, I immediately put on a
> happy face and expressed my thanks to her for having been invited
> to attend such a splendid affair. As the vulgar saying has it, "In the
> company of lunatics even a sane man can lose his wits." I have never
> before seen such an absence of morals between men and women,
> or lack of discrimination between noble and base. It was truly
> revolting.[11]

On the one hand, Japan was an Asian country, working to be recognized as such not only in Asia but in the world as a whole. The position (discussed above) of Japanese diplomacy with regard to the issue
of racial discrimination was related to this stance. Yet this self-assertion
as an Asian nation was bound to conflict with the other axis of Japan's
perception of itself as standard-bearer for the Western-led international
order. The solution then seemed to be to create a Japanese order in
Asia that could unite these two axes, and to secure international

recognition for it—yet this was one of the principal factors that set Japan on the course toward becoming the aggressor nation of Asia.

The future of recognition diplomacy

After World War II, Japan's pursuit of recognition diplomacy with regard to the countries of Asia also evolved along two distinct axes. The first was the effort to gain recognition within international society at large for Japan's contribution as a developed Asian democracy to the economic advancement and political stability of the region. The second was the desire for Japan to be acknowledged within Asia itself for its role as a kind of teacher and guide. Japan's use of official government aid to Asian countries as a lever, as well as its efforts to reflect the voice of Asia in forums such as the G7 and G8 summits, were expressions of this type of recognition diplomacy.

However, at this point many of the nations of Asia have now arrived, however imperfectly, at the establishment of democratic political institutions, and are also firmly on course with their economic development, with private sector trade and investment steadily increasing. In such an era, it would seem that Japan's recognition diplomacy in Asia has reached a significant turning point.

For virtually the first time in history, the time has come for Japan to define itself as a genuine partner of the other Asian nations and seek recognition of that fact. Yet in this case, it becomes a major issue as to whether the majority of the Asian countries desire to maintain the status quo of the present international order, or if they will opt for a fairly fundamental reorganization of it.

Apart from Japan and South Korea, there are no Asian nations that have signed closely binding defense treaties with the United States. Moreover, with the exceptions of Japan, South Korea and Singapore, the Asian countries assert their position both politically and economically as developing nations. In these circumstances, the formation of a partnership between Japan and the rest of Asia would seem to require that the Asian nations develop an awareness of their own global responsibilities and actively participate with Japan in crafting a vision of the world of the future.

The diplomacy of apology as recognition diplomacy

In Japan's diplomacy in Asia since the end of World War II, the issue of apology for Japan's acts of aggression in Asia has frequently been raised when Japan has sought recognition and understanding from the other Asian nations. This issue tends to get treated as one of popular national sentiment, but if we think of it in terms of diplomacy, one of the first things we must ask is why it did not develop into a major political and foreign policy issue immediately after the war, or indeed soon after the normalization of relations with South Korea (1965) and China (1972), rather than in the 1980s and 1990s.

As we can see from looking at the language of the various Japanese apologies presented on pages 58–62, in the period prior to what has come to be known as the Murayama Statement (1995), it was not necessarily clear who was apologizing, to whom they were apologizing, or precisely what they were apologizing for. Reviewing the texts of these pre-Murayama apologies, there is a lack of clarity surrounding such points as whether the nation of Japan has, by war, aggression, and colonial domination, visited great harm on the nations and peoples of China, Korea, and other Asian countries and violated their national dignity; the question of who might bear responsibility for this history; and whether or not the Japanese nation and its people as a whole have genuinely reflected upon and come to terms with these issues.

This vagueness of these statements might be said to reside in the fact that in the period following World War II, Japan was dominated by conservative political parties—primarily the LDP—that harbored significant numbers of former war criminals, and thus never made a complete break with their prewar and wartime past.

On the other hand, when prioritizing the strategic importance of their relationship with Japan, China and Korea have tended not to demand too much of this diplomacy of apology from Japan. China, especially during the period when it felt threatened by the Soviet Union, was apt to set aside demands for apologies from Japan. A similar tendency may be observed in the case of South Korea during periods when the relationship with Japan has been valued as a strategic counterweight in dealing with the threat of North Korea.

However, the issue of apology is likely to surface whenever such strategic considerations seem less pressing. Moreover, this is connected with both China and South Korea's own efforts to be recognized within international society. In other words, as both nations have gotten on track with remarkable economic development and have solidified their international standing, they have also begun to demand greater recognition of their status within international society. And it is in this context that they are prone to demand of Japan a settling of accounts for past humiliations.

But there is another, even more fundamental issue at stake here. If Japan wishes to be fully recognized by the other countries of Asia as an unquestioned economic leader and an established democracy, it must first of all clearly acknowledge the fact that in the past it trampled upon both democracy and liberty in Asia, and also make clear that it does indeed feel remorse for these actions. Herein lies the contemporary significance of both the diplomacy of recognition and the diplomacy of apology for Japan in Asia, as well as the real reason why the issue of apology has spilled over from the realm of foreign policy to become such a major domestic issue.

2. THE JAPAN WHICH TURNED ITS BACK ON ASIA

On the one hand, Japanese diplomacy has sought recognition and understanding from the other Asian nations, or pursued a foreign policy strategy of engagement with the Asian continent. But there is another aspect to Japan's Asian diplomacy; one that has tended to turn its back on Asia and seek isolation from it. This aspect is literally a withdrawal from Asia—a posture of distancing Japan from involvement in Asian affairs—and we need to examine historically why it emerged, and under what circumstances.

The blank sixth century
Probably the first example in Japanese history of the adoption of such a "withdrawal" from Asia as foreign policy was what has been called "the blank sixth century." After the fifth century BCE, during which the

I. Japan's major official apologies to South Korea

1. **Statement by Foreign Minister Kosaka Zentarō at a press conference upon his arrival in Korea, September 1960**

   I am aware of the hardship we have caused for you. But dwelling on the past will not bring happiness; let us join forces to open the way to a brighter future.

   > From the memoirs of Kosaka Zentarō, *Giin gaikō yonjyū-nen: Watashi no rirekisho* (Nihon Keizai Shimbunsha, 1994), 67.

2. **Statement by Foreign Minister Shiina Etsusaburō on his arrival at Seoul's Kimpo Airport, February 1965**

   Japan and South Korea are separated only by a narrow strip of water and have maintained close cultural and economic ties throughout the ages, not to speak of the contacts between the people of our two nations. We feel great regret and deep remorse over the unhappy phase in the long history of relations between the two countries.

   > *Asahi shimbun*, 17 February, 1965; translated in Wakamiya Yoshibumi, *The Postwar Conservative View of Asia: How the Political Right Has Delayed Japan's Coming to Terms with Its History of Aggression in Asia* (Tokyo: LTCB International Library Foundation, 1999), 236.

3. **Speech by Prime Minister Nakasone Yasuhiro at a luncheon for South Korean President Cheon Duhwan, September 1984**

   Japan caused great suffering to your country and your people during a certain period during this century. I would like to announce that the Japanese government and people express deep regret for the wrongs done to you and are determined to strictly caution themselves against repeating them in the future.

   > *Asahi shimbun*, evening edition, 7 September 1984; translated in Wakamiya, *The Postwar Conservative View of Asia*, 246.

4. Statement by the late Emperor Shōwa at a banquet welcoming South Korean President Cheon Duhwan, September 1984

> I feel great regret that there was an unhappy phase in relations between our two countries in a certain period of this century despite the close ties between us. I believe that such things should not be repeated.
>
> Asahi shimbun, evening edition, 7 September 1984; translated in Wakamiya, *The Postwar Conservative View of Asia*, 244.

5. Statement by Prime Minister Murayama Tomiichi: "On the Occasion of the 50th Anniversary of the War's End," 15 August 1995

> During a certain period in the not too distant past, Japan, following a mistaken national policy, advanced along the road to war, only to ensnare the Japanese people in a fateful crisis, and, through its colonial rule and aggression, caused tremendous damage and suffering to the people of many countries, particularly to those of Asian nations. In the hope that no such mistake be made in the future, I regard, in a spirit of humility, these irrefutable facts of history, and express here once again my feelings of deep remorse and state my heartfelt apology. Allow me also to express my feelings of profound mourning for all victims, both at home and abroad, of that history.
>
> Website of the Ministry of Foreign Affairs of Japan
> http://www.mofa.go.jp/announce/press/pm/murayama/9508.html

6. Statement by Prime Minister Kan Naoto, August 2010

> This year marks a significant juncture for the Japan-Republic of Korea relationship.
>
> In August precisely one hundred years ago, the Japan-Korea Annexation Treaty was concluded, marking the beginning of the colonial rule of thirty-six years. As demonstrated by strong resistance such as the Samil independence movement, the Korean people of

that time was [sic] deprived of their country and culture, and their ethnic pride was deeply scarred by the colonial rule which was imposed
against their will under the political and military circumstances.

I would like to face history with sincerity. I would like to have
[the] courage to squarely confront the facts of history and humility
to accept them, as well as to be honest to reflect upon the errors of
our own. Those who render pain tend to forget it while those who
suffered cannot forget it easily. [For] the tremendous damage and
sufferings that this colonial rule caused, I express here once again
my feelings of deep remorse and my heartfelt apology.

Guided by such understanding, I will build a future-oriented
Japan-Republic of Korea relationship by placing the next one hundred years to come in my prospect. I will continue in all sincerity
conducting such humanitarian cooperation as the assistance to
ethnic Koreans left in Sakhalin and the assistance in returning
remains of the people from the Korean Peninsula. Moreover, in
response to the expectations of the Korean people, I will transfer
precious archives originated from the Korean Peninsula that were
brought to Japan during the period of Japan's rule through the
Governor-General of Korea and [which] the Government of Japan
possesses, such as the Royal Protocols of the Joseon Dynasty.

10 August 2010 [Provisional Translation]
Website of the Prime Minister of Japan and His Cabinet
http://japan.kantei.go.jp/kan/statement/201008/10danwa_e.html

II. Japan's major official apologies to the People's Republic of China

1. Speech of Prime Minister Tanaka Kakuei at a banquet welcoming
   him to the Great Hall of the People, Beijing, 25 September 1972

   Japan and China are located in close geographic proximity to each
   other and share a two-thousand-year history of exchanges in many
   fields. Yet, regrettably, the relationship between the two countries

went through an unfortunate period over dozens of years in the past. So, once again, I would like to express my deep remorse for the huge trouble which Japan caused to the Chinese people.

> *Asahi shimbun*, 26 September 1972; Wakamiya, *The Postwar Conservative View of Asia*, 251.

(Addendum) Speech of Chinese Premier Zhou Enlai at banquet welcoming Prime Minister Tanaka, 25 February 1972

China and Japan had a two-thousand-year history of friendly personal contacts and cultural exchanges between their peoples. The people of both countries had maintained a close friendship. . . . However, Japanese militarists invaded China in 1894, and their invasion lasted for half a century, causing terrible damage to the Chinese people and inflicting huge losses on ordinary Japanese people as well. It is often said that we must not forget the past and learn lessons from it. So must we engrave these experiences and lessons deeply in our memories.

> *Asahi shimbun*, 26 September 1972; Wakamiya, *The Postwar Conservative View of Asia*, 251.

(Addendum) Remarks by Premier Zhou Enlai during talks with Prime Minister Tanaka Kakuei, 26 September 1972

We have a very positive assessment of remarks by the leaders of the Japanese government to the effect that they are seeking a political rather than a legal resolution to the issue of normalization of relations between our two countries. The lives of millions of Chinese people were sacrificed in the war. The damage done to Japan was also great. We must not forget the lessons of this history. We can accept Prime Minister Tanaka's expression of "remorse for the unfortunate events of the past." However, when Prime Minister Tanaka refers to "the huge trouble [*meiwaku*] which Japan caused to the Chinese people," this stirs resentment among the Chinese, because for us, the word trouble [*meiwaku*] is used only for trivial matters.

Ishii Akira, et al., eds., *Nitchū kokkō seijōka · Nitchū heiwa yūkō jōyaku tekei kōshō: Kiroku to kōshō* (Iwanami Shoten, 2003).

2. Joint Communique of the Government of Japan and the Government of the People's Republic of China, 29 September 1972

> The Japanese side is keenly conscious of the responsibility for the serious damage that Japan caused in the past to the Chinese people through war, and deeply reproaches itself. Further, the Japanese side reaffirms its position that it intends to realize the normalization of relations between the two countries from the stand of fully understanding "the three principles for the restoration of relations" put forward by the Government of the People's Republic of China. The Chinese side expresses its welcome for this.
>
> > Website of the Ministry of Foreign Affairs of Japan
> > http://www.mofa.go.jp/region/asia-paci/china/joint72.html

3. Statement by Prime Minister Murayama Tomiichi "On the Occasion of the 50th Anniversary of the War's End," 15 August 1995
   See I, no. 5 above.

"Five Kings of Wa (Japan)" conducted a high-profile diplomacy (see table 2–2), the sixth century followed as a kind of lacuna in Japanese foreign policy. After the mission sent by "King Bu of Wa" (Emperor Yūryaku) to the Liu Song court in 478, there is no sign of any close diplomatic contact between Japan and China or the states of the Korean

Table 2–2: Embassies to China of the "Five Kings of Wa (Japan)"

421	San (probably Emperor Nintoku)	tribute goods	official titles bestowed
425	Chin (probably Emperor Richū)	envoy, petition to Chinese emperor, tribute goods	General Pacifying the East, King of Wa
443	Sai (Emperor Hanzei or Ingyō)	envoy, tribute goods	General Pacifying the East, King of Wa
462	Kō (Emperor Ingyō or Ankō)	envoy, tribute goods	General Pacifying the East, King of Wa
478	Bu (Emperor Yūryaku)	envoy, petition	General Pacifying the East, King of Wa

Source: Ishihara Michihiro, et. al., ed. and trans., *Gishi Wajin den; Gokanjo Waden; Sōsho Wakoku den; Zuisho Wakoku den* (Iwanami Shoten, 1985).

peninsula until the mission dispatched by Prince Shōtoku to the Sui dynasty in 607.

This withdrawal is thought to have been influenced by several factors: the loss or drastic diminishment of Japan's territorial interests in the Korean peninsula (in the southern region known as Imna [Jpn.: Mimana] or Gaya [Kaya]), the rising power on the peninsula of the states of Silla and Baekje, and, even more significantly, the domestic power struggle in Japan over the establishment of the rule of the imperial house, symbolized by the rivalry between the Soga and Mononobe families and the assassination of Emperor Sushun. In short, the intensification of domestic political conflict and a (relative) diminution of Japan's overseas influence appear to have combined to inspire a foreign policy of withdrawal.

The suspension of embassies to Tang China

The next major point at which Japanese foreign policy strategy took a decisive inward turn was when Japan's embassies to Tang China (see table 2–3), which had continued over two centuries beginning in 630, were officially suspended in 894 as a result of Sugawara no Michizane's petition to the Japanese emperor.

Throughout the eighth century into the early ninth century, envoys were exchanged with some frequency not only between Japan and Tang China, but also between Japan and the state of Balhae (Bohai) that existed for several centuries in the southern part of Manchuria and the northern part of the Korean peninsula, but this situation underwent a radical alteration around the time of Michizane's petition. If we probe the background of the suspension of the missions to the continent, we find a variety of factors at work.

What is immediately striking when we look at the embassies to Tang China over time are the variations in frequency—the intervals between the dispatch of each mission and the next—that are apparent.

Table 2–3: Japanese Embassies to Tang China

Departure	Return	Envoys (and other remarks)
630	632	Inugami no Mitatsuki, Kusushi no Enichi
653	654,	Kishi no Nagani, Kishi no Koma
654	655	Takamuko no Kuromaro (died in China), Kawabe no Maro, Kusushi no Enichi
659	661	(Arrived at Tang capital of Changan in 659) Sakaibe no Iwashiki (shipwrecked and murdered on voyage), Tsumori no Kisa, Iki no Hakatoko
665	667	(Returning Tang envoy Liu Degao to China; bringing Tang envoy Sima Facong to Japan) Mori no Ōishi, Sakaibe no Iwatsumi, Kishi no Kimi, Kishi no Harima
667	668	(Taking Tang envoy Facong as far as Baekje; may not have gone all the way to China) Iki no Hakatoko, Kasa no Moroishi
669	uncertain	Kawachi no Kujira

Departure	Return	Envoys (and other remarks)
702	704 (707–718)	(Arrived Changan 702; some of the envoys did not return until 707 or 718) Awata no Mahito, Takahashi no Kasama, Kose no Ōji, Yamanoue no Okura
717	718	(arrived Changan 717) Tajihi no Agatamori, tomo no Yamamori, Fujiwara no Umakai
733	734 (739)	(arrived Changan 734) Tajihi no Hironari, Nakatomi no Nashiro
752	753 (754)	(arrived Changan 752) Fujiwara no Kiyokawa (who would remain in China), Ōtomo no Komaro, Kibi no Makibi
759	761	Kō Gendo, Kura no Matanari
777	778	(Arrived Changan 778. Were conveying Tang envoy Zhao Baoying back to Japan but he died en route.) Saeki no Imaemishi, tomo no Masutate, Fujiwara no Takatori, Ono no Iwane, miwa no Suetari
779	781	(Arrived Changan 780. Returning Tang envoy Sun Xingjin.) Fuse no Kiyonao
803	805 (804–806)	(Arrived Changan 804. Some members return 804–806.) Fujiwara no Kadonomaro, Ishikawa no Michimasa (who died in China)
836	838	(Arrived Changan 838. [Other sources say 839 or 840.]) Fujiwara no Tsunetsugu, Ono no Takamura (Ono remained in Japan, pleading illness)

Notes: 1. The first six embassies used the so-called northern route (via Korea) on both the outbound and return trips; subsequent embassies used the southern route (via the East China Sea and the city of Yangzhou in southern China) both ways, except for one which went via the Balhae Sea and one which returned using the northern route.

2. Embassies in 746 (headed by Isonokami no Osomaro) and in 894 (headed by Sugarawa no Michizane and Ki no Haseo) were cancelled. A 761 embassy (headed by Naka no Iwatomo) was terminated by damage to the ships; one in 762 (headed by Nakatomi no Takanushi) is believed to have been cancelled due to unfavorable weather.

3. The number of vessels sent was initially one or two; beginning with the ninth embassy, a convoy of four ships became the norm.

Source: Compiled by the author mainly from the tables on pages 28–29 of Tōno Haruyuki, *Kentōshi sen* (Asahi Shimbunsha, 1999) and other information contained in this work.

The gaps between them grow gradually longer: nineteen years between the embassies of 759 and 777; twenty-five years between the embassies of 779 and 803; and thirty-four years between 803 and 836.

Moreover, the time between the appointment of the envoys and their departure, initially about two years, gradually lengthened to as much as three or four years. In at least one case (that of Ono no Takamura, appointed as an envoy on the embassy of 836), an envoy even refused to make the voyage, using illness as a pretext. In addition, the northern sea route (via Korea) that had been used by the embassies through most of the seventh century was abandoned due to the changing situation on the Korean peninsula and in northern China, and especially the conflict between Japan and the Korean state of Silla, being replaced by a longer southern route across the East China Sea that drastically increased the likelihood of shipwreck.

Yet there were even more important factors influencing the dispatch of the embassies: the internal political situation in China and changes in the political climate in Japan itself.

In China, from the An Lushan Rebellion of the late eighth century onward, regional powers expanded under the so-called feudatory system, and in the ninth century major uprisings occurred, including those of Kang Quantai and Qiu Fu. In addition, the influence of Buddhism began to wane and that of Confucianism to reassert itself, as symbolized by the anti-Buddhist persecution initiated by Emperor Wuzong in 845. As a result of all of these developments, the Tang Empire gradually lost its international flavor and turned increasingly inward.

Meanwhile, changes were also taking place in Japan. First was the virtually complete remaking of the manners and customs of the Japanese imperial court following the Tang Chinese model, symbolized by the official adoption of Tang-style court dress in 818. There were also changes in the situation regarding economics and trade. As the volume of unofficial trading vessels plying the waters between Japan and Silla radically increased, the role played by the embassies to Tang China in stimulating trade with the continent declined in importance.

This was coincident with the rise of Silla as the dominant power on the Korean peninsula and at the same time a diminution of fears that the situation in the peninsula might exert a direct influence on domestic political conflict or Japan's foreign policy toward China. To put it another way, there was gradually less need for strategic dialogue between Japan and China regarding the Korean peninsula.

Domestic politics trumps foreign policy

As a result of the concatenation of all these factors, the significance of the embassies to Tang China shifted more in the direction of domestic politics than foreign policy. For one thing, there were signs that the dispatch to and reception of envoys from Tang China had been accorded importance as a ceremony accompanying the accession of crown princes to the imperial throne.[12] Moreover, as typified by the 804 embassy to the Tang court, which was accompanied by the monks Saichō and Kūkai, the domestic political considerations of the Buddhist clergy and their supporters had become involved in the dispatch of the embassies, as the Buddhist establishment sought to further solidify its position in Japan by sending monks along with the embassies to receive the political cachet that came with the voyage to China.[13]

The more the dispatch of the embassies became interwoven with domestic political ambitions, the greater the friction that arose among the members of the missions themselves, and there were some cases in which appointments as an envoy were met with de facto refusals. Such examples suggest, conversely, that the motivation had weakened for sending the embassies as a means to fulfill diplomatic or national strategy.[14] In this context, it seems an almost natural development that when Sugawara no Michizane was appointed chief envoy nearly sixty years after the last embassy was sent in 836, his memorial to the throne arguing for the termination of the embassies was officially approved.[15] It is probable that Michizane's appointment as envoy had been made for purely domestic political reasons, and the alacrity with which he refused it and petitioned the throne is indicative of this.

Michizane's memorial is well known for citing the decline of the Tang dynasty itself and the dangers of the ocean voyage as reasons for suspending the embassies, though these factors had already been more or less acknowledged for some time previously (with some room for argument over the situation of the Tang). Coupled with the fiscal difficulties experienced by the imperial court from the mid-Heian period onward, they make Michizane's memorial seem almost inevitable. In other words, there is reason to believe that Michizane's appointment as envoy was in itself "no more than a gesture," and one following a political scenario designed to elicit both Michizane's memorial and the termination of the embassies that it proposed.[16]

Others have suggested that, as in a previous campaign of slander directed at Michizane,[17] his appointment as envoy was a plot to remove him from the domestic political scene by sending him overseas, perhaps to meet with shipwreck or other misfortune on the voyage. In any case, with the decline in the diplomatic and strategic significance of the embassies to Tang China, the appointment of envoys became even more heavily influenced by domestic political factors.

Yet if we look at this process from a different perspective, it is also possible to conclude that the foreign policy issue of relations with China had actually become decoupled from domestic politics as a result of its waning political significance. The strategic relationship between Tang China and Japan disappeared with the termination of the embassies, but the embassies were also terminated precisely because the strategic rewards had become so insubstantial.

The inwardness of the Heian nobility

From the time of Sugawara no Michizane's memorial to the rise of Taira no Kiyomori, for nearly two centuries (the tenth and eleventh), the politics of the Heian court was characterized by a marked turning away from the outside world.

Many of the Heian court nobility regarded foreigners and contact with them as "unclean" (kegare). An episode from the "Fujitsubo" chapter of The Tale of Genji illustrates this tendency among the Heian nobility. The birth of an imperial heir occasions the desire to consult a (Song) Chinese diviner to read the child's physiognomy—but because inviting a foreigner within the palace grounds would "pollute" it, the child is taken outside the palace to be seen by the diviner instead. In another example, in 1170 Taira no Kiyomori invited the cloistered emperor

Go-Shirakawa to his villa at Fukuhara (present-day Kobe), and arranged a meeting between the former emperor and visitors from Song China, causing the Minister of the Right, Fujiwara no Kanezane, to lament that this was "the work of the devil."[18] This incident also suggests the xenophobic tendencies of the Heian nobility.

Such attitudes naturally enough influenced the realities of foreign policy. We see an example of this in the 1070s. In 1072 the monk Jōjin and his disciples went to Song China. When the disciples returned bearing an official letter and gifts from Emperor Shenzong, the Japanese court dithered over how to respond to this communication for five years before finally sending to China another Buddhist monk, Chūkai, to deliver a response (not in the name of the emperor, but that of a court official) and gifts in return. After dispatching Chūkai, the Japanese made no further efforts to maintain relations; it was the Chinese who followed up with communications from regional officials and a state letter from the Song court.[19] This situation continued until Kiyomori's era, even though Song merchants would repeatedly arrive in Japan bearing letters and gifts during the intervening years. What were the reasons behind this?

First of all, Japan seemed unable to cope with the major changes that were taking place on the Asian mainland as, at the beginning of the tenth century, the Tang dynasty collapsed, followed by the collapse of Balhae in 926, and Silla was supplanted by Goryeo. Yet perhaps even more significantly, the Song dynasty that arose to rule China adopted a stance of "cultivating literature and scorning the military"—firmly establishing a policy of civilian rule and a priority on economic activity. The Song aimed at maintaining peaceful relations with neighboring states and peoples (such as the Jin and Western Hsia) by fostering stability through the provision of trade incentives (supplies of silver, silk, tea, and other tribute goods). These Song policies were also applied to Japan, and while many Song merchants maintained trade relations (both official and illicit) with Japan, no official invitation came from the Song court for diplomatic or strategic relations at the governmental level.

In addition to this, the Japanese domestic political system had an influence. Heian court politics was rule by authority and status, the maintenance of which was enabled primarily by heredity and conservatism. By the tenth century the Heian court had more or less assimilated Tang-style culture and the *ritsuryō* system of imperial bureaucracy supporting it, and no longer felt any pressing need to keep importing customs and institutions from China in order to establish the authority of its rule.

The activities of Buddhist clergy

Even though diplomatic and strategic relations at the governmental level were almost entirely absent during the tenth and eleventh centuries, Japanese Buddhist clergy traveled to China with reasonable regularity, and were welcome at the Chinese imperial court. What are we to make of this?

Let's look at a few of the major examples of contact between Japanese Buddhist clergy and the Chinese court during this period.

983   Chōnen visits Song China, has an audience with the Emperor Taizong.

1008   Japanese monks reach the Song court, where they memorialize the Emperor Zhenzong, saying "to the east of the country an auspicious light appeared in the sky, which older people said was a marvelous sign that the Son of Heaven of the central realm was an enlightened ruler." The Emperor Zhenzong was delighted and built a temple for them.

1073   The monk Jōjin, accompanied by seven disciples, arrives in Song China. Five of the disciples return to Japan bearing a letter of state and official gifts from Emperor Shenzong.

1078   The monk Chūkai goes to China with a reply from a Japanese court official and gifts in return.[20]

Various historical factors were thus at work in the activities of Japanese monks,[21] but the passivity of the Japanese central government and the secular political designs of the Buddhist clergy were certainly both involved. From the perspective of the court nobility, faced with increased disorder in the provinces and aware that the illicit foreign trade of powerful local magnates was on the rise,[22] and aware that they did not have the power to control these developments, the most desirable thing was to minimize the impact of foreign affairs on domestic politics. As for the monks, the Buddhist clergy were at the time a kind of unofficial political force, and one path to enhancing their personal authority and expanding their power was to study abroad in China.[23]

The Heian period and the present

This history of the Heian court is not without relevance to the present day. Before mainland China and Japan took the momentous step of normalizing their relations in 1972, a variety of Japanese goodwill ambassadors had traveled back and forth to China. Andt whatever the subjective intentions of these individuals, from the perspective of the country as a whole they were a valuable means for gleaning intelligence about the internal situation on the Chinese mainland while strenuously avoiding any blowback on Japanese domestic politics.

Inwardness does not necessarily entail shutting down information channels, and in every age there are individuals who can serve in that capacity. Participation in and engagement with international society can be conducted in a variety of dimensions—political and strategic, commercial and economic, cultural and intellectual—and the depth or breadth of contact and the sharing of information in any of these dimensions at any given time depend on the overall international situation and domestic political circumstances. Also, the types of people who are active in foreign relations—politicians, scholars, journalists, diplomats, businesspeople, cultural figures, clergy, and so on—may change according to the distance or proximity of a country to international society and the forms of its relations to it, as we can see from the relationship between Heian Japan and Song China.

The fact that a variety of unofficial emissaries from the ranks of academia and business are still employed even today is consistent with efforts to carry out exchanges of information while maintaining a firewall between foreign affairs and domestic politics.

"Withdrawal" in diplomacy with the Qing Empire

A diplomatic posture of withdrawal, or what we might see as a turning of its back on Asia, is strongly apparent in Tokugawa Japan's relations with Qing China.

If we regard the political system under the Tokugawa shogunate as having reached maturity, then its advent almost overlaps with the supplanting of the Ming dynasty by the Qing in the 1640s. Given the fact that some Ming loyalists tried to appeal to the Tokugawa shogunate for military support, relations between the Qing court and the shogunate were delicate from the start, but in view of the dramatic increase in Japan-China trade from the latter half of the seventeenth century onward, and in terms of enhancing the prestige and authority of Tokugawa rule, it would seem that the establishment of formal diplomatic relations with Qing China would have been desirable to the shogunate. Why, then, did Japan turn its back on Asia, and refrain from establishing formal relations with the Qing?

For one thing, there was the reality that the sharp increase in trade with China was draining Japan of gold and silver bullion, and so copper was introduced as a settlement currency, which in turn led to domestic shortages of copper. Yet it is inconceivable that this alone led immediately to restrictions on trade with China and the deliberate rejection of the establishment of formal political relations. Instead, we should suspect that there were other strategic considerations at work.

One of these strategic considerations was related to the homeland of the Qing dynasty—in other words, the nomadic peoples of the Chinese northeast—and their relations with Japan. This in turn was connected to the policy of the shogunate with regard to the Ezo region (essentially present-day Hokkaidō and the other islands to the north).

From the middle of the seventeenth century the shogunate formally acknowledged the control of the Matsumae domain over southern Ezo. Trade with the indigenous Ainu people was institutionalized, and with this development came alarm over the "threat" posed by the nomadic tribes of northeast China. Some highly placed shogunal officials were even concerned that the Ainu resistance movement (against the domination by the Matsumae domain) might possibly enlist the military assistance of the nomads.[24]

In addition to this threat from the nomadic tribes of China's northeast, the other concrete concern felt by the shogunate with regard to the Qing dynasty during this period was the extent to which Western culture and the Christian religion appeared to be penetrating China. In 1583 the Jesuit priest Matteo Ricci began missionary work in Guangdong, and in 1601 was granted right of permanent residence in Beijing. After the establishment of the Qing dynasty, the Shunzhi and Kangxi emperors continued to adopt a tolerant attitude toward the Christian missionaries. During the reign of Shunzhi, the German Jesuit Adam Schall (who adopted the Chinese name Tang Ruowang) was given an official appointment as an astronomer to the Qing court. Given these circumstances, it is reasonable to assume that there was concern, albeit vague, within the Tokugawa shogunate that contact between Japan and China, through trade via Luzon and Macao, might lead to an importation into Japan of Christian thought and Western culture.

Such factors had implications for the stability of the Tokugawa regime. Trade between Japan and Qing China, which had flourished for a time, was limited to less than half its former levels by Arai Hakuseki's Shōtoku Shinrei of 1715—a set of trade regulations ostensibly intended to prevent the outflow of gold and silver from Japan, but which was also strongly colored by the motive of defending Tokugawa prestige and authority in the face of a burgeoning smuggling trade between Chinese merchants and their Japanese associates.[25]

The overlapping of all these aforementioned factors led the Tokugawa shogunate to treat (Qing) China in almost the same manner as the Western nations—as a "barbarian nation" subject to the *sakoku* seclusion policies. Thus, from 1621 onward, contact with the Chinese had been under the exclusive jurisdiction of the Nagasaki commissioner's office, and nearly a century later, in 1715, as a result of Arai Hakuseki's reforms and the Shōtoku Shinrei, Chinese ships calling at the port of Nagasaki were required to carry certificates (*shinpai*) issued by the Nagasaki commissioner—certificates which used Japanese era names rather than those of the Qing Empire, which was not referred to by its official name of "Great Qing" (Da Qing).[26]

Meanwhile, among shogunal officials such as Hayashi Razan, it even became fashionable to refer to the Chinese as "barbarians" (*ban'i*).[27] Behind this we may assume lay a political motivation of emphasizing that Japan stood outside the Chinese world order, and even an attempt, conceptually, to subsume China into a world order centered upon Japan.

Hideyoshi had intended to incorporate China into a Japanese world order with his planned invasion of the Ming. The Tokugawa regime went about this in a different—and converse—manner, by conceptually positioning China in their worldview as a nation subject to the exclusionary edicts of *sakoku*. This was because the ultimate goal of the Tokugawa regime was to maintain control over the daimyo and maintain a stable domestic political order. Ironically, the Tokugawa shogunate was attempting to ensure the stability of its regime by subjecting China to the *sakoku* regulations and thereby creating its own version of the traditional Sinocentric world order of East Asia, with China positioned within it as a peripheral state.

On the other hand, one of the reasons that these Japanese policies toward China were successfully implemented according to Japanese intentions or strategy was the fact that the Qing diplomatic posture toward Japan formed a complementary pairing with Japanese policy vis-à-vis the Qing.

As soon as the Qing dynasty had achieved the unification of China under its rule, it adopted a stance towards Japan demanding the latter's submission to the authority of China. In 1644 the Shunzhi emperor decided to return thirteen Japanese who had been shipwrecked on the Chinese mainland, and requested the king of Korea to provide safe passage for them through his country. The rationale given for taking this measure was stated as follows: "Having brought unity both internal and external and made the four seas into a single household, the people of all nations are now my beloved subjects, and I must exert myself to provide them with their proper place in the world, thus extending my imperial benevolence to all."[28]

Thus, while the Qing dynasty had been established by nomadic tribes from the north who had overthrown the ethnically Han Chinese rulers of the Ming dynasty, they sought to inherit and uphold the traditional Sinocentric worldview and ideology. One of the clearest formulations of this is the *Da Qing yitong zhi*, a comprehensive imperial geography published in 1764 that depicts the Western nations and Japan all as barbarian realms that should properly pay tribute to Qing China. When attempting to actually apply this Sinocentric vision to Japan, the Qing used Korea as their diplomatic conduit. Just as the Yuan dynasty had consistently used the Korean state of Goryeo in negotiations with Japan, the Qing used Joseon-dynasty Korea as intermediary.

What this signified was that both the Yuan and Qing dynasties, as non-Chinese rulers of China, were attempting to establish that rule in the form of the traditional Sinocentric worldview developed by the Han Chinese. In so doing they found it useful to enlist the support of Korea—a state clearly established as a vassal or tributary of China—to the fullest extent possible. Another way of putting this is to say that for China it was essential for reasons of geography and history to clearly situate the Korean peninsula inside the Chinese world order. Japan was seen *conceptually* as a state to whom the Chinese world order should also apply; but *in reality* it was not regarded as essential to bring it fully within the Sinocentric order.

For Japan under the Tokugawa shogunate, even if China was viewed *conceptually* as "barbarian," *in reality* China was not a tributary of Japan. Conversely, though the Qing dynasty might treat Japan *conceptually* as a tributary, *in reality* no such relationship had been established—a situation which the Qing seemed content to continue to ignore in their diplomatic posture towards Japan.

The real meaning of "leaving Asia and joining Europe"
This examination of the connection between foreign policy strategy and domestic politics in the Tokugawa regime's relationship to Qing China reveals that the real meaning of the well-known phrase "leaving Asia and joining Europe" (*datsu-A nyū-Ō*) is somewhat different than is usually understood. This phrase tends to be taken to signify, from a

diplomatic and political perspective, leaving the traditional Sinocentric world order to participate in the Western-style international system, and from a cultural perspective, to refer to the supplanting of Chinese culture by the assimilation of European culture.

Certainly, on a superficial level, it would be difficult to deny the appearance of such developments. Yet, as we have seen, in the Tokugawa period Japan did not maintain formal diplomatic relations with the Qing dynasty, and even China was subject to Japanese *sakoku* regulations. If this was the case, then the transition brought about by the Meiji Restoration (1868), in terms of foreign relations, was the opening of the country, not a "departure from Asia." This was because Japan had in fact already turned its back on Asia.

Herein lies one of the reasons why Japan, unlike the other East Asian countries, was able to come to grips so speedily with the process of modernization—it did not have to make a fresh effort to extricate itself from the traditional Chinese world order. In other countries, such as Joseon (Yi)-dynasty Korea or Vietnam, their response to the West was simultaneously enmeshed with the ways in which they coped with the traditional Sinocentric world order.

In other words, the Meiji Restoration was achieved along two axes: (1) a domestic political transformation and (2) a response to the West. In that process, concerns for Chinese suzerainty or for the integrity of the Sinocentric world order were essentially unnecessary (a point which is clearly illustrated by the differences in approach between Japan and Joseon-dynasty Korea in their diplomatic negotiations during the early Meiji period, discussed in greater detail in Part IV of this book).

Sakoku *as foreign policy*

In any case, if we are to consider the so-called policy of *sakoku*, or national seclusion, as an integral aspect of Japan's foreign policy during the Tokugawa period, then we must see it as a way of attempting to deal with the clash of values and ideologies between the outside world and Japan in a way that preserved both domestic political stability and the military and political security of the nation.

In today's world it would appear that only a very small number of countries—such as North Korea— are attempting to maintain similar foreign policies of seclusion. Yet viewed in terms of degree of involvement in international society, Japan's policy of "exclusive self-defense" (*senshu bōei*) is in a sense a policy of retreating, as it were, inside one's castle walls, and therefore shares some elements of the *sakoku* concept.

There is another point of correspondence between the concept of "exclusive self-defense" that forms the foundation of contemporary Japanese foreign policy and the traditional policy of *sakoku*. And that is the abandonment of any principle or concept of the exercise of military force overseas. In both cases, the premise is that the maintenance and strengthening of an established domestic order (in the Tokugawa period, the *bakuhan* system; in the present day, a liberal-democratic system based on the "peace constitution") require that the country refrain from the exercise of military force abroad.

Moreover, the maintenance of the domestic political order, connected with the contemporary Japanese conviction that sees a resort to warfare as evil except when absolutely necessary for the physical defense of the homeland, bears a peculiar resemblance to maintenance of the *bakuhan* system in its connection with the logic and ethos of samurai society. In this regard, there is contemporary significance in spending some time examining how the *sakoku* policies came into being, beginning with Hideyoshi's edict expelling the Christian missionaries.

The expulsion edict

Hideyoshi's expulsion edict, implemented in the summer of 1587,[29] may have come as a surprise to the missionaries themselves, but various factors—especially the thoroughness with which it was promulgated to the daimyo—make it clear that some time had been spent in its preparation. For precisely this reason, it seems unthinkable that Hideyoshi, who had long shown no signs of antipathy to the missionaries, should suddenly implement such a radical alteration of his foreign policy on a mere whim or shift in personal feeling. Rather, we should see his policies as based in careful consideration of political and diplomatic strategy.

First of all, it is significant that the year was 1587. In the fifth month of that year (Tenshō 15), Shimazu Yoshihisa of Satsuma capitulated to Hideyoshi, and within a few weeks' time the two Christian daimyo Ōmura Sumitada of Hizen and Ōtomo Sōrin of Bungo had both died—suddenly eliminating the need for Hideyoshi to show tolerance for Christianity in order to elicit the political support of the Christian daimyo against the Shimazu clan, the dominant power in Kyushu. Rather, having now brought Kyushu under his control, Hideyoshi not surprisingly became concerned that foreign powers might use the domains of the Christian daimyo in that region to foment internal disorder.

In addition, in an eleven-point edict issued by Hideyoshi at about the same time as the expulsion edict, it was explicitly forbidden to compel the peasantry to join either the Christian religion or the Ikkō sect of Buddhism, which suggests that the motivation was to prevent adherence of the common people to specific religious creeds that might lead them to challenge Hideyoshi's authority.

What should be noted here in connection with Japanese foreign policy in Asia is the fear that Christianity and other forms of Western thought might lead to the strengthening of subversive forces; in other words, that there was a strongly perceived apprehension regarding colonization by the West that was occasioned by the Western advance into Asia (even in Japan, certain of the daimyo made donations of land to the Christian church,[30] which may have been one of the factors fueling Hideyoshi's apprehensions regarding the advance of the incursions of the West).

In other words, *sakoku*—the closing of Japan—was a security policy implemented in an attempt to isolate the country from the outside world out of fear that external threats might ally with internal forces to challenge the established order.

Solidarity with Asia

If this is the case, then we must ask why Hideyoshi and the Tokugawa shogunate did not display any interest in cooperating with China to address concerns over the advance of Western colonialism into Asia—or at least why they did not clearly exclude China and Korea from their *sakoku* policies from the beginning.

The answer almost certainly is related to Hideyoshi's policies toward mainland Asia. Hideyoshi's intent was apparently to invade Korea and subjugate Ming China (or conversely, to establish stable relations with it). And, as we shall see later, this intent was not unrelated to the advance of Western powers into Asia and Japan. Hideyoshi's expansion into continental Asia was an effort to create a new order there in the face of the Western incursion. In short, Hideyoshi's Asian policies were tied to his policies for dealing with the "Southern barbarians"—the Spanish and Portuguese.

Yet the Tokugawa shogunate that followed Hideyoshi—no doubt in part because of the dynastic change from Ming to Qing that was occurring in China just as Tokugawa power was being consolidated—chose instead to pursue a policy of withdrawal from the Asian continent. Nearly four centuries later, similar circumstances led to war between Japan and China (1937–1945), followed by a break of over two decades in relations between the two countries.

The logic of trade restrictions

Regarding the *sakoku* policies, we should note that Hideyoshi was quite liberal with regard to trade, and did not attempt to impose any special restrictions upon it. In fact, his edict expelling the Christian missionaries explicitly stated that trade was quite a different matter. For a time, the Tokugawa shogunate strove to encourage foreign trade, even establishing an outpost in Taiwan for that purpose.[31]

Several factors were involved in the gradual evolution toward increasingly severe restrictions on trade. One (as noted earlier) was a perception of the danger that individuals ostensibly coming to Japan for trade might in secret be attempting to proselytize for the Christian faith. It is likely this was also tied to the shogunate's desire to monopolize the foreign trade that had until that time been divided among the various daimyo, as well as a desire to prevent the European merchants themselves from developing a de facto monopoly. In any case, the most important reason was probably fear of the social consequences of the expansion of trade networks and merchant activity that might destabilize the ideology and dominance of the samurai class.[32]

Here as well, we see a desire to maintain domestic stability strongly reflected in foreign policy.

Domestic politics and the diplomacy of withdrawal

As we have seen, in the diplomacy of withdrawal, security policy and the stability of the domestic political order were intimately connected. In the contemporary world as well, in the case of the North Korean regime, for example, the strict limitations it has imposed on not only political but also economic contact with international society are no doubt the product of the internal political necessities of maintaining and bolstering domestic order.

If this is the case, what has enabled China, also ostensibly a communist country, to proclaim reform and openness, and adopt more liberal economic policies? This is because the policies adopted position the Communist Party organization itself as an agent for economic growth and the efficient distribution of economic benefits, situating the legitimacy of the regime not in the pursuit of communistic equality but in economic development. Yet as a result today's China must struggle with issues of corruption and a growing disparity of wealth. To put it another way, there are no guarantees that a proper balance can be struck between the stability of the political situation in China and the extent and form of its openness to the outside world, so the degree of involvement China will maintain in international society is not easy to predict.

Moreover, if the goal is to encourage China's engagement with international society insofar as possible, then, the first factor to be considered is the country's domestic political stability. In short, if a so-called policy of engagement with China is to be implemented, then considerable care must be exercised in terms of external demands regarding democratization or human rights issues in China. Conduct of a "moral diplomacy" insisting that China share the values generally recognized by international society can be one aspect of a policy of engagement, but we should be aware that if this threatens to damage the internal political stability of the country, China, rather than becoming more engaged, is instead likely to withdraw entirely from engagement with the outside world.

3. THE DILEMMA OF INTERNAL AND EXTERNAL: JAPAN'S RESPONSE TO FORCES FOR REFORM IN ASIA

Cooperation with antigovernment forces

In Japan's Asian diplomacy there have been times when the relationship between governments has been close to collusion, or when they have used each other for political purposes; but there have also been times when Japan has linked itself with antigovernment or even insurgent forces in its relations with the countries of continental Asia.

In ancient times, Japan's expedition in support of the restoration of the Korean kingdom of Baekje, down to the defeat in the Battle of Baekgangu (Jpn.: Hakusukinoe) in 663 could be seen, depending upon one's perspective, as an alliance with pro-Baekje insurgent forces against the Korean kingdom of Silla and Tang China. Later, on the eve of the attempted Mongol invasions of Japan in the thirteenth century, there was a revolt, known as the Sambyeolcho (Three Elite Patrols) Rebellion, against Mongol domination of Korea and the capitulation of the Goryeo dynasty to the invaders. The insurgent forces sought support from Japan, and the question of how to respond to the matter was debated at both the imperial and shogunal courts, but no support was forthcoming.[33] During the transitional period in the seventeenth century between the Ming and Qing dynasties as well, Ming loyalists appealed to the Tokugawa shogunate for assistance, which is another case in which insurgent forces at least believed there might be a possibility of gaining the cooperation of Japan in their cause.

In modern times, the concept and nature of cooperation between Japan and antigovernment or anticolonial forces in Korea, China, Vietnam, India, and elsewhere has been at various times an extremely delicate diplomatic and political issue involving Japan's relations with the other countries' governments and/or their colonizers.

Virtually the first example in which Japan became involved in a major way in a reform movement on the Asian continent was in its response to the activities of the Independence Association (Dongnip Hyeophoe, 1896–98) and its successor, the Iljinhoe (1904–10). The Association denounced the corruption of the government of the Joseon

81

dynasty and sought to secure independence for Korea centered around the monarchy of King (later Emperor) Gojong.

There is evidence that among Japanese military officials there was interest in utilizing such political developments in Korea for strategic purposes in the war with Russia,[34] but foreign policy officials were less enthusiastic about cultivating ties to such dissident elements, fearing that as they developed into mass movements they would invite unrest and disorder and create a general destabilization of the political situation in Korea. Because of this, Japanese diplomatic officials felt it was desirable to encourage a suppression of these movements.[35]

As far as relations with China were concerned, Japan had to respond to the eruption of the so-called Boxer Rebellion (or Yihetuan Movement, 1898–1900), a popular movement based in martial arts and folk religion that spread rapidly through Shandong province to Beijing, under the slogan "Support the Qing, Eliminate the Westerners." In response to efforts by the Qing dynasty to utilize the rebellion as a means to drive the Western powers from China, the Japanese government chose to cooperate with the Western powers in implementing sanctions and working to prevent the movement from spreading to central and south China, where the foreign economic interests were then concentrated.[36]

This policy was completely devoid of any insight into the historical significance of the Boxer Rebellion. In other words, there was little or no appreciation or consideration of the long-term consequences of the fact that while the Yihetuan Movement had clearly ethnic and nationalistic elements, popular antipathy toward the incursion of the Western powers into China had reached such heights that the Manchu rulers of the Qing dynasty had no choice but to support the movement.

In addition, the stance adopted by the Japanese authorities was motivated not only by a desire for cooperation with the Western powers, but also by issues related to Japanese colonial management of Taiwan. By the late 1890s a Taiwanese resistance movement against Japan had arisen.[37] Wishing to suppress it, Japanese officials were concerned that the repercussions of the Boxer Rebellion might reach South China, and particularly the vicinity of Fujian province opposite Taiwan.

If the Yihetuan Movement is seen as a manifestation of Chinese nationalism, then the intentions of Japan's leaders to "control" this nationalism through cooperation with the Western powers and compromise with the Qing government were connected to the Japanese response to the nationalist movement in South China and Japan's colonial enterprise in Taiwan. Moreover, at the time Russia was taking a somewhat different approach than the other great powers, attempting to expand its own interests in North China by supporting the Qing government, and this also had an impact on Japanese policy.

Japan's betrayal of progressive forces in Asia: The cases of Kim Okgyun and of Kim Daejung

In 1881, a "Korean Courtiers' Observation Mission" led by Kim Hongjip was dispatched by Joseon-dynasty Korea to visit Japan, where its members met with Japanese leaders and intellectuals and made an inspection tour of the country. Among the members of the mission was Kim Okgyun, a staunch advocate for reform in Korea. At the time of the mission Kim Okgyun was not yet a leader of antigovernment forces, but in 1882 the reactionary Daewongun, the former regent to King Gojong, seized power in a coup d'état known as the Imo Incident. This had the effect of deepening Qing China's interference in Korean affairs, and in an effort to counter that, Kim Okgyun planned and executed a countercoup, the Gapsin Coup of 1884. This three-day coup by pro-Japanese reformists aimed at replacing the king's closest advisors and seizing the initiative for the modernization of Korea by breaking off relations with the Qing and drawing closer to Japan. Its failure resulted in increased Chinese domination of Korea in the decade from 1885 to 1894.

Then, nearly a hundred years later, in 1973, there was the Kim Daejung incident, in which Kim, leader of the democratization movement opposing what might be called the military regime of Park Jeonghui, was kidnapped by Korean intelligence operatives while on a visit to Japan and forcibly returned to Korea.

If we compare these two cases, we can see a certain similarity in the Japanese attitude toward reform and democratization movements in neighboring Korea, despite the passage of a century and the differing nature of the two incidents — similarities that are bound up with the issues of morality and ideology in Japanese diplomacy toward Asia.

First of all, what was the response to the Gapsin Coup and Kim Okgyun's subsequent political activities? On the eve of the Gapsin Coup in 1884, the officials of the Japanese legation in Seoul proposed two different plans for dealing with the situation to their superiors in Tokyo. The first was to avoid a direct confrontation with Qing China, offering only safe haven to Kim Okgyun and his "Japan faction." The second was to give full cooperation to Kim and his allies and touch off a full-fledged revolt, which might result in war with Qing China. (It should be noted that there was an addendum to this communication from Tokyo warning that even if Japan exercised caution at this juncture, if matters were left as they were, Korea would continue to regard Qing China as a great power upon which it was dependent, and that Japan must do something to combat the Qing influence; if it did not, the "Japan faction" would be forced into a desperate position, and might resort to terrorist activities).[38]

The response of the Japanese government to this was a policy of advising Kim Okgyun and his associates to restrain themselves and not prematurely launch an uprising, ostensibly because ". . . it would be to our advantage if, for the time being, we worked to induce those persons calling themselves the 'Japan faction' to exert themselves, using peaceful methods, to bring about the enlightenment of their country."[39]

However, given the fact that Japan was at that time providing both direct and indirect support to Kim Okgyun and his associates, the policy articulated above was really for nothing more than external consumption. Japan needed a pretext or rationale for supporting the Korean reformers with the use of force, and it did not have one (while, on the other hand, China possessed such an excuse for intervening in Korean affairs as Korea was officially a tributary of the Qing Empire).

Because of this, in dealing with the failure of the Gapsin Coup, the Japanese government blamed the involvement of Japanese troops on an overreach of authority by the Japanese minister in Korea, Takezoe Shin'ichirō, and swept the matter under the rug, settling with the Korean government the damages to Japanese nationals and to the legation itself through the conclusion of the Treaty of Hanseong (the present-day Seoul), by which Korea made an apology for the incident and paid reparations.[40] The Japanese government also took the stance that it was not responsible for the escape of Kim Okgyun and his associates aboard the *Chitose Maru*, a Japanese ship anchored in Incheon harbor, and their flight to Japan.[41]

In fact, it is believed that Japanese minister Takezoe initially agreed to a demand by Paul Georg von Mollendorff, a German advisor to the Korean government stationed in Incheon, to hand over the nine Koreans, including Kim, who had boarded the *Chitose Maru*, but that the fugitives were not remanded to Korean custody because the ship's captain, Tsuji Katsusaburō, stubbornly insisted that no such persons had come aboard his vessel.[42] In short, the fundamental official position of the Japanese government, Minister Takezoe included, was to strenuously deny that it had been supporting Kim and his comrades.

There followed a lengthy series of negotiations between the Japanese and Korean governments over the repatriation of Kim, now a refugee in Japan. Initially the Japanese government staunchly refused to deliver Kim to Korea. When the Korean envoy So Sangu, with Mollendorff as his assistant, came to Japan in March 1885, he requested the Japanese to arrest and deport Kim and the members of his "band of rascals." But Foreign Vice-Minister Yoshida Kiyonari and other officials of the Japanese government responded that while there were rumors in the newspapers that Kim and company had fled to Japan, the government was unable to confirm this. When the Koreans responded by suggesting that perhaps the government should investigate the newspapers' sources, Japanese officials pushed back, saying that there were no grounds in international law (*bankoku kōhō*) obliging them to hand over the Korean refugees.[43]

However, with the signing of the Tianjin Convention in April 1885 between Japan and Qing China, Japan's right to station troops in Korea in time of emergency was recognized. Moreover, at about the same time, the British Navy occupied Geomundo (Port Hamilton), a small group of islands off the south coast of Korea, on the pretext of protecting the Korea Strait from Russian naval activity. Faced with the perceived need for cooperation with the Qing against third parties in the region, the Japanese government became even more concerned with maintaining relations with China.

On top of all this, there was the so-called Osaka Incident of January 1885, led by Ōi Kentarō and Kobayashi Kusuo. They intended to go to Korea with a small band of a score or so of like-minded popular rights activists and foment a revolt there, hoping in turn to bring about the resignation of the Japanese government or even trigger a full-scale revolution in Japan. But there was dissension in the ranks of their supporters, and word of the plot leaked out, leading to a series of arrests. Ōi Kentarō was a member of the more radical wing of the Jiyūtō, or Liberal Party. The failure of a series of attempts to foment uprisings among the poorer peasantry appears to have led him to the conclusion that the Korean issue could be utilized to effect a change in the domestic political situation. Kim Okgyun was a close acquaintance of Kobayashi's, and while there is no concrete evidence that Kim was directly involved in their plot,[44] Japanese officialdom was being confronted with the reality that the presence of Kim Okgyun in Japan was problematic not only in terms of the Korean issue but because of possible domestic political repercussions as well.

Given these circumstances, the attitude of the Japanese government toward Kim gradually cooled, and he was eventually shipped off to the Ogasawara Islands. After two years there, he was sent to Sapporo in Hokkaido, and then to Shanghai, where he was murdered by an assassin dispatched by the Korean government.[45]

This convoluted history of the Japanese government's treatment of Kim Okgyun reveals three significant points concerning the nature of Japanese foreign policy. The first is the issue of official government involvement. In the case of both Kim Okgyun's failed coup and his flight to Japan, the involvement of the Japanese legation and the Japanese government itself was an undeniable fact; yet the government denied this, attempting to evade direct diplomatic and political responsibility by blaming any Japanese involvement in the coup attempt on the legation officials having exceeded their authority.

Second, behind the adoption of such a stance (as we have seen in connection with the Osaka Incident), lay concerns that foreign affairs would have a major impact on the domestic political situation.

And third, a strategy of cooperation with the Korean government, and behind it, the Qing Empire—albeit temporary in nature—was what seems to have in the end sealed the fate of Kim Okgyun as far as Japan was concerned.

If we hold this mirror of history up to the Kim Daejung incident of the 1970s, we see three similar points. First of all, the fact of the kidnapping of Kim from a Tokyo hotel by KCIA operatives, an illegitimate act by an official government authority (and thus a violation of Japanese sovereignty), was denied to the end by both Korean and Japanese governments, who dealt with the issue as a "private" matter involving individuals such as Kim Dong Un (the first secretary of the Korean embassy in Tokyo at the time), whose fingerprints were found at the scene.

Second, behind this was a political resolution reached as a result of a visit by Korean prime minister Kim Jong Pil, former head of the KCIA, to Tokyo, suggesting that both the Japanese and Korean governments were operating out of a concern for preventing the incident from having an impact on domestic politics that might destabilize the political base of either government.

Third, we must consider the international situation at that time. In 1973, the year of the Kim Daejung incident, the process of normalizing relations between Japan and China and between the United States and China had just commenced, while at the same time tensions between China and the Soviet Union were deepening. In this context, maintaining the stability of relations between Japan and South Korea was of particular strategic importance.

Thus the treatment of Kim Okgyun and the handling of the Kim Daejung incident were both characterized by an evasion of responsibility based on domestic political concerns and a resolution based on bilateral strategic interests—in which one can detect almost no definite moral or philosophical commitment on the part of Japan to Korean modernization or democratization. This in turn provides us with a glimpse of the betrayal of progressive forces by Japan's Asian diplomacy.

A tale of two Boses and Japan's view of Asia

If Japan's rationale for support for Korean activists such as Kim Okgyun had been predicated morally or philosophically on the ideal of assisting Korea's modernization, the spirit of the anticolonial independence movements was another Asian ideal that required a Japanese response. Among the leaders of such movements who drew close to Japan in pursuit of the ideal of independence were Rash Behari Bose and Subhas Chandra Bose of India.

R. B. Bose was born in 1886 in an agricultural village near Chandannagar, north of Calcutta. While working as a minor official for the colonial government, Bose led a double life, secretly devoting himself to agitation against British rule. World War I proved to be a turning point, however, and in 1915 he was involved in plotting an uprising in Lahore that failed when plans leaked prematurely.

As a result of this incident, British surveillance of Bose and his comrades grew more intense, and his range of action was greatly restricted. Realizing that weapons would be needed if another uprising were to be attempted, Bose traveled to Japan with the primary goal of purchasing arms. He arrived in Japan in June of 1915, traveling under an assumed name.[46]

As Bose established a base for himself in Japan, and labored to establish connections with anticolonial movements in other Asian nations, several of his comrades were arrested in Singapore by the British, who discovered from captured documents that the Indian national residing in Japan under the alias Thakur was actually the R. B. Bose sought by British colonial authorities.

Hence, the British informed the Japanese government that Mr. Thakur was wanted for crimes committed in India, and requested his immediate arrest and deportation to Singapore.[47] The Japanese government maintained a cautious and deliberate attitude toward this request. It did not immediately comply, but neither did it wish to damage its alliance with Britain. A series of negotiations ensued between the two countries over whether Bose should be deported or permitted to remain in Japan. The British desired Bose to be deported, either to Shanghai or (preferably) Hong Kong.[48] They were considering a plan to have him taken into custody by the British navy while en route. The British informed the Japanese government that, if Japan were to be unwilling to go along with such a scheme, rather than Japan deporting Bose to Shanghai, they would prefer him to be allowed to remain in Japan but to be kept under close surveillance.[49]

The Japanese government, which from the beginning had been unenthusiastic about forcibly deporting Bose, took this stance of the British into consideration and allowed Bose to remain in Japan while monitoring his activities. So it was that on 27 November 1915, Bose attended a banquet of Indian residents in Japan at the restaurant Sei-yōken in Ueno. The atmosphere of this gathering had a pronounced anti-British tinge, with some of the Japanese attending it speaking openly of independence for India.[50] As a result, the day after the banquet Bose was served an order of deportation by the Japanese police. But the reason given was that Bose had been associating with German spies and engaging in espionage activities for Germany.[51]

On the one hand, the Japanese government had been reluctant to deport Bose; but behind the sudden decision to expel Bose from the country after his participation in the anti-British assembly of Indian residents was the government's concern for honoring the terms of the Third Anglo-Japanese Alliance (signed in 1911), one of the objectives of which, as stated in the third clause of its preamble, was

> c. The maintenance of the territorial rights of the High Contracting Parties [viz., Britain and Japan] in the regions of Eastern Asia and of India, and the defence of their special interests in the said regions.

Pursuant to this, Article 1 of the treaty read:

> It is agreed that whenever, in the opinion of either Great Britain or Japan, any of the rights and interests referred to in the preamble of this Agreement [i.e., items a, b, c above] are in jeopardy, the two Governments will communicate with one another fully and frankly,

and consider in common the measures which should be taken to safeguard those menaced rights or interests.

This article was in turn based on articles 3 and 4 of the Second Anglo-Japanese Alliance (signed 1905), in which the two powers, Japan and Great Britain, mutually recognized one another's imperialist special rights and interests in Korea and India, respectively. However, by the time of the third alliance in 1911, Japan had already annexed Korea, so in the revised treaty the reference to Korea was replaced by the vaguer wording of "Eastern Asia."

In other words, one of the key elements of the Anglo-Japanese Alliance (in all three of its versions) was that it was based on a deal between Japan and Britain in which the two pledged to protect one another's rights in Korea and India. If one read between the lines this also meant a tacit agreement that Japan would assist in suppressing the Indian independence movement and anti-British agitation, while for its part Britain would cooperate in controlling anti-Japanese activities among the Koreans.

If Japan's annexation of Korea is considered to be a "betrayal" of Asia, then it could also be said to have led to a second betrayal in the cold shoulder Japan showed to Indian anticolonial activists—and one catalyst for these betrayals was the Anglo-Japanese Alliance.

Another "Asia"

In examining Japan's response to the Indian independence movement, particularly in regard to the Anglo-Japanese Alliance, we find evidence, as already mentioned, that Japan's honoring of the terms of the alliance was connected to an indecisive stance toward the question of Indian independence. But there is a further question we need to ask in assessing this from the perspective of Japan's overall foreign policy in Asia. And that is whether or not, in its diplomatic response to Britain and the Indian independence movement, Japan actually considered India to be, like itself, a part of Asia.

In order for us to definitively state that the mutual recognition of special interests in the Anglo-Japanese Alliance implied a betrayal of Asia, and that the Japanese response to the Indian independence movement was a manifestation of this betrayal, a crucial premise must be fulfilled: i.e., that Japan regarded India as part of Asia in the first place. This might seem at first to be an obvious premise, but in fact the matter is not so simple. For example, we should recall the Japanese attitude—and the Indian assessment of it—when Captain Mohan Singh formed the Indian National Army in 1941, raising the flag of revolt against the British, and requested the Japanese to inform him what their "Greater East Asian Co-Prosperity Sphere" meant in concrete terms. Japan gave no clear response to Singh's query. And Singh, seeing this attitude on the part of Japan (and sensing that India was not to be included in Japan's "Co-Prosperity Sphere"), sardonically remarked that all the prosperity from this new order would accrue to the Japanese and that the other nations of Asia would have to content themselves with the leftovers.[52] This might be said to hint at the dual betrayal of Asia by Japanese foreign policy.

Subhas Chandra Bose and Japanese diplomacy

This type of betrayal might also be seen in Japan's treatment of Subhas Chandra Bose.

Bose had for many years based himself in Germany engaging in anti-British activities, and Nazi Germany had protected him as a valuable asset in its operations against Britain, but as the tide of war turned against the Germans in Europe, Bose shifted the focus of his activities to Japan. In other words, Bose was first of all a clandestine operative in Germany's war against Britain, and not a figure that Japan had supported from the beginning. It is well known that from 1943 onwards, Japanese army intelligence began to perceive the potential military value of the anti-British movement in India and began to plan and take concrete steps towards utilizing Subhas Chandra Bose, especially in his military capacity as one of the leaders of the Indian National Army. Yet as of the summer of 1942, even the Japanese army was not very enthusiastic about the idea of summoning Bose to Japan from Europe, out of concern for what Germany might think.[53]

Then, after the failure of its campaign in North Africa in November 1942, Germany began to lose interest in Indian operations, and sent representatives to the Japanese ambassador to Germany, Ōshima Hiroshi, to sound out the Japanese on the idea of sending Bose to Japan. But the Japanese foreign ministry was unenthusiastic about giving him permission to enter or remain in the country—"If [Bose] really insists on coming to Japan we might admit him, but we should avoid any commitment prior to his arrival."[54]

Later, Subhas Chandra Bose was invited (although only as an "observer") to attend the Greater East Asian Conference held in Tokyo in November 1943, where he vowed to join forces with the Japanese army. That encouraged Japan (and especially the military) to make use of Bose and the Indian National Army in the ill-fated Japanese operations against Burma and India, culminating in the disastrous Imphal campaign. Yet throughout this time, the interest of the Japanese government officials in Bose was almost exclusively in relation to the military usefulness of the Indian National Army, and there were at least three major points of divergence between Bose and the Japanese.

The first concerned interference by the Japanese military in the internal affairs of the Indian National Army, for strategic and tactical reasons, that appeared to compromise the INA's autonomy and aroused discontent among its members.[55]

The second was both a philosophical and strategic rift. Bose believed that in order to overthrow British rule in India, it was important not only to have military assistance from Japan but also to mobilize support from the Soviet Union and China for India's independence movement. Japan did not agree with this strategy.

The third point is related to the second. Bose intended to expand the scope of not just military but political activities by securing international recognition for an Indian provisional government headed by himself and his associates. In contrast, the Japanese showed no enthusiasm for this, right down to the period of the Imphal campaign, offering various legalistic objections to the recognition of a provisional government and arguing that it did not yet deserve such status.[56]

The way in which the physical transport of Bose's person from Germany to Japan was arranged is symbolic of all these rifts. At the beginning of 1943, the passage of Bose to Japan was agreed upon in discussions between Germany and the Japanese military authorities. Since a land voyage would have been difficult if not impossible given the state of relations with the Soviet Union, it was agreed that Bose would be transported by a German submarine, and his transfer to a Japanese navy submarine would take place at sea. Yet even so, there were objections to this by the Japanese side on the grounds that Bose was a civilian, and agreement was reached only after the Germans had overcome these objections by pointing out that, as the commander-in-chief of the Indian National Army, Bose could properly be considered a member of the military.[57] Japanese foreign ministry officials seem to have had no discussions of this matter with their German counterparts, noting, "We were informed of this plan to bring Bose to Japan only on the eve of his departure from Germany."[58]

These episodes and events all hint at the following conclusion. Subhas Chandra Bose's movement for Indian independence was a philosophical, political, and military action. With the outbreak of the Pacific War Japan found itself sympathetic to his anti-British stance and eventually embarked on joint military operations with him, but Japan never possessed the political will or ideology that would have permitted it to lend enthusiastic support to his political doctrine or activities.

Is India part of Asia?

As may be seen in Japan's response to Subhas Chandra Bose, India has continued to possess a certain vagueness in the context of Japan's Asian diplomacy. Unlike China, Taiwan, Korea, or the countries of Southeast Asia, at times India has not fit within that policy—either in theory or in practice. Even today, for example, India—along with Pakistan and Bangladesh—is not included in the vision of an East Asian Community.

That India has been peripheral rather than central to Japan's Asian foreign policy is not simply a matter of geographical distance. The fundamental reason that India has been perceived as "foreign" to Asia by the Japanese is that Japan's relations with India, whatever their strategic importance, have not been accompanied by mutual interest and cultural exchange on the part of the general population of either nation. And by extension, in contrast to East Asia, the issues of the Indian subcontinent have almost never been directly connected to Japanese domestic politics. As a result of this paucity of interest at the popular level and the lack of a domestic political connection, relations between India and Japan have tended to be a matter of convenience or else a subject of strategic consideration by a certain segment of the leadership, but have never become a focus of general national interest. However, precisely because of this, the relationship between India and Japan can provide a valuable opportunity for cooly examining the respective position of the two nations in the world and thinking about their roles in Asia from a lucid historical perspective.

We also should not forget that it was individuals from the Indian subcontinent, like Justice Radhabinod Pal at the Tokyo war crime trials, who expressed a more objective response, from an Asian perspective, to the views of the Allied powers concerning the origins of World War II and the issue of war responsibility. This is perhaps related to the spiritual qualities of Indian civilization.

The solidarity of the Asian nations has, historically speaking, been founded on anticolonialism and largely sought in common manners and customs and the depth of economic ties among them; rarely has it embodied a clearly defined system of values or an Asian ideology. Occasionally a Confucian or a Buddhist spirit has been alluded to, but it has never been clear how such a spirit actually connects with political solidarity. However, when India speaks of Asia, there is a connotation of a kind of antithesis to the materialism and utilitarianism of modern civilization. This philosophical or spiritual quality has the potential to transcend Asia and be globally shared. One might say that India ha the potential to serve as an effective catalyst for the globalization of the Asian spirit. In this sense, the meaning that contemporary India holds for Japan's diplomacy in Asia is far from insignificant.

Asian radicalism and foreign policy: The case of Sun Yat-sen

Sun Yat-sen (Sun Wen) was a key figure in the Chinese Revolution of 1911 and was appointed provisional president of the Republic of China when it was founded in 1912. Sun's relationship with Japan was profound, principally through his ties to Japanese activists (*shishi*, "men

of high purpose") and a handful of prominent politicians who sympathized with his movement. In fact, the outlines of this history are well
known to the general public in Japan. Yet if we examine Sun's relationship with Japan from the perspective of how those in charge of Japan's
foreign policy dealt with this Chinese revolutionary, his presence and
activities in Japan, and his movement in general, a somewhat different
picture emerges. This raises the question of how the Chinese revolutionary movement was perceived from the standpoint of foreign policy
strategy, and how this radical and revolutionary thought was received as
a political ideology.

Sun Yat-sen first arrived on Japanese soil in November 1895, but
soon left for Hawaii; his longest period of residence in Japan was from
1897 to 1903. During this period, Sun assumed the identity of a medical student and the Japanese name of Nakayama Shō; this has been
seen as evidence that he was already under surveillance by agents of
the Qing dynasty, but there is nothing to suggest that the Qing government had lodged a formal request with the Japanese authorities to deal
with Sun. Nor did the Japanese have any particular plans to make use
of him for purposes of foreign policy, since he was still not regarded as
a significant political figure.

Ideologically speaking, certain Japanese officials such as Ōkuma
Shigenobu and other members of the Kenseitō (Constitutional Party)-led
cabinet were comparatively sympathetic to the Chinese revolutionary
movement, but leaned more toward Kang Youwei and the advocates of
a constitutional monarchy than they did to Sun and his associates, who
called for the establishment of a republic, though they made some efforts
to arrange a meeting between the two Chinese activists.

Meanwhile, there were others in the Japanese government who
began to see the possibility of utilizing Sun Yat-sen's movement for
their own strategic purposes. For example, in the Amoy Incident[59] in
August and the Huizhou Incident[60] in October of 1900 there were some
efforts on the Japanese side to support revolutionary activities in southern China, attempting to use these events to consolidate Japanese rule
over Taiwan and to extend Japanese influence along the South China
coast. Somewhat later, around 1908, there were also overtures made to

enlist Sun Yat-sen in behind-the-scenes efforts to suppress a Chinese boycott of Japanese products.[61] However, as the situation in China grew increasingly unstable, and Sun Yat-sen's activities began to receive international attention, the Qing government requested the support of foreign governments in maintaining its monarchical political system and in suppressing the revolutionary movement against it. As a result, Japan became more cautious in its dealings with Sun.

The way in which Japan handled the permission for Sun's 1910 visit to Japan is an excellent illustration of this. In November 1910, Sun convened a secret meeting in Penang with Huang Xing and other leaders of the Tongmenghui (Revolutionary Alliance) to finalize plans for an armed insurrection in Guangzhou. Sun had hoped to use Japan as his headquarters for leading the insurrection, stopping briefly in Japan for several weeks in June 1910 before heading for Penang. Sun was using the alias "Takano" when he arrived at the port of Yokohama; the Japanese authorities discovered this immediately, but allowed him to enter the country under this assumed name on the condition that he would stay only briefly.[62]

Meanwhile, thanks to the efforts of political activist Miyazaki Tōten and his friends, Sun was able to stay in Tokyo for a while. The Japanese government initially ignored articles in the press carrying rumors of Sun's presence in Japan, and then even went so far as to issue a disclaimer that "the individual calling himself Takano" was not Sun.[63] From this we can see that the Japanese government did not prohibit his contact with Japanese supporters in Tokyo, and in fact deliberately glossed over Sun's presence in Japan.

It should be noted that in the meantime Sun requested official authorization for his stay in Japan, using Miyazaki Tōten and other supporters as intermediaries, but the Japanese government appears to have been unwilling to grant this request.[64]

How was Sun treated by the Western powers during this period? The British refused to grant him permission to stay in Hong Kong, and France would not allow him entry into Indochina. Despite (or perhaps because of) being denied official permission to remain in Japan and being hemmed in by the great powers in this way, Sun embarked on the path leading to the revolution he commenced on October 10, 1911. One might say that one of the factors setting Sun more firmly on the path to violent revolution was the cooperative diplomacy (overt and covert) with the Qing dynasty engaged in by Japan and the Western powers.

International cooperation in response to radical forces

The intensification of efforts by the Qing government to suppress the Chinese revolutionary forces centered on Sun Yat-sen, as well as the cooperative or collaborative stance taken toward this by the great powers, engendered greater solidarity among Sun and his revolutionary movement (both among the masses and among the radical activists). This further radicalized the movement, which in turn inspired more concerted efforts and greater cooperation among the powers to suppress it. One can glimpse a similar process at work today in political movements and radical activities in the Islamic world and the response of powerful nations to them.

We should understand that once reformist forces in a country have taken on a violent revolutionary coloring, the more the violence is condemned, the greater the tendency for the movement to resort to further violence. Or, to put this another way, cooperation among governments may be effective in maintaining the status quo, but it is extremely rare for it to work toward the reform of the status quo.

Japan's schizophrenia with regard to Asian revolutionaries

When the developments discussed above eventuated in the 1911 Revolution in China, Japan was confronted with the questions of whether to provide arms to the Qing government or send troops in its defense, or to provide the revolutionaries with weapons and financial assistance.[65] Generally speaking, the Japanese response involved four main efforts, some of which conflicted with each other in both intent and effect: (1) cooperation with the Western powers, particularly Britain; (2) protection of Japan's interests in North China, centered on Manchuria; (3) utilization of the revolutionary movement to create a sphere of Japanese influence in South China and thereby strengthen Japanese colonial rule in Taiwan; and (4) tacit permission or indirect encouragement of private-sector efforts to provide arms and financial assistance to the revolutionaries in order to cultivate influence with them.

Overall, these approaches suggest that Japan's perspective was less that of attempting to deal philosophically or politically with the rise of Chinese nationalism and its historical consequences, and more that of how to skillfully balance and manipulate the great powers, the Qing dynasty, and the revolutionaries in order to secure Japan's special interests and concessions in China. However, the fact that Japanese governmental leaders chose not to directly provide even clandestine support to the revolutionary movement centered on Sun or the nationalist impulses underlying it should not be understood simply as a failure on their part to adequately understand the importance of Chinese nationalism. For one thing, while the Chinese revolutionary movement had by 1910 begun to demonstrate a certain amount of unity under Sun's leadership, it was still riven by internal conflict and dissension.

Initially there had been the conflict between Kang Youwei and supporters of a constitutional monarchy on the one hand, and Sun and the advocates of a republic on the other; then there was conflict within the republican camp between Sun's supporters and other groups. In addition, the movement for the overthrow of the Qing dynasty tended to overlap with ethnic slogans calling for expulsion of the Manchus and restoration of the rights of the Han Chinese. Nor could the issue of relations with the Western powers be ignored. The attitudes of Britain and France to the revolutionary movement were subtly different,[66] and the United States (and Germany) were more sensitive than the other powers to the advances of Japan into China. All these factors meant that Japan had to exercise caution in dealing with the Chinese revolutionary movement.

What was behind the schizophrenic response

In contrast to the Japanese government, whose ambivalent stance toward the Chinese revolutionary movement stemmed largely from a concern for relations with the Western powers and the Qing dynasty, activists in the private sector in Japan were both sympathetic to the Chinese revolutionary movement and unstinting in offering concrete assistance to it. Why was this so?

The historian Suzue Gen'ichi provides two reasons. The first is that Japan's own experience of being victimized by colonialism (in the form of the unequal treaties) led to sympathy for China's effort to restore its national sovereignty; the second is that the Japanese economic penetration of China tended to be hindered by the entrenched interests and influence of the Western powers, which meant that many in the Japanese business world adopted a sympathetic attitude toward China's anticolonial struggle.[67]

These were certainly factors that help to explain the difference in official and private sector Japanese responses to the Chinese revolutionary movement. Yet at an even deeper level, it would seem that criticism and resentment of the Japanese ruling clique (dominated by men from the former domains of Satsuma and Chōshū), represented in Japanese domestic politics by the popular rights movement and other oppositional forces, was also subtly linked to the Chinese revolutionary movement in the form of the involvement of Japanese grassroots activists in Chinse politics.

This situation was similar in some respects to the Japanese response to Chinese socialist forces in the period after World War II. The cold response of the Japanese government to Asian socialist movements is commonly understood as a consistent element of its strategic response to the East-West conflict; but in fact, as was the case in the early twentieth century, deep discontent and resentment of the monopoly of power enjoyed by Japan's conservative elites fostered a connection between popular political forces at home and the Asian socialist movement. The fact that anti-Chinese sentiment rapidly arose at the popular level in Japan as the conservative monopoly on government collapsed in the 1990s is an indicator of the limitations of seeing Sino-Japanese relations solely in terms of the international formula of East-West conflict.

4. FOREIGN POLICY AND DOMESTIC POWER STRUGGLES

Foreign policy can most easily become connected to domestic politics when it is utilized as a weapon in internal power struggles. One example of this is when the dispatch of a diplomatic mission is undertaken out of domestic political considerations. Back in the days of the Soviet Union, a key Soviet leader named Dmitry Polyansky was appointed ambassador to Japan, but it was rumored that this was a ploy to expel him from the centers of Communist party power. And in the early days of the Park Jeonghui regime in South Korea, a number of prominent military men were appointed to ambassadorships overseas; Park, a former military officer who had come to power in a coup d'état, was said to have used this as a means to prevent these well-known senior military figures from engaging in domestic political activity.

In Japan as well, it is well known that internal power struggles were heavily involved in the selection of personnel for the Iwakura embassy, an eighteen-month-long official mission to the United States and Europe that was one of the major diplomatic initiatives of the early Meiji period. This lengthy overseas voyage would confer considerable prestige on the key figures participating in it, but it also threatened to displace them from their positions in the central government. Precisely because of this, the question of who would remain in Japan and who would go abroad on the mission became a major issue among government leaders such as Ōkuma Shigenobu, Ōkubo Toshimichi, and Iwakura Tomomi. The result was the signing of an agreement that no major domestic issues would be decided during the period that the members of the embassy were absent from Japan.

The embassies sent from Japan to Tang-dynasty China are another fine example in Japan's diplomacy in Asia of the link between diplomatic missions and domestic power struggles, as we see in the case of Takamuku Kuromaro, who was sent to China in 654, where he died shortly thereafter. Kuromaro had long been active in attempting to improve Japan's relations with the Korean state of Silla, and had previously voyaged there on a diplomatic mission. But as Japan's relations with Silla deteriorated, a political struggle also took place within the Japanese imperial court, and some scholars believe that as a result Kuromaro's mission to Tang China was actually close to a sentence of exile.[68]

There is a bizarre legend associated with Kuromaro which took the form of a poem entitled "Kentōshi Takamuko no Kuromaro no tōdaiki,"[69] in which he is said to have been bewitched in some fashion by officials of the Chinese court and transformed into a human torch, grieving for his lost homeland as he was slowly consumed by the flame burning atop his head. The story hints at the agonies experienced by a political exile barred from returning to Japan.

Kuromaro's was not the only case in which a mission to Tang China was entangled in domestic power struggles; we observe the same pattern in the case of Sugawara no Michizane. Before Michizane's petition for the suspension of the embassy to the Tang that he had been appointed to lead, he appears to have been the target of various political intrigues, including a campaign of slander against him.[70] Thus it is likely that his appointment as ambassador to the Tang court was a political plot to absent him from the country and, perchance, to meet with some disaster on the long and dangerous voyage.

Domestic political entanglements surrounding the dispatch of diplomatic missions can also be observed in the case of envoys sent by the Chinese imperial court to Japan. One example is that of Gao Biaoren, who arrived in Japan in 632. Historical chronicles inform us that Gao "had no diplomatic skills and disputed with the Japanese court over protocol, returning to China without delivering the imperial decree." In other words, it appears that Gao complained of his reception by the Japanese and thus failed to fulfill his mission. But there are problems with taking this assessment at face value. Why did Gao feel it necessary to engage in a dispute over diplomatic protocol? And what was the "imperial decree" he failed to deliver?

One theory is that the imperial decree was an effort to officially incorporate Japan into China's tribute system, and that Gao was so overbearing in his efforts to force this upon the Japanese that they rejected it. But this interpretation is difficult to accept. In evaluating the reason why, we must consider Tang China's attitude toward Japan. Taizong, second emperor of the Tang dynasty, who dispatched Gao Biaoren to Japan, informed Inugami no Mitasuki, the Japanese envoy to his court, that while Japan's tribute was appreciated, Japan was a distant country and would not be expected to render it on an annual basis.[71] In other words, it is unlikely that at this time the Tang court was making strong demands on Japan with regard to its incorporation within the hierarchy of nations tributary to China (if that were the case, then presumably the same demands would have been conveyed to Inugami no Mitasuki). Thus it is difficult to believe that this was the origin of Gao's "dispute over protocol" with the Japanese.

Gao Biaoren was a descendant of prominent officials of the Sui dynasty, but was made governor of a remote region known as Xinzhou (now part of Guangdong Province), believed to be a way of removing him from the centers of power. It is quite conceivable that his assignment as envoy to Japan was also tantamount to exile.

In any case, the conclusion to be drawn, based on these assumptions, is that Gao's appointment was probably a reflection of political intrigue and power struggles within the Tang court, just as the selection of Japanese envoys to the Tang court had arisen out of similar considerations and pressures.

The power struggle over the Sino-Japanese Aviation Agreement

The influence of domestic power struggles on foreign policy formulation can also be frequently observed in the course of Japan's Asian diplomacy in the period since World War II. Issues of relations with China and Korea have almost always become domestic political issues in Japan, and the instruments or the objects of power struggles between opposing Japanese factions sympathetic to either Taiwan or the Chinese communists, or to North or South Korea.

The negotiations concerning a Sino-Japanese aviation agreement that took place between 1972 and 1974 might be cited as one of the most revealing and intense examples of the way in which diplomatic negotiations can become entangled with domestic political infighting. The negotiations for the agreement were the first working-level talks to take place after the normalization of Sino-Japanese relations, and concerned both the creation of regular airline routes between Japan and the People's Republic of China and the question of how existing air traffic between Japan and Taiwan should be handled.[72]

The main reason that these negotiations became the object of a domestic political struggle in Japan was that there was already conflict within the ruling Liberal Democratic Party (LDP) between factions sympathetic to Taiwan or to mainland China—conflict which should properly have emerged during the process leading to the normalization of relations with China, which should have been the focus of this power struggle. However, the normalization of relations took place within a rapidly changing international context that included the rapprochement between the United States and China and the decision of the United Nations to expel Taiwan and seat the mainland as the official Chinese delegation. Meanwhile, the cabinet of Tanaka Kakuei, the motive force behind the drive toward normalization, had just emerged victorious from the LDP party elections and was at the height of its power. In the context of these circumstances, Japanese public opinion strongly favored normalization of relations with China. It was not an opportune time for the pro-Taiwan faction within the LDP to make normalization the object of an internal power struggle. Moreover, the push toward normalization happened with breathtaking speed in a month or two during the summer of 1972, giving its opponents almost no room to maneuver.

The negotiations for the aviation agreement were a different matter. Commencing toward the end of 1972, they immediately ran into difficulties over the issue of how to deal with air routes to Taiwan—which, because they involved entrenched economic rights and interests, sparked intense political argument within the LDP itself. There were also three additional political factors that came into play.

The first was that the normalization of relations with China had been negotiated so precipitously that it was open to criticism for not having allocated sufficient time for consideration or debate concerning the issue of how to deal with Taiwan. This, combined with the frustration of the pro-Taiwan faction over the way that normalization had been pushed through, led to a concerted effort to assert and protect interests associated with Taiwan in the working-level negotiations.

A second point (related to the first), was fallout from the election for LDP party president in the spring of 1972. Fukuda Takeo's faction had lost the election, and its members thought that one reason for the defeat was China's cold attitude toward Fukuda, who had served as foreign minister in the pro-Taiwan cabinet of Prime Minister Satō Eisaku.

The Fukuda faction also felt antipathy at the popularity the Tanaka cabinet garnered through its startlingly rapid normalization of relations with China. The result was that the Fukuda faction and those sympathetic to it generally felt that the pace of normalization was far too radical, and were increasingly critical of the lack of consideration given to Taiwan in the process. Because of this, the Fukuda faction and other anti-mainstream groups within the LDP used the negotiation of the aviation agreement as a tool for attempts to destabilize the Tanaka cabinet.

Another tendency within the LDP that was also a factor in linking the aviation negotiations with internal political struggles was a generational struggle taking place between younger members and the party leadership. The Seirankai[73] was a group that embodied this "young officer's revolt" against the established factions—a revolt which was itself occasioned by a sense of crisis among younger members regarding the direction the party seemed to be taking. The bitter struggle between Tanaka and Fukuda for the presidency of the party actually stimulated the rebelliousness of younger party members toward the factionalism splintering the party. And all of this was connected to some extent with the issue of Japan's relations with China, as evidenced by the following criticism voiced by one Seirankai member: "In the general elections the LDP seemed to be intent on winning on the strength of the China boom, even to the extent of bringing a pair of pandas from China."[74]

Yet at an even deeper level the crisis consciousness of the young party members involved the very identity of the Liberal Democratic Party. They connected the issue of Sino-Japanese relations in general with the issue of freedom of expression in China and the related issue of what they saw as the pro-Chinese prejudices displayed by Japanese journalism in its reporting on China. For example, Nakao Eiichi and Ishihara Shintarō formed an organization called "The Association for the Defense of Freedom in the Mass Media," commencing a debate that included questioning the LDP's commitment to the liberal democratic principles it claimed to espouse.

In this manner, as a result of the intimate entanglement of diplomatic negotiations with domestic power struggles, a tacit accommodation between Japan and Taiwan to protect the real interests of both countries became almost impossible. Eventually, Taiwan and the pro-Taiwan faction in Japan, both striving to save political face, were forced in the direction of a temporary termination of air routes between Japan and Taiwan.

A *perfect storm of power struggles*

As we have seen, a domestic power struggle in Japan cast a significant shadow over the negotiations for the Sino-Japanese aviation agreement. But the negotiations also took place during a period when an intense power struggle was roiling the political waters in China, and what we might call the perfect storm of these two internal power struggles operated to make the course of the negotiations even more problematic. In China, the pragmatists led by Zhou Enlai who had engineered the normalization of relations with Japan were under assault by the dogmatic leftists known as the Gang of Four—a conflict that deepened into an even more violent power struggle after the downfall of Mao Zedong's erstwhile successor Lin Biao left the succession issue in question. Japan's stance on Taiwan seems to have been powerful ammunition for the Gang of Four in their criticism of the pragmatists.[75]

In the history of Japan's relations with its Asian neighbors, management of foreign policy issues has frequently been attended by such complex interactions among domestic power struggles in both Japan and the other countries. For historical reasons, relations among these nations have been susceptible to linkage with domestic political issues and the stirring up of popular sentiment; it is precisely for this reason that in dealing with matters of foreign policy, attention must be paid to the internal politics of the other country, and especially to the state of domestic power struggles in that country.

In order to minimize the negative synergy that such power struggles can exert over diplomatic negotiations, negotiators on both sides, and particularly the heads of state, must try to achieve an understanding of the internal political situation confronting their counterparts that transcends mere diplomatic strategy. The reason that the establishment of personal relations of trust between heads of state is often emphasized is not so much to affirm relations of amity between the two countries, but rather to insulate matters of diplomacy from the influence of domestic power struggles.

5. CONSIDERATIONS OF HONOR AND "FACE"

Particularly among Asian nations imbued with the Confucian tradition of "rites" (*rei*; Ch. *li*), issues of honor and "face" in diplomacy are more than mere formalities of protocol. They can occasionally develop into problems capable of undermining the entire edifice of foreign relations. We might say that the negotiations between Tokugawa Japan and Joseon (Yi)-dynasty Korea over the dispatch and reception of embassies were more concerned with the forms in which the dialogue was to take place than with any specific matters of content. Even today, though it is not often publicly acknowledged, more attention is often paid to the details of venue, schedule, and procedure in negotiation or talks between Japan and the United States, or Japan and China, than is given to the actual content of the discussions—which leads us to observe that even though there may be differences in form and extent, issues of national honor and face are still operative in these encounters.

Let us then examine these issues of honor and face using historical examples and focusing on the aspects of initiation, mutuality, and prestige.

Initiation of diplomatic contact—who invites whom?

The initiation of diplomatic contact or negotiations—the question of who makes the first move or tenders the first request for action—can in itself sometimes become a major political and diplomatic issue. Particularly in cases in which customary protocols have not been adequately established governing contact between the two countries, the question of who makes the first move, and for what reasons, can become the subject of subtle maneuvering related to issues of honor and face.

Immediately after the establishment of the Tokugawa regime, the question of formal diplomatic relations between Japan and Korea emerged as a major foreign policy issue. In the wake of Toyotomi Hideyoshi's attempts to conquer Korea, the Koreans remained quite wary of Japan, while as a newly established government, the Tokugawa shogunate wanted to establish relations of amity with Korea. Moreover, the domain of Tsushima, which had benefited politically and economically as a trading intermediary between Korea and the main islands of Japan, desired to see stable relations established as soon as possible between the central Tokugawa government and that of Korea. In the years after 1600, Tsushima acted repeatedly on behalf of the Tokugawa shogunate to repatriate Korean prisoners of war taken by Hideyoshi and to propose the formal reestablishment of diplomatic relations between the two countries. The Korean response to these overtures was cool.[76] However, in 1607 Korea finally decided to send Yeo Yugil to Japan as its formal envoy. Yet before it would do so, it demanded a formal letter of state from Tokugawa Ieyasu requesting the dispatch of a mission.

This was to frame it so that it was clear that Japan had initiated the process—so that Korea could save face by responding to a request by the Japanese. Conversely, from the Japanese perspective, there was no doubt some resistance to things taking this form, no matter how much Ieyasu wished to establish a new relationship between them. However the domain of Tsushima, eager to serve as intermediary, is said to have "forged" a state letter that skillfully balanced the intentions of the shogunate and the Korean court, and delivered it to the Koreans.[77]

Even today, such issues of who made the first request or who initiated action can still sometimes develop into delicate issues in East Asian diplomacy. For example, in the mid-1980s, after South Korean president Cheon Duhwan had come to power in what amounted to a military coup, the issue of a personal summit meeting between Cheon and Japanese prime minister Suzuki Zenkō came to the fore in the course of negotiations that were underway regarding massive amounts of economic assistance from Japan to Korea. The question of who should visit the other country first, and who should extend the invitation or express the desire to make such a state visit, became a matter of considerable internal debate on both sides.

At one point, a Japanese cabinet member visiting Korea reportedly asked why Cheon, who had made a state visit to America relatively soon after assuming office, had not yet visited Japan, and Cheon responded "Because there has been no invitation from Japan."[78] When, somewhat later, Prime Minister Suzuki sent a personal letter to President Cheon, it left deliberately vague the question of who should visit whom, saying only, "I look forward to the honor of seeing you sometime soon."[79]

It is quite easy to imagine how question of initiative—the order in which a request or invitation is made—could influence a nation's prestige or standing. Taking the initiative in making a request could be one way of saving the other's face, while at the same time giving the country responding to it a rationale for doing so. In the past, there have been cases in which Japan camouflaged its own desire to take military action in Asia by creating the pretext that it was acting on the invitation or request of another country.

In December 1903, as the likelihood of war between Russia and Japan escalated, Japan found itself in a situation in which it had to ship large amounts of military supplies to the Korean peninsula—and prepare to land troops—in anticipation of military operations in Manchuria. But Japan needed a pretext for taking such action, and so it became important to have Japan's military operations in Korea take the form of a "request" from the Koreans. At the time Korea's domestic political situation was unstable, still roiling with the repercussions of popular unrest, and the Japanese seized upon this as a way of inducing the Korean authorities to acknowledge the legitimacy of Japan's intended operations.

Hayashi Gonsuke, the Japanese minister to Korea, urged the Koreans to "request the sincere assistance of Japan with regard to maintaining the security and independence of the [Korean] imperial house."[80] On this basis the Japanese further proposed a secret agreement that would authorize Japan to take necessary security measures in the event of a military conflict. The Koreans, however, still had keen memories of the assassination of Queen Min in the Eulmi Incident of 1895, making them quite wary of the nature of the protection to be offered by the Japanese military to the Korean imperial house. In addition, the Korean government was locked in an internal power struggle that also worked to thwart the signing of such a secret agreement.[81]

Today as well, with regard to the stationing of US troops in Japan, congressional leaders and other American political figures frequently express the opinion that this is taking place at the request of the Japanese, and that matters would be different if Japan objected to their presence. But this is disingenuous, and borders on hypocrisy. The

American military presence in Japan follows on from the Allied Occupation, with the 1952 US-Japan Mutual Security Treaty stating in its first article that the United States had been granted "the right . . . to dispose United States land, air and sea forces in and about Japan," and later, in Article 6 of the 1960 revision of the treaty, "the United States of America is granted the use by its land, air and naval forces of facilities and areas in Japan." Nowhere in the text of these treaties is there language directly stating that Japan has requested this presence. The treaties imply that the United States is demanding the stationing of its forces in Japan, though Japan might also desire it. Despite this, the frequent deployment of rhetoric claiming that the US military presence in Japan is based on a request by the Japanese is no more than a pretense — an effort to make it appear less self-serving. Here, too, we see a "request" being used as a convenient formal device in diplomacy.

Mutuality and equality

In examining the mechanics of how face or prestige are established in diplomatic affairs, one aspect of this is the establishment of mutuality. If both parties in a diplomatic relationship behave in a similar fashion with respect to each other, a basic equality is manifested.

One example from Japanese diplomatic history in which such mutuality was explicitly created was in Arai Hakuseki's management of relations with Korea. Hakuseki was particularly concerned with giving the Korean embassies dispatched to Japan a reception equivalent to that received by Japanese missions to Korea. Hakuseki wrote of his own intentions in the following terms:

> Recently, their envoys were borne into the guesthouse in palanquins without dismounting, and there was no ceremony of welcome upon their arrival, nor later one of departure. This does not at all comport with ancient custom. Moreover, it differs from the way that our envoys to their country have been received in the past. So the daimyo of Tsushima has been given the following shogunal order: "From this time hence, when the envoys are about to enter the diplomatic

guesthouse, they shall disembark from their palanquins and shall be greeted and seen off with ceremony at the entryway, following the example of the way that past envoys of ours to their country have been received."[82]

The establishment of mutuality can extend into many areas—the details of visits by heads of state (who goes, who comes), the choice of language to be used in talks, and so on. In the case of Japan, the establishment of mutuality has not been so problematic with the United States and the European nations, but it has frequently been a source of concern in relations with the Asian nations. This suggests that with regard to neighboring countries, the general public is more aware of and concerned with the issue of mutuality.

The establishment of mutuality may actually be seen, in its broadest sense, as a means for the establishment of equality. In other words, it would be no exaggeration to say that the issue of face in Asian diplomacy is at base an issue of how to achieve equality.

One famous example in Japanese diplomacy in which great care was taken to achieve such equality was in Prince Shōtoku's dealings with the Sui dynasty in China. As we have already seen, in the year 600, Ametarishihiko (Prince Shōtoku) dispatched an embassy to the Sui court. When the Sui emperor inquired, through his subordinates, concerning the manners and customs of the Japanese, the Japanese envoy was said to have replied, "The sovereign of Japan regards heaven as his elder brother and the sun as his younger brother."[83] In this assertion we can sense something of the envoy's eagerness for equal standing with the Chinese.

Similarly, the famous letter of state that envoy Ono no Imoko, also sent by Prince Shōtoku in 607, bore with him to the Sui court opened with the salutation, "From the Son of Heaven in the land where the sun rises to the Son of Heaven in the land where the sun sets." Whether or not this followed established protocol, it is difficult to deny the assertion of equality it exudes. Particularly if taken together with a second state letter carried by Ono no Imoko on a return mission to Sui China the following year that began, "The Son of Heaven in the east respectfully addresses the Son of Heaven in the west," we can surmise that Prince

Shōtoku was particularly concerned with establishing a position of equality vis-à-vis the Sui court.[84]

Today, in talks between Japan and China or Japan and Korea, the Japanese interpreters tend to make a point of saying "China-Japan relations" or, sometimes, "Korea-Japan relations" when speaking Chinese or Korean, while the standard Japanese terms place Japan first. In contrast, even when speaking Japanese, Chinese and Korean interpreters place their own country first—indicating a subtle difference in sensibility with regard to the establishment of equality.

Maintaining prestige

Precisely because diplomacy that prioritizes face is so closely tied to the issues of national prestige and the authority of specific regimes or governments, it is difficult to make a categorical statement regarding its merits or demerits. If we examine historical examples, there are those in which an overemphasis on face has proven to be a minus diplomatically; but conversely, there are numerous cases when the abandonment of diplomatic face (primarily from domestic political considerations) has also invited undesirable diplomatic outcomes.

Among cases in which Japan has been intimately involved, the way in which the Qing court handled its foreign relations in the period leading up to the Sino-Japanese War might be cited as an example of the former. In the mid- to late nineteenth century the Qing dynasty was troubled by the rising power of regional military cliques and local commanders in the wake of the suppression of the Taiping Rebellion, while at the same time being threatened by the incursions of Western colonialism into Chinese territory. Consequently, the Qing rulers were obsessed with maintaining the status and prestige of the imperial court and central bureaucracy.[85]

The more the Qing court concerned itself with defending its status and prestige, the more desperately it tried to control its minority populations and maintain its suzerainty over its satellite states.[86] Qing policies aimed at maintaining the status of Joseon Korea as a tributary of the Qing Empire were clearly part of these efforts. And in fact, during the 1880s the Qing court embarked on a program of reaffirming its suzerainty over Korea.

As a counter to increasing Japanese economic penetration of Korea, the Qing urged Korea to sign commercial treaties with countries other than Japan. This was intended to maintain and enforce Qing suzerainty over Korea by demonstrating China's influence in the signing of the treaties and working to ensure that this was acknowledged by the treaty signatories.[87] Meanwhile, powerful Qing statesman Li Hongzhang stationed his trusted aide Yuan Shikai in Seoul, seeking to maintain and strengthen trade and economic ties between China and Korea through a variety of means, including a joint telecommunications project.

In response to these policies on the part of the Qing dynasty, the Korean court sought to strengthen its relations with the Qing in order to bolster its own position and rule; this infuriated the Korean reform faction and led to an increasing alienation of the royal court from the reformers, which in turn encouraged the reformers to ally themselves with Japan—eventually ending in deep domestic divisions in Korea and a decisive showdown between Japan and China. Viewed in this light, one of the underlying causes of the Qing dynasty's defeat in the Sino-Japanese War might be said to be its adherence to a foreign policy oriented towards saving face.

Here is another example of failure from overemphasis on face. In the process leading up to Japan's entry into World War II, the obsession of the Japanese Army and Navy with matters of honor and face to the detriment of attempts at realistic problem-solving were unquestionably one of the factors leading to the failure of Japanese diplomacy in negotiations with the United States and in its relations with China.

On the other hand, in the quest to bring about an end to the war, the willingness of Japanese diplomats to cast aside the issue of national pride—in their attempts to broker a peace using the Soviet Union as an intermediary— ironically became a factor that served to deepen the tragedy. Even if one accepts the formal relationship of neutrality established by the treaty with the Soviets signed by Japan in 1941 (and the utility of this strategy as a way of leading the Japanese military towards ending the war), this appeal to a nation that had been waging war against Japan's ally Germany to broker peace negotiations was a diplomatic move tantamount to abandoning national prestige.

Merits and demerits of a diplomacy ignoring face

Another fascinating case in Japanese diplomatic history in which issues of face or prestige were deliberately ignored or minimized in pursuit of specific strategic and political goals was that of shogun Ashikaga Yoshimitsu's relations with Ming China.

From 1373 to 1380, Yoshimitsu invited Ming envoys to Kyoto and sent Japanese Buddhist monks as emissaries to the Ming,[88] but as a result of the conflict with the southern imperial court and power struggles within the Ashikaga family itself, for nearly twenty years thereafter formal contacts with the Ming dynasty were interrupted. However, at the beginning of the fifteenth century, Yoshimitsu initiated a deliberate effort to restore relations with the Ming. In 1401, he dispatched a mission that, along with a state letter in which he claimed to have personally unified the country under his rule, bore with it a thousand *ryō* of gold, fourteen horses, a hundred fans, and other items of tribute, as well as a number of shipwrecked Chinese sailors for repatriation.

In response to this overture from Yoshimitsu, a Ming embassy arrived the following year, carrying with it a personal letter from the Chinese emperor to the shogun. In it he wrote that "Japan has been known from antiquity as a land of poetry, and has been much on my mind, though attention to domestic military affairs has prevented me from sending greetings until now." He expressed gratitude for Yoshimitsu's mission to his court, addressed him as "Minamoto no Dōgi, Sovereign of Japan" and pronounced him to be a loyal subject, conferring upon him a copy of the Ming calendar and confirming the legitimacy of his status as ruler of Japan in what amounted to a declaration of investiture (by which an emperor entrusted a vassal with a domain and the authority to rule it).[89] Traditionally this letter has been criticized as an outrageous affront to the national honor and Yoshimitsu's acceptance of it as a submission to a relationship of vassalage to the Ming empire.[90]

Then, in 1403, Yoshimitsu dispatched Zen monk Kenchū Keimitsu of the temple Tenryūji as his envoy to the Ming court, bearing with him items including twenty-four horses, ten thousand *kin* of sulfur, three golden folding screens, one thousand spears, and one hundred large swords. In the state letter presented on this occasion,[91] Yoshimitsu styled himself "Sovereign of Japan, Your Vassal, Minamoto," an act that has been criticized by many commentators, beginning with Zuikei Shūhō, compiler of the diplomatic chronicle *Zenrin kokuhōki* (1470).

From this, it would appear at first that Yoshimitsu's diplomacy toward the Ming took the issue of Japan's national prestige rather lightly, focusing instead on using these diplomatic initiatives for his own strategic purposes, which were to monopolize trade (and trading rights) between Japan and Ming China (as well as bolstering his own domestic political legitimacy, as noted earlier). In that case, we should note that Yoshimitsu's deferential behavior was adopted of his own volition, not forced upon him by the Ming, although the latter were obviously gratified by it. In other words, we can see that Yoshimitsu was clearly pursuing a foreign policy strategy.

In fact, Yoshimitsu's efforts to control the trade with Ming China had a variety of strategic implications. The profit from the trade ships sent to the Ming in the year 1407 was said to be 200,000 *kan* of copper—while the expense of building Yoshimitsu's Kitayama palace was rumored to have been a million *kan*. In short, the money to be made on trade with the Ming was considerable, and there is every reason to believe that a good portion of it went into Yoshimitsu's construction projects or donations to Buddhist temples.[92] Yet monopolizing the China trade meant more to Yoshimitsu than mere personal financial gain, for it would also serve the national goal of establishing a monetary economy through the importation of copper coinage, while at the same time solidifying the power of the Ashikaga shogunate by enabling it to control the circulation of currency.[93]

This suggests other purposes behind this drive to secure profits from the China trade: preventing powerful regional clans within Japan from subsidizing their political independence through covert or overt connections with the *wakō* pirates and trade with the Ming, as well as preventing forces still loyal to the southern imperial court from connecting with the *wakō* or certain forces in China.[94]

At the same time, Yoshimitsu's interest in the profits of the China trade was also spurred by its usefulness in displaying his mastery of the aristocratic culture of the imperial court nobility—which in turn was an aid to establishing the legitimacy of his rule. Yoshimitsu's diligence in absorbing court culture, and his lavish expenditure on projects such as the construction of the Kinkakuji, was in part compensation for the fact that he could not himself boast of a noble pedigree.

This was also tied up with the factors leading Yoshimitsu to pose himself as "Sovereign of Japan." Yoshimitsu turned his private residence (the Kitayama Palace) into the de facto seat of government in Japan, and treated members of the highest court nobility (*sekkan-ke*) as if they were his own retainers—as for example when at a poetry gathering in 1395 he made the regent (*kampaku*) Ichijō Tsunetsugu, who held court rank superior to his own, hold the train of his robe as if the latter were a personal attendant. He also appointed his own sons and daughters as heads of important state-sponsored Buddhist temples that had traditionally been headed by members of the imperial family. All of these actions have been cited as examples of Yoshimitsu's presumption of sovereign power.[95] It was this thinking that led him to set his mind on being recognized as a sovereign by foreign powers as well, and not to concern himself overly much if that meant Japan as a whole must then appear to have accepted the hegemony of the Ming dynasty.

Some might feel the disregard for face or national prestige displayed by Yoshimitsu to be virtually impossible in modern international society, where national sovereignty—at least in name and form, if not always in fact—is a foundational assumption. Modern nation-states are equals, at least in theory, and any overt action in pursuit of particular interests that might injure the national pride is normally avoided. Yet practical economic and trade negotiations between modern nations are not always in the hands of government representatives. And there are numerous cases in which formal diplomatic relations between states do not exist, or in which significant diplomatic and political rifts have taken place, and international negotiations proceed through a kind of separation of politics from economics.

For example, for quite some time after World War II, trade negotiations between Japan and Communist China were conducted by so-called "friendship associations." At these meetings a tacit deal was struck: the Japanese representatives were asked to express sympathy for the political demands of the Chinese—sometimes overtly critical of the official stance of the Japanese government—and in return, they would be granted certain trading rights and concessions. The fact that the Japanese representatives at these meetings were not representatives of the Japanese government itself meant that as a general rule they could treat issues of face rather lightly, and tolerate the political assertiveness shown by the Chinese.

Concerns with matter of national prestige cast a long shadow over how the issue of Taiwan was handled in the process of normalizing Sino-Japanese relations and in the so-called working-level talks that followed between Japan and China. In the negotiations for the Sino-Japanese aviation agreement that were part of these working-level discussions, the Chinese (the Beijing government) demanded that if Taiwan were to continue to maintain air routes to and from Japan, it would have to change its national flag and the name of its national flag carrier (China Airlines). Taiwan refused to comply, as a matter of national prestige. So we can see that conflicts between practicality and prestige have continued to be problematic issues into modern times.

Some years ago, a representative of the Interchange Association, Japan (the organization representing Japan's interests in Taiwan), made remarks that were interpreted to mean that Japan's official position was that the international legal status of Taiwan was undecided, and ended up having to leave the country. In this case, we must make a clear distinction between two different issues regarding Taiwan's legal status: the issue of what Japan should state publicly on the matter, and the issue of what Taiwan's status should be in international law (or from the perspective of the United States and the other Allied nations of World War II). There are a number of complex legal factors involved here, but looking at the problem from a political perspective, we can consider it as one involving certain issues of prestige or face. In other words, it is not difficult to understand why the Taiwanese might have felt their national pride to be wounded when—regardless of Taiwan's actual status in international law—a "representative" who was the de facto ambassador of Japan seemed to publicly state that Taiwan's legal status was undecided.

National pride or face is manifested and perceived with particular impact in the person of heads of state, foreign ministers, and envoys. The fact that summit conferences between heads of state generally tend to be conciliatory in nature probably has much to do with the fact that both leaders are conscious of the ways in which issues of national prestige are involved.

Diplomatic face in the contemporary world

It should be noted that the issue of face in contemporary foreign policy, particularly with regard to relations with China, has the potential for transcending normally conceived boundaries and tying into issues that can cause serious conflict between the two countries. One example is the issue of official visits by Japanese government leaders to Yasukuni Shrine. It tends to be seen in Japan as demonstrating the contrast between Chinese and Japanese national sentiments, or as a conflict between genuine feelings on the part of the Japanese toward the war dead enshrined at Yasukuni and the political stance adopted by the Chinese. Or, conversely, as the result of prioritizing Japanese domestic political factors, such as concern for the families of the war dead, or those associated with the shrines.

Say one assumes hypothetically that at some time in the past there was an understanding between the Japanese and Chinese governments or leading diplomats to the effect that, in view of wartime history, Japan's top government leaders (such as the prime minister and foreign minister) would not, while in office, pay either official or unofficial visits to the shrine, and that in return China would not lodge complaints against the behavior of other Japanese politicians. Even so, visits of Japanese government leaders to the shrine would have more impact as a direct affront to the political face of the Chinese leaders than as a breach of any previous understanding. Political face is of great significance to China, and we would do well to give serious consideration to it in the conduct of contemporary foreign policy.

This also applies, to a certain extent, to the current issues surrounding national territory. If China were to claim that there was at one time a tacit political agreement reached between China and Japan to defer the resolution of such territorial issues to the wisdom of future generations, then regardless of the validity of that agreement, Japan should take care not to injure the "face" China has invested in such an interpretation—as this is an issue that should be carefully distinguished from Japan's defense of its own territorial rights. Even if the Japanese position is perfectly legitimate—in fact, all the more so if that is the case—we must give careful consideration to whether words or actions that might damage China's national prestige are truly in Japan's long-term national interest.

We should recall how deeply China's pride was wounded when Japan confronted it with the Twenty-One Demands as well as what serious consequences this had for subsequent relations between the two countries, and ask ourselves whether or not anyone in Japan at that time called for deeper consideration and restraint.

PART II

FOREIGN RELATIONS OF JAPAN, CHINA, AND KOREA IN HISTORICAL PERSPECTIVE

CHAPTER THREE

The History of *Seikanron* Thought

Today it would be virtually impossible for Japan to undertake the direct exercise of military force in the Korean peninsula, even if this could be legitimated in terms of a commitment to international peace in accordance with the U.S.-Japan Mutual Security Treaty and the United Nations Charter. Yet at times Japanese policy towards North Korea possesses elements that suggest it would not be adverse to military action by the United States and South Korea, and in this sense, the potential use of "indirect" military force has still not been eliminated from Japan's policies regarding the peninsula.

Historically, direct military action by Japan against the armies of states located on the Korean peninsula has in every case been against combined forces of both the Korean state and of China (Silla and the Tang, Goryeo and the Yuan, Yi-dynasty Korea and the Ming); it might be said that no large-scale military engagements have taken place solely between Japan and any of the Korean states.

On the other hand, in the history of Japanese diplomacy, military expeditions against Korean states of a punitive or intimidating nature have been seriously proposed and considered on more than one or two occasions. An investigation of the historical lineage of *seikanron* (debates over punitive action against Korea) will reveal the domestic circumstances and international conditions that have invited such responses on the part of Japan, and provide us with a better benchmark for judging whether contemporary Japanese policy toward the Korean peninsula is in some way distorted or aberrant.

1. THE YAMATO COURT AND THE DEBATE OVER
AN EXPEDITION AGAINST SILLA

The first attempt at a punitive military strike against Korea that takes us out of the realm of myth and into clearly recorded history was the planning for an expedition against Silla around the year 601. The Yamato court in Nara is believed to have begun planning military action against Silla toward the end of the sixth century, after Silla had conquered the southern Korean region of Mimana (Imna), which had been under strong Japanese influence.

Specifically, the arrest in Tsushima of a spy from Silla named Gamada appears to have occasioned the dispatch of a military force to northern Kyūshū under the leadership of an imperial prince, Kume, in preparation for a punitive mission against Silla. This expedition never departed for the Korean peninsula, however, as Prince Kume died at his encampment in Tsukushi.[1] Nevertheless, it is obvious that the purpose of the intended military action was to restore Japanese influence in the Mimana region (or to reestablish some form of Japanese sovereignty over the region in the south of the peninsula formerly controlled by the Gaya confederacy). But the real question is why the Yamato court was so eager to restore its authority in Mimana.

The most immediate reason was that Japanese authority in Mimana was directly connected to the legitimacy of the rule of generations of Japanese emperors since the last recorded words of Emperor Kinmei, who implored his son the crown prince to make war against Silla and establish Mimana as a feudal dependency. But why did Emperor Kinmei leave this deathbed request, and why was it honored by succeeding generations? This was because the legitimacy of the Yamato court itself was intertwined with the court's involvement in the affairs of the Korean peninsula. In short, we may surmise that the imperial court and the leadership group surrounding it (the Soga family, for example) had familial connections to the Mimana region and the southern part of the Korean peninsula, connections which were seen as symbolic of its authority and power.[2]

However, the expedition against Silla, so fervently intended to restore Japan's position in Mimana, was terminated after the sudden death of Prince Kume, which was followed by the death of Princess Toneri, wife of Kume's elder brother Prince Tōma (Taima), who had been appointed to lead the expedition after his brother's demise. The question is why the expedition was called off. Some scholars argue that the imperial court was experiencing difficulty in controlling powerful local clans in the Kyūshū region and was concerned for the effect this might have upon the military discipline of the expeditionary forces stationed there.[3]

Yet it seems unlikely that this important expedition for the restoration of Mimana, so intertwined with the legitimacy of the imperial house itself, should be so quickly abandoned in the face of what were no doubt predictable difficulties with local magnates. Instead, it is conceivable that the expedition itself was intended, at least in part, as a means for consolidating control over the powerful local clans of Kyūshū, which tended to operate with a considerable degree of independence even after the Iwai Rebellion in Kyūshū was put down by the Yamato court in the early sixth century. Moreover, the expeditionary army, headed by an imperial prince and incorporating the forces of a number of powerful clans such as the Soga, might have been mobilized, like the forces for Hideyoshi's invasions of Korea, for the purpose of establishing the authority of the central government.

In any event, it seems most natural to assume that the expeditionary army never reached Korea because changes in the situation on the peninsula itself influenced Japanese strategy. At the beginning of the seventh century, Silla faced increasing military pressure from Goguryeo on the one hand and Baekje on the other, probably resulting—at least temporarily—in a somewhat more pliant attitude toward the Yamato court (and in fact, one or two years later, Baekje would attack Silla in North Jeollabuk-do, and in 603 Goguryeo would attack Silla's border outposts).

In other words, the expeditionary army Japan had planned to send against Silla was not intended as an army of occupation, but as a punitive strike or a show of force. Because of this, it is likely that changes in the situation on the Korean peninsula and in Silla's attitude toward Japan, coupled with the domestic circumstances attendant upon the deaths of the imperial prince and princess, worked together to bring about a suspension of Japan's plans for military action.

2. FUJIWARA NO NAKAMARO'S PLAN FOR A PUNITIVE EXPEDITION AGAINST KOREA

In the mid-seventh century, Japan developed close trading relations with the state of Balhae, which had established itself in northern China, and relations between Japan and Silla, which dominated most of the Korean peninsula, became even more strained.

In 735 an envoy from Silla was rejected when he announced that his country had changed its name to "Royal Castle State"; the Japanese side was offended because the change of names had been made without notice; perhaps in reaction to this a Japanese mission dispatched to Silla in 737 was refused recognition for "failure to observe protocol." Following this, in 743 envoys from Silla were sent home after arriving in Kyūshū because the goods they brought were described as "gifts" rather than tribute. And in 752 the Silla envoy was reprimanded for attempting to deliver an oral message rather than an official letter of state, and told that unless his king were to come to Japan in person to pay his respects, an official letter was mandatory. In 753, this sparring between Japan and Silla eventuated in a dispute over precedence in their positions at the Tang Chinese court.[4]

In the meantime, there are indications that a punitive expedition against Silla was being debated in Japan,[5] while Korean sources (the *Samguksagi*) go so far as recording that a Japanese fleet of 300 troopships attacked the east coast of Silla, where it was repelled by Silla forces. At precisely this time, the groundwork was being laid domestically in Japan for implementation of the *ritsuryō* system, a system of centralized imperial government modeled on that of Tang China, and with the establishment of this new national government the entanglement of marriage politics with the issue of imperial succession grew more prominent, intensifying the conflict among the clans making up the court nobility, and ending in the founding of something close to a dictatorship by Fujiwara no Nakamaro in 757.

About this time, the central government was also waging a campaign to conquer the provinces of northeastern Honshū, and Nakamaro was also intent on subduing the Ezo people of northern Japan. These northern strategic concerns naturally directed Nakamaro's attention toward China. Coincidentally, the Tang dynasty was being thrown into disorder by the An Lushan Rebellion and, fearing that the repercussions of this might even reach as far as Japan, Nakamaro's government ordered the Dazaifu, the imperial office governing the Kyūshū region, to strengthen the defenses of the region.

Nakamaro's concern with foreign policy was also directed against Silla, toward which he took a hard line, attempting to confirm its relationship to Japan as a tributary state. The envoy sent from Silla in 760 was chastised for his country's breach of protocol in failing to communicate with Japan since the last mission, sent in 752. Then, from 759 to 761, Nakamaro ordered the powerful western clans to construct troopships and dispatched a specially created commandant to the region to oversee preparations for an expedition against Silla.

Simultaneously, Nakamaro embarked on diplomatic overtures toward the state of Balhae. In 758 he selected Ono no Tamori, whose mission several years earlier to Silla had been rebuffed, as an envoy to Balhae, and on the eve of Ono's departure gave a farewell banquet for the envoy at his own residence, underlining the importance of the mission to Nakamaro's diplomatic stance.[6]

About the same time—in 759, 760, and 761—envoys were exchanged between Japan and Balhae, indicating a significant intensification of relations between the two countries. Then, in 762, the year in which the expedition against Silla was expected to be launched, a succession of imperial supplications for victory in battle were made at major shrines and temples, suggesting that its dispatch was imminent. But in the end, the expedition was cancelled. The reasons for this are not entirely clear, but domestic politics seems to have been linked to foreign policy. The domestic instability occasioned by the rise of anti-Nakamaro forces at court, led by the influential monk Dōkyō, as well as the antagonism between Empress Kōken and Emperor Junnin, probably led to the termination of the expedition.[7] If such was the case, this would also provide evidence that the plans for an expedition against Silla were motivated less by foreign policy strategy than they were by Nakamaro's desire to strengthen his domestic power base.

On the other hand, by this time there were also changes in Balhae's diplomatic stance towards Japan, as seen in the fact that, as a result of improvements in relations between Tang China and Balhae, the envoy from Balhae who arrived in 762 was unenthusiastic about the prospect of joint military action with Japan.[8] It is conceivable that this also had an adverse influence on Japanese plans for the expedition against Silla.[9]

Table 3-1: Number of Missions between Japan and Silla or Balhae from the Battle of Hakusukinoe to 920

Decade	Silla		Balhae		Decade	Silla		Balhae	
	From Japan	To Japan	From Japan	To Japan		From Japan	To Japan	From Japan	To Japan
670	3	10	0	0	800	3 (6)	0	0	1
680	3	9	0	0	810	0	0	1	4
690	3	5	0	0	820	0	0	0	4
700	3 (4)	4	0	0	830	1	0	0	0
710	3	2	0	0	840	0	0	0	2
720	2	3	1	1	850	0	0	0	1
730	2	3	0	1	860	0	0	0	1
740	1 (2)	2	1	0	870	(1)	0	0	2
750	2	1	1	3	880	(1)	0	0	1
760	0	4	3	1	890	0	0	0	2
770	1	2	3	5	900	0	0	0	1
780	0	0	0	1	910	0	0	0	1
790	1	0	3	2	920	0	0	0	1

Source: Compiled by the author from information in Kodama Kōta, ed., *Nihonshi nempyō · chizu* (Yoshikawa Kōbunkan, 2013) and Yoshino Makoto, *Higashi Ajia shi no naka no Nihon to Chōsen* (Akashi Shoten, 2004).

Note: Numbers in parentheses represent those found only in Korean sources, as cited in Yoshino's text.

3. THE MONGOL INVASIONS AND "A PUNITIVE EXPEDITION AGAINST FOREIGN LANDS"

Not long after the attempted Mongol invasions of Japan in 1274 and 1281, the Kamakura shogunate ordered its vassals in Shikoku and Kyūshū to prepare for mobilization for military action in "a punitive expedition against foreign lands" (*ikoku seibatsu*) — in other words, an assault on Goryeo. The vassals obliged to respond to this call for mobilization were those not engaged in construction of domestic defenses, and while some scholars believe the mobilization was abandoned because of a sudden increase in the number of vassals who found themselves so occupied,[10] there is reason to believe that the real intent of the mobilization order was not actually to send troops to Korea, but primarily to achieve a higher level of domestic unification and to strengthen control over provincial vassals.

In fact, it is difficult to find any reliable historical sources that indicate an invasion by Japanese forces against the Korean peninsula during this period,[11] and sporadic reports of Japanese "military" activity appear to have been acts of piracy by the so-called *wakō* pirates and not organized military actions controlled from the Japanese home islands.[12]

In sum, the arguments for "a punitive expedition against foreign lands" during this period were based upon a desire to punish Goryeo for its role in the attempted Mongol invasions of Japan, but were also probably motivated by domestic concerns for achieving greater national unity and strengthening central control over the provinces.[13]

4. HIDEYOSHI'S INVASIONS OF KOREA

As noted earlier,[14] in the late 1580s, as Hideyoshi consolidated his control over Kyūshū his concept of "Japan" as the area under his personal control began to gradually expand. This conjunction of Hideyoshi's awareness of foreign policy with his campaign to unify Japan internally was most clearly manifested in his demand that the Korean king present himself at the imperial palace in the same manner as the Japanese daimyo.

Another way of looking at this is that Hideyoshi's pacification of Kyūshū, whatever merits it might have on its own, was intended to solidify his unification of the country by ordering the daimyo of Honshū to send troops to Kyūshū and thereby establish a wartime regime throughout Japan. By advancing up the Korean peninsula to attack Ming China, he aimed to further strengthen his regime, including his dominion over Kyūshū.[15] In any case, for Hideyoshi, the pacification of Kyūshū signified the completion of the unification of Japan, and, with it, his conception of the outer periphery of "Japan" began to gradually expand. Hideyoshi clearly had designs on foreign conquest, but even so this did not mean an immediate resort to force of arms. Hideyoshi's strategy was, in a sense, quite calculated.

For his campaign against Korea, Hideyoshi first brought the domain of Tsushima into play, making it clear that the continuing rule of its daimyo would be predicated on the latter's conduct of negotiations with Korea. In June 1586, Hideyoshi sent the lord of Tsushima, Sō Yoshishige, a letter divulging the former's intention to personally lead a force to Kyūshū for the invasion of Korea, and that in the near future he would be sending further instructions to Tsushima.[16] The letter basically confirmed the Sō family as the lords of Tsushima, but in turn demanded their fealty to Hideyoshi and ordered them to demonstrate their loyalty by working to convince the king of Korea to pay a state visit to Japan.

After receiving these instructions, Sō Yoshishige dispatched one of his retainers, Tachibana Yasuhiro (Yuzuya Yasuhiro) to Korea with credentials as an official envoy of Japan. But Tachibana did not demand a visit by the Korean king to Japan, instead requesting that the Koreans send a mission in celebration of the unification of Japan by its new king (i.e., Hideyoshi).[17] However, the Koreans refused to send such a mission, arguing that Hideyoshi's claim to kingship was not legitimate, and that the long sea voyage to Japan was too difficult.[18]

Not long afterward, in 1589, Hideoyoshi ordered Yoshitoshi, who had succeeded to the headship of the Sō family upon the death of his father Yoshishige, to travel in person to Korea and persuade the Korean king to come to Japan. Receiving these instructions, Yoshitoshi made a renewed and even more formal effort to engage in negotiations with the Koreans. He organized a mission comprising 25 members, led by the monk Keitetsu Genso, who had resided at the temple Seizanji in Tsushima and served as an advisor to the daimyo since 1579, as chief envoy, with Yoshitoshi himself serving as deputy envoy. The Koreans received this mission led by Keitetsu and agreed to send a comparable mission to Japan on one condition: the forcible repatriation of the "out-law"Sa Eulbaedong, originally of the island of Jindo in Jeollanam-do, along with his piratical accomplices.[19]

This might be seen as a calculated move on the part of Korea (perhaps in part to test the sincerity of the Japanese), but given that during the period of these negotiations the powerful western daimyo Konishi Yukinaga and the Hakata merchant Torii Sōshitsu were also actively in communication with the Koreans, we can see how, in the complex negotiations between the Japanese and Korean sides, the issue of the repatriation of pirates was used as a bargaining point in the dealings over the dispatch of a Korean envoy to Japan. In other words, economic interests in Tsushima and Hakata (keen on the profits that could be made in trade with Korea) overlapped with the political interests of Konishi and the Sō family (who wanted to maintain special diplomatic and political connections with Korea) to set the negotiations on course.

As a result of these developments, in July 1590 a Korean mission arrived in Japan, and in November of that year Hideyoshi received the Korean envoys at his Jurakudai palace in Kyoto. The arrival of the Korean envoys made it possible for Hideyoshi to see this as evidence of Korea's acceptance of a tributary relationship to Japan. So Hideyoshi responded to the state letter brought by the Korean envoys, and dispatched an embassy of his own to accompany the Koreans on their homeward journey, with Yanagawa Shigenobu and Keitetsu Genso as his envoys. Their mission was to persuade the Koreans to serve as guides and possible allies in his planned conquest of Ming China.

This time, Keitetsu and the other Japanese envoys, in part out of consideration for the Korean position, delivered a somewhat different message, telling the Koreans that Japan wished Korea to serve as an intermediary in reopening the tribute trade with Ming China, and that if this request were refused Hideyoshi was likely to send troops to the peninsula; they had altered Hideyoshi's original demands to a negotiating stance that only asked for "temporary passage" for Japanese forces through Korea on the way to attack the Ming.

The Koreans are believed to have responded to these demands with a polite written refusal they entrusted to Keitetsu and his associates that spoke of the history of friendly relations between Korea and Ming China and said that it was therefore impossible for the Koreans to participate in an attack on the Ming. There is nothing to indicate, however, that the envoys ever delivered this letter to Hideyoshi, so it appears that the Japanese delegation deliberately destroyed it.

Thus, through the efforts and wisdom of his intermediaries, Hideyoshi's Korean strategy was conveyed in a considerably softened form to the Koreans (at least publicly; what was said privately we cannot know). Because his intentions were softened in this way by the Sō family and other intermediaries, the Korean response to Hideyoshi's strategic ambitions was somewhat hesitant at this juncture, and a serious difference of opinion emerged between advocates of soft and hard lines in Korea.

This problem first clearly emerged when the Korean envoys Hwang Yungil and Kim Seongil returned from their November 1590 audience with Hideyoshi and reported their opinions to the Korean court concerning Hideyoshi's character and temperament and what Japan was likely to do in future. Hwang Yungil commented on the sharpness of Hideyoshi's gaze and expressed the opinion that he would eventually send troops against Korea; in contrast, Kim Seongil reported that Hideyoshi was not worthy of fear and that there was no sign that he was in fact preparing an invasion force.[20]

The conflict between these two men, whatever the differences in their personal perceptions of the situation, also reflected the conflict that existed at that time within the Korean court. At the time, the Korean court was divided into two main factions, the Dongin (Easterners) and the Seoin (Westerners), who were locked in a fierce struggle involving marriage relations with the royal family, control over personnel decisions within the government bureaucracy, differing political philosophies and ideals, and academic factionalism. Hwang was a Westerner; Kim an Easterner, and their conflict with each other was a direct reflection of the divisions that already existed within the government.[21]

However, the conflicting Korean perceptions of Hideyoshi and Japan's Korean strategy were not merely a product of factional divisions within the Korean court; it should also be viewed as a reflection of divisions that existed on the Japanese side as well, especially between the goals of the Tsushima domain and the intentions of Hideyoshi. Viewed in terms of the results, the buffering effect of the Japanese intermediaries combined with the factionalism of the Joseon court caused the latter to underestimate the seriousness—and belligerence— of Hideyoshi's intentions toward Korea.

If we consider these developments, we must conclude that Hideyoshi's aggressive intention to treat the Korean peninsula in the same way he had brought the domains of Japan proper under his control was not the only factor underlying his invasions of Korea; in fact, what helped precipitate military action on his part was a complex combination of subterfuge on the part of the Japanese intermediaries and factional infighting among the Koreans themselves. In short, domestic political considerations and conflict on both Japanese and Korean sides led to distortions in the diplomatic process that served as one of the fuses igniting the exercise of military force.

5. *SEIKANRON* IN THE LATE TOKUGAWA AND MEIJI PERIODS

Seikanron *as a defense of Asia against the "Western barbarians"*
Toward the end of the Tokugawa period, from the 1840s to the 1850s, Qing-dynasty China suffered from both internal disorder (the Taiping Rebellion) and the incursions of Western colonialism (the Opium Wars with Great Britain). Japanese intellectuals of the era were aware of this situation (Japan would soon face its own "black ship" crisis with the arrival of Commodore Perry in 1853), and could not remain unconcerned by developments on the Asian mainland. Some even began to argue that for the purposes of its own national security Japan should

expand into continental Asia and fulfill the mission of defending Asian values against the encroachment of the West.

One such individual was Yamada Yasugorō, a Confucian scholar from the domain of Matsuyama in Shikoku. In 1861, Yamada proposed that Japan should divide its forces into three armies: one to be sent to attack Taiwan, one to invade Korea, and the third to seize the Shandong region of China. The purpose, according to Yamada: "chiefly to pacify these areas and to restore the manners and customs of ancient China."[22]

Here, *seikanron* becomes an expression of Asian resistance against Western colonialism, but Japanese intellectuals did not conceive of this in terms of making common cause with Joseon Korea or Qing China against the West, and instead advocated a Japanese invasion of the continent, because they did not have any faith in the capacity of Korea or China to resist the Western threat. In the 1860s, when clashes occurred between Korea and the French and Americans, it was reported that rumors spread throughout the Far East that certain Japanese Confucian scholars were calling for an invasion of Korea.[23] Here as well, we see how the rise of *seikanron* accompanied Western incursions into East Asia during the late Tokugawa period.

This mode of thought, as exemplified by Yamada Yasugorō, did not go beyond a Confucian conception of the defense of Asian values against the West, and thus shared a certain commonality of logic with Toyotomi Hideyoshi's invasions of Korea.

The modernization of Japan and calls to "chastise" Korea

Not long after this, Japan experienced the Meiji Restoration and set itself on the path toward modernization. Naturally, this was reflected in its foreign policy as well, and negotiations were initiated to establish "modern" diplomatic relations with neighboring Korea.

The first step, following the precedent set in the Tokugawa period, was to use the domain of Tsushima to convey the news that a new government had been established in Japan, and to transmit a letter of state informing the Koreans that this new government wished to establish formal diplomatic relations with Korea.[24] But the Joseon court refused to accept the official Japanese letter, on the grounds that in its formalities (specifically, use of the term "emperor" to refer to the Japanese sovereign, which the Koreans felt should be reserved to refer to the emperor of China) it violated established usage.

Japan made several subsequent attempts to negotiate with Korea, but the Korean stance remained firm, and the Japanese negotiators began to call for a military expedition against Korea.[25] Despite this, the Meiji government sent several more missions to Korea, but without success. In the meantime, the xenophobic sentiment that had been building for some time in Korea began to come to a head, and there were provocative incidents directed against the *waegwan*, the official Japanese residence in Busan.[26]

Around the same time, agitation for a punitive expedition against Korea—so-called *seikanron*—gathered strength in Japan. One of its advocates was Kido Takayoshi, a hero of the Meiji Restoration of 1868, who argued

> Associating with others with a sense of public justice is the way of the world; and since it is the way of the world, other nations cannot accept one which refuses it. Since such a nation must be regarded as incapable of grasping the trends of the world, it may be that we must resort to force to move it.[27]

Yanagiwara Sakimitsu, who at the time occupied the post in the new Meiji government equivalent to that of foreign minister, also argued that since the nations of Europe and the United States were resorting to military force in other parts of the world, Japan should send troops to Korea to protect its own security.[28]

Such statements were arguments for an expedition against Korea essentially as chastisement or punishment for its having so strenuously refused Japan's diplomatic initiatives.

Seikanron *as an external diversion of internal contradictions*

Paralleling this emergence of an argument for a punitive campaign against Korea were issues related to the collapse of Japanese feudal society, which had created a large pool of disaffected samurai who were quite ready to listen to advocates of foreign military adventures. Some politicians thought that diverting the energies of these disaffected elements overseas might reduce the possibility of domestic unrest, while others sought to utilize the situation to bolster their own authority and power. In this sense, it can be argued that *seikanron* served as an external diversion of internal contradictions. A typical example of this was the case of Maruyama Sakura, a high-ranking official in the Ministry of Foreign Affairs, who was arrested and imprisoned in 1871 for an alleged plot to purchase arms, organize disaffected samurai, and lead them in an assault on Korea.[29]

Saigō Takamori, doubtless the most famous advocate of a campaign against Korea, also suggested the importance of this diversion of internal discontent as a motive for *seikanron* in a proposal he made to Sanjō Sanetomi, grand minister of state, in which Saigō remarked that it would be "an indirect strategy for building the nation by externally diverting sentiment that might breed internal disorder."[30]

Japanese perceptions of Korea as seen in the history of seikanron

Viewed historically, the lineage of *seikanron* gives us a glimpse of a set of perceptions or attitudes toward Korea that Japan tends to fall into rather easily.

First of all, there is the fact that Japanese governments have tended to connect the legitimacy of their own domestic rule with the maintenance of power and influence in the Korean peninsula. In part this is due to Korea's geographic proximity as a neighboring country, but it also suggests how easy it is for Japan to assume that as a member of a shared cultural sphere, Korea should also possess similar ways of thought and perception. Precisely because of this, at times when nations on the Korean peninsula have embraced a perception of the international situation considerably different from that held by Japan, the Japanese stance has tended to be to try to rectify that perception and, if that is not heeded, to resort to punitive action.

If the present strain in Japanese public sentiment toward North Korea harbors a desire to see Pyongyang punished for its policies towards Japan — including the so-called abduction issue — then it may tread a familiar historical path.

Moreover, if Japanese and Korean opinions differ considerably with regard to the present and future of Asia—including the role of the United States and the position of China in the region—we must acknowledge that historically, when relations with Korea have been tense, this has often spilled over from the strategic dimension into heightened tensions at the level of popular sentiment.

All of these elements, in sum, suggest a strong tendency for the issues of the Korean peninsula to be deeply implicated in Japanese domestic politics. Even more than is the case with China, feelings of insult and the desire to punish come readily into play, and there is always the danger that such sentiments will be echoed and amplified in a vicious cycle of domestic and international politics.

Divided Korea and Japan

In examining *seikanron* we are essentially examining choices concerning the potential for the exercise of military force in Japan's policies toward the Korean peninsula. Looking from this perspective at past Japanese policy toward the Korean peninsula, we can see something significant about the relationship between Japan's policies and the multiple kingdoms or polities that have existed on the peninsula.

In periods of fragmentation, when a unified polity has not existed in the Korean peninsula, Japan has established friendly relations with one of the states and either distanced itself from or become an enemy of the others. In other words, when disunity has prevailed on the Korean peninsula, Japan has tended to "intervene" in one form or another. This was of course related to Japan's desire to maintain its sphere of influence on the Korean peninsula, but was also a reflection of extreme sensitivity to the exercise of influence in the region by third parties—primarily China until the nineteenth century, and afterwards, the nations of the West.

On the other hand, in periods when a unified state did emerge in the Korean peninsula, it was almost always under the strong political and military influence of China, and the biggest diplomatic issue was the extent to which Japan would acknowledge this in its actions. Today, whether or not Japan should regard the unification of Korea as strategically desirable is hugely dependent upon what sort of relationship such a unified state would enter into with a resurgent China (setting aside for a moment the issue of US involvement), and what China's political and diplomatic strategy might be at the time.

6. TOWARD MAKING KOREA A "PROTECTORATE"

The Japanese policies towards Korea deriving from *seikanron* found their concrete expression in Japan's establishment of a "protectorate" over Korea, followed by outright annexation.

Here there are three issues we must examine, at least from the standpoint of foreign policy. The first is the motivation and background for Japan's concept of a protectorate in Korea; the second is the response to this move by the major powers, particularly Great Britain and the United States; and the third is the forms of Korean resistance to Japanese policy.

Origins of the protectorate concept

The concept of a Japanese protectorate over Korea is generally thought to have first been formally articulated as government policy in the "policy platform" issued by the Katsura Tarō cabinet when it took office in June 1901, which spoke of "achieving the goal of making Korea a protectorate (*hogokoku*)."[31] If this is the case, why had the Japanese government come to embrace the idea of a protectorate in Korea by this time, even if it was still seen as a goal for the future?

One element of the context was the contemporary international situation; that is, Qing China's loss of political and international prestige as a result of the Boxer Rebellion, and the concomitant intensification of the Russian presence in Manchuria, which strengthened arguments that Japan must take international responsibility for the stabilization of the Korean peninsula.

A second element was the breathtaking development of Japan's basic industries in the period following the Sino-Japanese War, and the growing desire to advance into overseas markets—developments that were accompanied by the formation of a new political party in Japan, the Seiyūkai, and a strengthening of interconnections between government, the political parties, and financial interests.

A third element that cannot be ignored was the domestic political situation in Korea. On the one hand, there was a deepening of ties between Russia and Emperor Gojong of Korea; on the other, the political climate was extremely unsettled, with frequent uprisings among the peasantry and the urban poor (aggravated by suddenly rising rice prices as a rest of the export trade) and increased agitation by organized groups such as the Hwalbindang and the Yeonghakdang from the late nineteenth century onward.[32]

Thus we can see that the context for the emerging concept of a Japanese protectorate in Korea was formed by a conjunction of three separate factors: the international situation, the Japanese domestic economic and political situation, and domestic political circumstances in Korea.

The Russo-Japanese War and negotiations with Korea

From the time of the Katsura cabinet onward, the Japanese government had a protectorate over Korea in sight as a long-term goal, but concrete manifestations of this in Japan's policy toward Korea did not emerge until 1903, as the possibility of war with Russia grew stronger.

As war with Russia loomed, the biggest task facing Japanese diplomacy was how to keep Korea within the Japanese sphere of influence and secure the freedom of action it needed to transport troops and supplies through Korea to the front. To seek Korea's agreement in this regard, the Japanese opened diplomatic negotiations, hoping to conclude a pact that would authorize Japanese military action in defense of Korea. But the Koreans resisted and opposed this diplomatic campaign and the rising pressure from Japan.

In January 1904, in the midst of negotiations for a Japanese-Korean agreement, the Korean government issued a formal declaration of neutrality in the event of war between Japan and Russia (this declaration was accepted by Great Britain, China, and other great powers, but not by Japan or Russia). It is reasonable to assume that the dominant thinking in the Korean court leading up to this declaration was that "as far as the independence of Korea is concerned, the safest thing to do is to maintain neutrality. Today, should Korea ally with Japan it would incur the wrath of Russia and be most injurious to Korean independence."[33]

However, with the outbreak of the Russo-Japanese War in February 1904, Japan commenced military operations in Korea, landing troops at the port of Incheon. At the same time, it suppressed Yi Yongik and other uncooperative Korean hard-liners and sent them to Japan. Thus, under heavy military and political pressure from Japan, Korea signed a protocol that promised to "give full facilities to promote the action of the Imperial Japanese government."[34]

Postwar Aims

As the Russo-Japanese War unfolded toward a Japanese victory, the Japanese government strongly felt the necessity to establish a postwar order in which Korea's domestic stability was secured and at the same time the country was prevented from tilting toward Russia. To this end, a policy program with regard to Korea was drafted on May 31, 1905, the principal points of which were that (1) Korea should be induced to permit the stationing of Japanese troops even in time of peace; (2) Japan should supervise Korea's diplomatic relations; (3) Japan should supervise Korea's fiscal affairs; and (4) Japan should control Korean railways and communications.

Behind these policies lay a deep distrust on the part of Japan with regard to the state of Korea's internal administration. Japanese opinion was that corruption among government officials and the volatility of popular sentiment would make it impossible to maintain the country's independence, which would in turn invite the intervention of other foreign powers.[35] At about this time, Japan dispatched Itō Hirobumi as a special envoy to Korea for face-to-face talks with the Korean emperor.[36] These were an effort to make the Korean court approve Japanese intervention in Korea in return for a Japanese promise to guarantee "the peace and security of the Imperial House of Korea"; Japan thereby sought to promote its protectorate of Korea from above, i.e., through the authority of the Korean emperor.

There were two currents underlying this. One was Japan's distrust of the Korean imperial house. In other words, the Japanese felt a pressing need to surround the Korean emperor—who in 1896 and 1897 had taken refuge in the Russian embassy for an entire year to escape factional infighting within the Korean court—with reliable advisors who could both keep an eye on him and serve as liaison officers. But there was a second, and deeper, undercurrent. And that was internal conflict and strife in Korea itself, and the Korean emperor's lack of confidence in his own retainers. For in fact internal conflict and feuding had penetrated the imperial court itself, and in his talks with Itō Hirobumi, the Emperor Gojong at several points complained that "my ministers have little competence in helping and advising me, and thus we as yet have no definite policy."[37] In these circumstances, Itō exerted himself to unify Korean public opinion "from above," that is, using the leadership and authority of the Korean emperor to move it in a direction favorable to Japan.

On the other hand, in the talks with Itō the Emperor Gojong repeatedly referred to the need for "reforms of internal administration," which ironically made Itō more cautious about trusting the emperor. Itō was privately concerned that if the emperor carelessly undertook political action under the aegis of internal reform, this might prove even more disruptive of the country's internal administration and threaten Korea's political stability. Such apprehensions would develop into arguments for the necessity of even deeper Japanese involvement in Korean domestic affairs.

As the political situation in Korea grew more opaque and suspicions deepened that Korea's stance toward Japan, despite a surface appearance of cordiality, was actually becoming more uncertain, the Japanese policy line on Korea hardened. These developments eventuated in a cabinet resolution to dispatch a Japanese financial advisor and a foreign diplomatic advisor to the Korean court. On August 22, 1904, the following agreement (the First Korean-Japanese Convention) was signed by the two countries:

> Article I. The Korean Government shall engage as a financial adviser to the Korean Government a Japanese subject recommended by the Japanese Government, and all matters concerning finance shall be dealt with after his counsel has been taken.

Article II. The Korean Government shall engage as a diplomatic adviser to the Department of Foreign Affairs a foreigner recommended by the Japanese Government, and all important matters concerning foreign relations shall be dealt with after his counsel has been taken.

Article III. The Korean Government shall consult the Japanese Government previous to concluding Treaties or Conventions with foreign Powers, and in dealing with other important diplomatic affairs such as granting of concessions to or contracts with foreigners.

This agreement not only established Japan's right to intervene in Korea's foreign policy decision-making process; it also inserted Japan directly into Korea's domestic (fiscal) administration.[38]

Meanwhile, as the victory of the Japanese forces in the Russo-Japanese War became increasingly certain, Japan's war aims and diplomatic strategy expanded and grew more forceful. The original goal of defending the Korean peninsula from the incursion of third powers such as Russia hardened and broadened into a determination to completely eliminate Russian influence from the region, supplanting it with a foreign policy offensive grounded in active intervention by Japan in Korea and the transformation of the country into a Japanese protectorate. This led, in November 1905, to the signing of the Second Korean-Japanese Convention,[39] which was not only a de facto usurpation of Korea's diplomatic rights by Japan, but also installed a Japanese resident-general within the court of the Korean emperor to monitor and supervise its affairs.

Yet the establishment of this postwar order had in fact been preceded by the development, even before the outbreak of the Russo-Japanese War, of a kind of understanding between Japan and other powers, particularly Great Britain, concerning the governance of the Korean peninsula—an understanding that, in tandem with Japan's victory over Russia, greatly facilitated Japan's actions in Korea.

Anglo-Japanese talks on the issue of Korea

Fundamentally, the Anglo-Japanese Alliance of 1902 was a cooperative effort by the two countries to oppose the Russian advance into the Far

East, but from the standpoint of Japan's foreign policy in Asia, it is no exaggeration to say that it was also a tradeoff in which Japan secured British support for the Japanese position in Korea by offering Japan's cooperation in protecting British concessions and interests in Qing China. Previously, in April 1901, when the Japanese minister to Great Britain, Hayashi Tadasu, initiated informal talks with the British foreign secretary, Lord Lansdowne, Hayashi remarked, "If Russia develops the resources of Manchuria, they will end by occupying Korea. This is something Japan must exert itself to the utmost to prevent." Later, he added, "The Koreans are incapable of governing themselves, and therefore.... the question arises: who is to govern this country?"[40]

This was not the personal opinion of Ambassador Hayashi; it represented the thinking of the Japanese government at the time. In fact, the government had given Hayashi the following instructions prior to his exchange of views with the British: "Preventing Korea from suffering the fate of being gradually whittled away and absorbed by another power is a fundamental principle for Japan; one which the Japanese government must ignore all hardships and exert every effort in order to maintain and defend."[41]

This was clearly understood by the British in their dealings with Japan. In August 1901, Foreign Secretary Lansdowne remarked, "The major goals [of the Anglo-Japanese Alliance] are to maintain the Open Door and the territorial integrity of China, and to maintain Japan's interests in Korea."[42] If we read between the lines here, one of the most important purposes of the alliance was to induce Great Britain to acknowledge Japan's political position in the Korean peninsula (and its intervention in the affairs of the Korean government).

Yet we should also note that British experts and Far East specialists (like their Japanese counterparts) tended to hold a strong belief that stability of Korean domestic politics and administration was something the Koreans would have great difficulty in achieving on their own. This was typified by the remarks of George Curzon quoted in chapter 1.3. This opinion was also shared by the writer Isabella Bird, who travelled widely through Japan and Korea at the time, and was more or less prevalent among most Britons with some experience of the Far East.

After a series of negotiations between Japan and Britain,[43] the result was a treaty of alliance, signed on 30 January 1902, whose first article read:

> The High Contracting Parties, having mutually recognized the independence of China and Korea, declare themselves to be entirely uninfluenced by any aggressive tendencies in either country. Having in view, however, their special interests of which those of Great Britain relate principally to China, while Japan, in addition to the interests which she possesses in China, is interested in a peculiar degree politically as well as commercially and industrially in Korea, the High Contracting Parties recognise that it will be admissible for either of them to take such measures as may be indispensable in order to safeguard those interests if threatened either by the aggressive action of any other Power, or by disturbances arising in China or Korea, and necessitating the intervention of either of the High Contracting Parties for the protection of the lives and property of its subjects.

The Second Anglo-Japanese Alliance and the Korean question

Later, in the spring of 1905, Japan and Great Britain worked to strengthen their alliance, in part as insurance against Russia. Korea was a key issue for Japan in the negotiations for this Second Anglo-Japanese Alliance. The Japanese proposed the following clause for insertion in the main text of the treaty:

> The right of Japan to take such measures as she may deem right and necessary in order to safeguard her special political, military, and economical interests in Corea [sic], is fully recognized by Great Britain.

In addition to this, the Japanese wished to add a separate, secret note to the treaty:

> In case Japan finds it necessary to establish [a] protectorate over Corea in order to check [the] aggressive action of any third Power, and to prevent complications in connection with [the] foreign relations of Corea, Great Britain engages to support the action of Japan.[44]

In response to this, the British (while rejecting the idea of any secret codicils) were willing to assent to Japanese actions in Korea, but only insofar as such actions did not infringe upon the treaty rights of other powers. Moreover, the British insisted on adding a similar clause in which Japan recognized Britain's special interests in the regions in proximity to the Indian frontier, as well as measures that Britain must take to safeguard these interests.[45]

But the British insistence on respect for the treaty rights of other powers should be seen as predicated on the knowledge—and acceptance—of the fact that Japan intended to make Korea a protectorate, and thus an expression of concern for protecting Britain's own interests (chiefly economic and commercial) in Korea. The end result of this process of negotiation was essentially that Japan, in return for its acknowledgement of Britain's right to defend its colonial interests in India and adjacent regions, induced Great Britain to assent in the implementation of a Japanese protectorate over Korea.[46]

In this fashion, the establishment of Japanese interests in Korea was founded upon a deal involving Japanese support for British rule in India—a strategic balance of interests. Even so, the reason that the British overcame their initial hesitancy and ended in almost complete acknowledgment of Japan's right to intervene in Korean affairs was that securing the stability of the Korean peninsula was a crucial part of protecting British interests not only in India but throughout Asia; the British perception was that placing it under Japanese control was the best method for attaining this. In other words, the British saw Korean independence as an impossibility, and feared that if it were not placed under Japanese protection its instability could have a disruptive impact on the Far East.[47]

One might say that in addition to striking a balance of strategic interests between Japan and Great Britain regarding Korea and India, the alliance represented a commonality of interest with regard to the political stability of Korea and a common perception of the political situation on the peninsula.

Japan's Korean protectorate and talks with the United States

Japan's move to turn Korea into a protectorate required the understanding of the United States as well as Great Britain. This was not only necessary in terms of the bilateral relationship between Japan and the United States, but also because Britain wanted to avoid friction between the United States and Japan on this issue and did not want to be placed in an awkward position as a result.[48]

For some time, the Japanese embassy in Washington had been meeting with representatives of the US government concerning a negotiated settlement to the Russo-Japanese War, and during these talks had repeatedly explained the Japanese position on Korea. For example, in January 1905, Ambassador Takahira Kogorō sought President Theodore Roosevelt's understanding of Japan's position on Korea.[49] Takahira told the president that in order to ensure the political stability of Korea and protect the peninsula from harmful external influences, Japan believed it necessary to bring Korea into its own sphere of influence and exercise protection, supervision, and guidance over it. The first manifestation of a clear understanding between Japan and the United States in this regard was the so-called Katsura-Taft agreement.

On July 25, 1905, William Taft, a former US governor-general of the Philippines who was then secretary of war in Roosevelt's cabinet arrived in Tokyo with a delegation of members of both houses of Congress, and met with Japanese prime minister Katsura Tarō. In their conversation, Prime Minister Katsura said that Korea's ability to enter into treaty relations with other powers, inviting international disputes, was one of the causes of the Russo-Japanese War, and that Japan therefore felt it essential to take measures to prevent a recurrence of such problems now that the war was over.[50] In response, Taft—while making it clear he was stating his personal opinion rather than that of his government—said that "the establishment of a suzerainty by Japanese troops over Corea [sic] to the extent of requiring that Corea enter into no foreign treaties without the consent of Japan was the logical result of the present war and would directly contribute to permanent peace in the Far East." A memorandum of this conversation was drawn up and, with Roosevelt's approval, became a sort of unofficial understanding between the two countries, known as the Katsura-Taft agreement.

What we should note here are the circumstances of Taft's trip to Japan. He was visiting Tokyo after an inspection tour of the Philippines, and his major goal was to sound out Japanese policy towards the Philippines in the wake of the Russo-Japanese War. At the beginning of the conversation with Katsura, Taft alluded to "some pro-Russians in America who would have the public believe that the victory of Japan [in the Russo-Japanese War] would be a certain prelude to her aggression in the Philippines," and received assurances from Katsura that Japan had no such intentions.

Thus, it is possible to see the Katsura-Taft agreement as a diplomatic trade-off in which the United States assented to a Japanese protectorate over Korea in exchange for Japanese acknowledgment of America's colonial domination of the Philippines—much as Great Britain and Japan had mutually acknowledged each other's political domination of India and Korea, respectively. One might say that Japan's exercise of a protectorate or of suzerainty over Korea was based on a mutual acceptance among the great powers—Japan included—of each other's colonial rule, and in that sense was made possible by a common commitment to maintaining the status quo of the international order of the day.

Toward the Third Korean-Japanese Convention
In November 1905, after the Russo-Japanese War ended, the Second Korean-Japanese Convention was signed, allowing Japan to establish a protectorate over Korea and put a Japanese resident-general in charge of much of Korea's affairs, foreign and domestic. The convention, however, still contained limitations on how deeply Japan could intervene in the internal affairs of Korea, particularly in terms of internal security and police administration. It also remained unclear to what extent the Japanese resident-general would limit the powers of the Korean emperor.

Meanwhile, as we shall see in greater detail later, a Korean movement against the Japanese protectorate arose, and Emperor Gojong irritated the Japanese by sending secret emissaries to other foreign powers in an effort to defend Korea's sovereignty. The result was that establishing internal order in Korea and restricting the activities of the emperor became pressing issues for Japan.

The background of this situation was shaped by Emperor Gojong's role in Korea's modernization and the deep political contradictions it had engendered. The first of these was that the advent of Gojong's government—the Empire of Korea (1897–1910)—was not, like the Meiji Restoration in Japan, the advent of a completely new regime, but rather a continuation of Joseon Korea, retaining the concentration of power in the hands of the emperor and doing nothing to end the continual power struggles within his court and government—and leading some Koreans, such as Yi Wanyong, to believe that the emperor should abdicate the throne. Moreover, Emperor Gojong depended heavily upon Confucian thought as a means of establishing the legitimacy of his authority as emperor, and the seriousness with which he regarded the memorials to the throne by his Confucian advisors[51] was one factor in the contradictions underlying Korea's modernization and efforts to maintain its sovereignty.

The contradictions in the Korean situation, as well as Emperor Gojong's diplomatic campaign to preserve Korean sovereignty, inflamed Japanese public opinion. In addition, Itō Hirobumi's gradualist policies as Japan's first resident-general with regard to establishing internal stability in Korea were met with hostility at home in Japan, and actually fanned the flames of hard-line rhetoric.

Thus a vicious circle was initiated: Emperor Gojong's intensified efforts to maintain sovereignty—radicalization of Korean popular movements and increased political unrest—hardening of Japanese public opinion—articulation of hard-line policies toward Korea—renewed Korean efforts to defend sovereignty. The upshot of all this was that Japan seized on Emperor Gojong's dispatch of confidential emissaries to the Hague Peace Convention of 1907 to force his abdication and the signing of the Third Korean-Japanese Convention,[52] which ceded to Japan even greater control over Korea's internal administration.

Thus we can say that Japan's establishment of a protectorate over Korea was driven by three main currents: Japan's diplomatic designs with regard to the situation in the Far East, Japan's assessment of Korean domestic administration, and the attitude of great powers such as Great Britain and the United States toward Japan's diplomatic and military actions. But quite naturally the Koreans attempted political and diplomatic resistance to these currents. What was the nature of this resistance, and why did it fail?

Korea's initial reaction to the Anglo-Japanese Alliance

A major impetus behind the establishment of Japan's Korean protectorate was the Anglo-Japanese Alliance, but Korean reaction to this was lukewarm. Japan gave Korea official notice of the alliance in February 1902, accompanied by assurances that one of the goals of the alliance was the independence and territorial integrity of Korea (and China) and requesting the Korean government not to be deceived by the efforts of third powers to alienate Korea and Japan from one another. The Korean emperor and government purportedly harbored certain misgivings regarding these Japanese assurances, but in the end made no special protests or requests (to Japan) regarding the Anglo-Japanese Alliance, nor were there any overt manifestations of popular protest in Korea.

Why was it that the Anglo-Japanese Alliance and its provisions regarding Korea—which garnered global attention at the time and were without question of major concern to Korea—did not induce any overt expression of protest from the Korean side? Fundamentally, this was because the governmental structure of Korea at the time (the Empire of Korea, established in August 1899) was one in which power was concentrated in the person of the emperor. And the Emperor Gojong, though past circumstances led him to feel a certain friendship for Russia (he had once taken refuge from popular disturbances in the Russian legation), and certainly no hostility, was also concerned to maintain a balance of power in the Korean peninsula between the influences of Japan and Britain on the one hand and Russia on the other, believing this to be the best basis for maintaining his personal rule over the country and advancing Korea's modernization. In short, the Korean government of the time felt Japanese and British involvement in Korea to be a useful restraining force against Russia, while also believing that Russia could be used as a check against the Japanese.

The blunted nature of the reaction in Korean intellectuals and popular opinion was heavily influenced in domestic politics, especially the reactionary mentality of many intellectuals grounded in traditional Confucian thought (who wanted to restore traditional hairstyles and the lunar calendar, for example). Another factor was the repression by Korean authorities of the movement against foreign concessions in Korea led by the Independence Association, out of fear that it might develop into a more broadly based popular movement for a constitutional monarchy.

In any case, Korea had already become a tool in Japan's great-power diplomacy, while Korea itself was attempting to achieve its modernization by increasing the power of a despotic imperial system, and attempting accommodation with the powers by playing them off against one another. The result was that the Anglo-Japanese Alliance did not become a major diplomatic or political issue between Korea and Japan.

Korean resistance

However, after the conclusion of the Anglo-Japanese Alliance, the Koreans offered a variety of forms of diplomatic and political resistance to Japan's actions in the process of the negotiations, from 1903 to 1907, that resulted in the Japan-Korea protocol of February 1904 and the three Korean-Japanese conventions. The principal tactics of Korean resistance against the protocol were efforts to buy time and drag out the negotiations. For example, at the beginning of 1904, Yi Jiyong, an acting foreign minister, conveyed to Japanese minister to Korea Hayashi Gonsuke that the Korean emperor was moving toward approval of the terms of the protocol, but attempted to put off the signing of it by stating that "there was no choice but to defer this as we are presently in a state of national mourning."[53] Then, after the protocol had actually been signed, Yi Jiyong refused to participate in the exchange of documents that was part of the formal procedures for its public promulgation, and fled to the outskirts of Seoul.[54]

When such efforts by the top government officials at stalling brought no success, and with Japan's victory in the Russo-Japanese War rapidly strengthening its position, Emperor Gojong and his supporters mounted a vigorous international appeal in resistance to Japan. Immediately before the signing of the protocol, the Korean government dispatched I Seungman, recently released from prison, to the United States to make a direct appeal to President Roosevelt regarding the Japanese pressure on Korea. Then, in November 1905, taking advantage of a home leave on the part of an American tutor to the imperial court, Homer B. Hulbert, the Koreans induced him to act as a secret emissary to Secretary of State Elihu Root, protesting to him Japan's oppressive actions. But the US government would not deal with Hulbert, saying that he was not properly and formally credentialed as an envoy. Later, in consultation with Hulbert, Emperor Gojong orchestrated the famous dispatch of a secret Korean mission to the Hague Peace Convention in June 1907. The emperor sent former high government officials Yi Sangseol, Yi Jun, and Yi Wijong, along with a personal letter to Tsar Nikolai II of Russia, appealing for Russia's support in getting this delegation seated at the Second Hague Peace Conference then underway in the Netherlands, so that an appeal might be made there regarding the danger of Korea's loss of sovereignty.

In addition to this international appeal, a variety of protest actions took place within Korea itself. For example, Min Yeonghwan, chief aide-de-camp to Emperor Gojong, committed suicide in 1905 to protest the Second Korean-Japanese Convention establishing the Japanese protectorate over Korea, as did Jo Byungse, another top government official, who swallowed poison. Then, in the spring of 1906, a former government official named Min Jongsik and the famous Confucian scholar Choi Ikhyeon led armed uprisings of Confucian students and peasants. Such protests continued into 1907 and 1908. But this resistance met with repression by Japanese authorities and dwindled as time went on. As it did, the protest movement turned toward terrorism. Durham Stevens, an American who had formerly been an advisor to the Korean Foreign Office, was shot to death in San Francisco by Korean assassins in 1908, and in October 1909 Itō Hirobumi was assassinated by Ahn Junggeun.

A primary reason for the failure of the Korean resistance movement was its suppression by Japanese authorities, but another was the fact that its ideological wellsprings were primarily anti-Western and anti-Japanese sentiment and support for the Korean imperial house—in other words, maintenance of the status quo or the ancien régime. Another crucial factor was that with the conclusion of the Anglo-Japanese Alliance and the Treaty of Portsmouth, signed to end the Russo-Japanese War, Korea had come to be recognized internationally as a sphere of Japanese special interests, making it much more difficult for the Korean domestic resistance to enlist international support.[55]

Behind the colonial mentality

Through an analysis of the progression of Japanese foreign and military policies that brought about Korea's conversion into a Japanese protectorate (and eventually its outright annexation by Japan), we can see that several major factors were involved.

The first was a strong distrust of Korea's domestic politics and capacity for self-government. There are really no easy answers as to why this distrust deepened, but it is clear that the pace and methods of modernization in Korea, the social reactions to it, and the international assessment of the Korean situation all came into play.

The fact that not only Japan itself, but the Western powers as well, shared a common belief that because of its geographical proximity Japan bore significant responsibilities with regard to Korean modernization and the stability of its internal affairs was another aspect of the overall context. The ideological limitations of the resistance movement and its lack of international support can be identified as factors in the failure of Korea to adequately counter these developments.

Moreover, we must note that at this time Japanese political thought and institutions possessed many of the attributes of imperialism, while the forces that might have found common cause with the Korean resistance movement remained terribly weak and undeveloped in Japan itself. In addition, Japan's aggressive foreign policy toward Korea was accepted by the Western powers insofar as they saw it as being fundamentally in accordance with preserving the international status quo founded upon a balance among the powers, and Japan had laid the diplomatic groundwork to achieve that acceptance and understanding. In this respect, Japan's Asian diplomacy was in fact a diplomacy oriented toward the Western nations—and Asia was reduced to little more than its instrument.

CHAPTER FOUR

Two Millennia of Sino-Japanese History:
Five Wars and Their Antecedents

J apan's relations with China have a history of more than two millennia—a history which has fundamentally been one of friendly and peaceful contact. The only truly unhappy period in this history came with the twentieth-century warfare between Japan and China—or so we often hear. Then positive examples of cultural communication between the two countries are usually cited, such as the Japanese embassies to the Tang dynasty and the pilgrimages of Japanese Buddhist monks to China in various eras.

Yet we must also turn our attention to another aspect of the two-thousand-year history of Japan and China—the reality that this unique relationship was profoundly influenced by the political and diplomatic strategies of the two countries during every era of their mutual involvement. It is also necessary to examine the significance of the warfare between Japan and China in the modern era in the context of the long history of previous relations between the two countries.

And there is another reason, and a different perspective from which to engage in such an examination: it is by looking at the Sino-Japanese relationship within the context of the long history of bilateral relations, rather than merely from within the Western international system, that the truly unique characteristics of this relationship will be more clearly exposed.

With such considerations in mind, let us take up the subject of five military conflicts between Japan and China—the Battle of Haku-sukinoe (seventh century), the Mongol Invasions (thirteenth century), Hideyoshi's Korean campaigns and his battles with Ming forces (six-teenth century), the First Sino-Japanese War of 1894–95, and the Sec-ond Sino-Japanese War of 1937–45—in reverse chronological order. Depending upon one's point of view, the dispatch of Japanese troops to China at the time of the Boxer Rebellion might also be seen as a military conflict between Japan and China, but I have removed it from consideration here because it was not an immediate product of bilateral diplomatic and political relations between Japan and China.

1. THE ROAD TO THE SECOND SINO-JAPANESE WAR

The road to the Second Sino-Japanese War (1937–45) is commonly regarded as having begun with the so-called Manchurian Incident. On the night of 18 September 1931, a section of railway track was blown up on the outskirts of Mukden (Fengtian, now Shenyang) in Manchu-ria, leading to a full-scale clash between Chinese and Japanese troops. Behind the incident lay a deep and fundamental division between the positions of the two countries: on the one hand, Japan's determination to defend its special interests in Manchuria to the bitter end (even if it meant the use of military force); and on the other, the acute sense on the part of the Nationalist government that it must move to extend its revolution and the recovery of China's sovereignty beyond the borders of China proper to include Manchuria.

But why did it prove to be impossible to maintain Japan's position in Manchuria through negotiation and compromise with the Chinese, rather than a resort to military action? One reason was that the Chinese had decided to contain Japanese influence in the region by construct-ing a parallel rail line to compete directly with the South Manchu-rian Railway that was the cornerstone of Japan's interests. In addition, it was difficult for the Chinese to take a flexible approach to the nego-tiations with Japan because of the mutual constraints imposed upon one another by Zhang Xueliang (son of Zhang Zuolin), the warlord who was the de facto ruler of Manchuria, and the Nationalist government of Chiang Kai-shek (Jiang Jieshi), which had gradually extended its sphere of influence northward from its base in South China. The intransigence of the Chinese and the instability of China's internal politics worked to encourage forces in Japan arguing for a hard-line approach to China and a military resolution to the conflict.

This being the case, we might ask why Japan did not adopt a more conciliatory attitude on the restoration of Chinese sovereignty before the wave of the Chinese nationalist revolution swept over Manchuria, why it did not take the lead among the powers in moving toward the return of colonial concessions to China. In fact, during the 1920s there had been a time when Japan adopted a policy of cooperation in North China with Britain, whose interests were principally situated in South China, and the British (acknowledging the limitations of their own power) gradually began to support Japan's leading role in maintaining order in North China. This ironically became a factor encouraging Japanese military intervention in the region. In other words, Japan's cooperation with the other great powers encouraged it to move toward an alliance to contain Chinese nationalism. Moreover, in the 1920s a movement against Japanese immigration flared up in the United States, creating a situation in which coordination of Japanese and American policies towards China—especially if initiated by the Japanese—had become very difficult. Added to this was the globalization of the communist movement. The establishment of the Soviet Union and the development of the Chinese Communist Party were linked (at least indirectly) with the rise of a socialist movement within Japan; and the presence of communist elements within the Chinese nationalist movement also narrowed the possibilities for diplomatic negotiations.

All of these currents served to expand the interference of the military in Japanese politics and diplomacy. The Shandong Expeditions (1927–28) might be seen as the tipping point between a diplomacy predicated on restraint in the exercise of military force and one which had shifted to an active utilization of force as a means to secure the upper hand in diplomatic negotiations. Since these expeditions lit the fuse for the Second Sino-Japanese War, we must examine their background in some detail.

It is commonly believed that the 1928 assassination of Zhang Zuolin in a plot engineered by Japan's Guandong Army in Manchuria—as well as the character of the military that covered up responsibility for the incident and the structure of Japanese politics and government that tacitly accepted such a cover-up—set Japan upon the path toward war with China and, by extension, with the United States and its allies. Certainly, from the perspective of the connection between the Second Sino-Japanese War and Japanese domestic politics, this is a valid and important point. But if we look at this from the dimension of foreign policy, by the mid-1920s—even before the flames of revolution had reached Manchuria—Japanese military intervention in China had already become an issue that at times severely divided the opinions of the Japanese military, the domestic public, Japanese expatriates in China, and diplomatic officials, generating a dysfunctional cycle. From this perspective as well, there is a need to examine the Shandong Expeditions and the logic of Japanese military intervention in China that served as their antecedent.

The Northern Expedition and the dispatch of Japanese troops

In May 1927, the northern advance of the National Revolutionary Army (NRA), established by the Chinese Nationalist Party (Kuomintang, or KMT) under the leadership of Chiang Kai-shek in 1925, threatened to reach Jinan in Shandong Province, where there happened to be many Japanese residents.

In response, Japan dispatched troops to nearby Qingdao, where a small force was already stationed in the foreign concession. As local tensions heightened, Japanese leaders realized it was impossible to send a large enough contingent of troops to completely guarantee the safety of Japanese nationals in the region, and that such a large-scale intervention would in any case be undesirable. So they resigned themselves to an evacuation of Japanese residents to Qingdao, if necessary. In order to accomplish this, however, the rail line linking the port of Qingdao with the interior city of Jinan would have to be thoroughly secured—so in the end troops were sent as far as Jinan for this purpose. This expedition was the first large-scale unilateral dispatch of Japanese troops to the interior of China, and greatly alarmed the Chinese, but in the end there was no collision between Japanese and Chinese forces, the local situation was stabilized, and in August the Japanese decided upon—and executed—a troop withdrawal.[1]

Localization of the conflict and repercussions

Thus the First Shandong Expedition ended without a direct confrontation with China, and a peaceful status quo was maintained locally. There were several factors behind this.

First of all, the Japanese residents of the area remained calm, and avoided unreasonable demands or rash action.

Second, in the region surrounding Shandong Province, a variety of Chinese forces—the Shandong-based warlord Zhang Zongchang; Zhang Zuolin, warlord of Manchuria; and the NRA pushing up from the south—had stalemated one another, preserving a balance of power. The dispatch of Japanese troops was perceived as helping to maintain that balance, and even among the Chinese there was secretly little desire to oppose it, whatever might be said for public consumption.

Added to this was the response of other foreign powers. At the time, Britain had a major stake in and influence over the situation in China, and the British were troubled by the activities of the NRA in the south, primarily out of concern for British interests and concessions in South China. Moreover, with anti-British sentiment running high in China, the British were relatively happy to have Japan take the lead role in a military intervention in North China.[2] This attitude on the part of the British influenced the Japanese decision to send troops, and was probably not unrelated to the initial stabilization of the situation.

However, the First Shandong Expedition had various repercussions, as it was the first major deployment of Japanese troops to the interior of China proper (Manchuria being a different matter). The first repercussion was to greatly exacerbate a rapid shift—from Britain to Japan—as the principal target of the radical anti-imperialist forces based in Shanghai and other urban centers.

Moreover, and related to this trend, the KMT became convinced that Japan was throwing its weight behind the warlords of the north. This was because the Japanese military intervention had resulted in preserving the position of this northern faction, and the Japanese military had shown increasing interest in utilizing Zhang Zuolin, in particular, to protect Japanese interests and concessions in Manchuria.

In addition, as the perception spread that the Shandong Expedition had proven effective in normalizing the local situation, this influenced the thinking and attitudes of Japanese residents towards the idea of military intervention, encouraging a tendency to overestimate both the authority and power of the Japanese Army.

Domestic political developments

Behind these repercussions and aftershocks lay even more profound developments in the Japanese domestic political situation.

In April 1927, a Kenseikai government that had come to power on a platform of "democratization" (*minpon shugi*) was replaced by a conservative Seiyūkai cabinet. In a domestic political environment characterized by intensifying polarization between left and right, this heralded a sharply conservative tilt on the part of the so-called "bourgeois" political parties. This was matched on the other end of the political spectrum by the reestablishment of the Japan Communist Party in 1927, and its publication of its "1927 Theses" declaring that the preconditions for a socialist revolution in Japan were already in place. The intensified polarization of left and right, coupled with the rise of the international communist movement, fueled fears of international revolutionary alliances and spurred on the increasing conservatism of the established political parties.[3]

Moreover, the situation in China was suddenly interacting with developments in Japanese domestic politics. First of all, the advancing power of the Chinese Communist Party (CCP) and the activities of the left wing of the KMT began to profoundly influence Japan's China policies.

Second, with the Nanjing Incident (1927; to be discussed below) as a turning point, Japanese national sentiment hardened around injuries to Japanese expatriates, and agitation for the use of military force in China grew more vocal, creating a situation in which domestic political conflict over this issue became almost inevitable.

We might conclude that the First Shandong Expedition was a decision driven by all of these currents, and in turn became a major factor in intensifying them.

The road to the Second Shandong Expedition

Then, in April 1928, Chiang Kai-shek commenced his second Northern Campaign, with the NRA driving the northern warlords from the Shandong region, and Zhang Zuolin's army retreating to Beijing.

Japan, concerned for the welfare of Japanese residents in the area,[4] dispatched troops to Jinan to guard the area and keep the peace; but on May 2, with the arrival of Chiang's forces and as a result of negotiations between the Japanese and the NRA, Japanese troops were withdrawn from the city. Immediately afterward, there were incidents in which Japanese residents were murdered and Japanese shops looted. Japanese forces in the area, having failed in their mission to protect Japanese nationals, acted quickly and almost unilaterally to restore the prestige of the army and prevent further outbreaks of anti-Japanese violence, demanding from the Chinese harsh and immediate punishment for the offenders. Dissatisfied with the Chinese response, they mounted an assault on the old walled city of Jinan, which the NRA had occupied. This resulted in a full-scale clash between Japanese and Chinese forces that produced several thousand casualties on the Chinese side.

The Chinese strongly protested this turn of events, lodging a formal appeal with the League of Nations, but the response of the great powers was noncommittal. On May 18, Japan issued a communiqué calling on both the Northern and Southern armies (under Zhang Zuolin and Chiang Kai-shek, respectively) to engage in talks aimed at preventing further armed clashes, while at the same time warning that if the repercussions of any such military actions on the part of Northern or Southern Chinese forces reached Manchuria, the Japanese army would be ordered to intervene.[5] The Chinese intensified their appeal to global public opinion, insisting that Japan's actions were a violation of international norms. But the Japanese worked to engineer an understanding with Zhang Zuolin concerning railway rights in Manchuria, and in the meantime commenced efforts to mediate between Zhang's and Chiang's armies.

These initiatives by Japan signified that it had begun to intervene in a major way, both diplomatically and militarily, in China's civil war. Moreover, this intervention was essentially a unilateral action on the part of Japan, unsupported by adequate consultation or understandings with the other major powers.

What Japan hoped to accomplish with these actions was blown to pieces with the bomb that killed Zhang Zuolin, planted by Colonel Kōmoto Daisaku of Japan's Guangdong Army on the railway on the outskirts of Mukden. From that point onward, Japan's China policy slipped into a quagmire of military intervention eventually leading to all-out war with China.

Perspectives on the Second Sino-Japanese War

Reflecting upon the events outlined above, a present-day observer cannot help but realize that the war between Japan and China from the 1930s into the 1940s was fundamentally occasioned by Japan's diplomatic and military intervention in China's internal conflicts and political affairs, and by the ways in which this intervention became entangled in Japan's own domestic politics. Moreover, it must be noted that the failure of Japan to consult or coordinate with the other great powers was a major factor in rendering its China policy almost recklessly unilateral. And finally, although the linchpin of Japanese foreign policy after the Russo-Japanese War (1904–5) was to secure Japan's interests in Manchuria, a lack of national understanding regarding the increasing difficulty of achieving that goal in the face of the rising tide of Chinese nationalism was one of the major factors, on the Japanese side, leading to the war with China.

Looking back, the Shandong Expeditions might be regarded as the first step in Japan's China policy toward overt use of military force to intervene in China's civil war; but from another perspective, it was also around this time that Japan began to part ways with the Nationalists, whom Japanese diplomats had been praising as "Young China." The real turning point in this farewell to "Young China" can be said to be the Japanese response to the Nanjing Incident, which preceded the Shandong Expeditions.

160

The Nanjing Incident and the Japanese Response

On March 24, 1927, the Nationalist army, or NRA, was in the
of the first Northern Expedition. After skirmishing with forces
Northern warlords, it entered Nanjing, where some elements
army ran amok, assaulting and murdering foreigners, forcing the
into the Japanese consulate and elsewhere, and committing v
other acts of looting and violence.[6] Similar violence was also di
against other foreign nationals, such as the British and Ame
resulting in many injuries, unlawful detentions, and looted shops

Local representatives of the Japanese government interprete
background to these events in the following manner:

> It is increasingly clear that the present violence was deliberate, pr
> meditated, and organized anti-foreign violence, initiated by politic
> cadres and officers of the Chinese Communist Party attached to th
> regular forces of the Southern Army [NRA], based on a plot to haste
> the downfall of Chiang [Kai-shek] and his faction.[7]

Japanese civilian and military officials on the scene responded t
outbreak of the Nanjing Incident calmly and deliberately, despit
rioting in the streets and the temporary incursion into the Japa
consulate. Partly in response to entreaties from the Japanese civi
taking refuge in the consulate, Japanese military personnel kept
profile, removing their badges of rank and their caps, and refrai
from overt action in the city. The machine guns that had been s
for the defense of the consulate were removed, and Japanese gunl
at anchor in the river did not fire a single shot.[8]

It is particularly noteworthy that Japanese military personnel :
lowed their pride and exerted themselves to the utmost to coope
with a policy of nonresistance. In fact, one of them, Lieutenant A
Kameo of the Japanese navy, attempted suicide on March 29 on b
one of the gunboats, having followed orders to refrain from action
taking responsibility for the injury he felt had been done to the pres
of the Japanese Empire.[9]

Perhaps the most significant factor that might be cited as enab
this unanimity between foreign policy officials and military person

was the strong desire of the resident Japanese community to avoid a repetition of the tragedy of the Japanese massacred in the Nikolayevsk Incident during the Russian Civil War, an event still etched in the minds of Japanese residents, officials, and military personnel alike.[10]

The Japanese government's response to the Nanjing Incident, after consultations in Beijing with British and American officials, was a decision to present the Chinese with a list of four demands: the punishment of those responsible for the violence and looting; a promise that steps would be taken to prevent a recurrence of such incidents; a formal apology; and the payment of an indemnity.[11]

However, partly because the Japanese had refrained from a bombardment of Nanjing, they were reluctant to engage in complete cooperation and coordination with the Western powers.[12] In particular, the Japanese were opposed to the idea of demanding a time limit for the Chinese response, as successfully implementing the evacuation of large numbers of Japanese civilian residents would be time-consuming.

At the same time, the Japanese government (which as noted earlier, was sensitive to the activities of the Communist Party from the outset) was convinced that the Nanjing Incident had been the product of a Communist plot, and that there was a need to do what was possible to bolster the position of Chiang Kai-shek and his faction, with some officials feeling it would be a mistake to be too precipitous in presenting the Chinese with an ultimatum.[13]

On 14 April 1927, the Chinese presented the foreign powers with a similar set of responses. However, their response to Japan, while accepting the payment of an indemnity for damage caused to Japanese persons and property and promising to work to prevent future incidents, also proposed that a joint commission of China and the "foreign powers" be formed to investigate the violence to determine appropriate punishments and apologies. They also called for negotiations to address the fundamental issue of the unequal treaties.

What is especially noteworthy in these developments is the interaction between China and Japan. The Chinese, particularly Chiang Kai-sek, hoped that in dealing with the Nanjing Incident the Japanese government would draw a line between itself and the other foreign

powers—especially the British, who had been the object of greatest popular denunciation—in negotiations with China, and that this would give Communist elements less chance to exploit the negotiations.[14] The left-leaning KMT faction in Wuhan took a similar tack, deciding "at this time we should join with Japan in working toward a resolution of the present situation,"[15] and at one point even prepared a special "Declaration Concerning Policies toward Japan" that expressed gratitude for the fact that Japan had refrained from participating in the bombardments of Nanjing and Hankou and stated that the Nationalist government would guarantee the legitimate interests of Japan and the welfare of Japanese residents. It then proposed that Japan and China should enter a new dimension of mutual dialogue.[16]

Within the Japanese government, and especially so among its China-based personnel, opinion was running strongly in favor of accepting these overtures from China and taking the Nanjing Incident as an opportunity for Japan to join hands with "moderate elements" in China to help bring about a unification of the country. Yet the overall government position, while recognizing that Japan should exert itself to contribute to a stabilization of the political situation in China, remained committed to joining the other foreign powers in adopting a hard line with China, for the following reasons.

The first was that the Nanjing Incident was perceived as a simultaneous, calculated action against the foreign powers, and thus as a grave threat to the international order in China. The feeling was that if the foreign powers did not join together in adopting a rigorous attitude toward China, there was a danger that their interests and concessions in China might be encroached upon. The second reason was the belief that there was a "dark side" to the Chinese revolutionary movement that needed to be rectified if the nationalist movement in China was to be set upon the correct path. Intertwined with these two reasons, however, were two even more subtle factors.

One was that indignation against the Chinese government—beginning with the British—was widespread, and there was apprehension that unilateral action on the part of Japan might cause the British to adopt an even more hard-line position toward China; it was thought that there was some need for Japan to maintain a united front with the other powers, in part to serve as a restraining influence on Britain.

The second factor was the domestic situation in Japan. The opposition parties called for a buildup of Japan's defenses, criticizing the government's handling of the Nanjing Incident for "dragging the nation's flag and reputation through the mud" with a policy of "passive non-resistance" that invited a "loss of national honor."[17] While it is undeniable that these attacks by the opposition were based more on political opportunism than a genuine ideological position, they seem to have led foreign policymakers to the conclusion that if Japan broke ranks with the other foreign powers and embarked on unilateral action, it would play into the hands of domestic hard-liners and make calm and rational policy-making even more difficult.

In short, the slogan of "cooperation with the powers" enunciated by the Japanese government was an effort to restrain hard-line domestic opinion. Thus, the principal goal of Japan's China policy became cooperation with the other powers to make the Chinese authorities acknowledge the wrongdoing that had taken place, apologize for it, promise that measures would be taken to prevent further incidents, and follow through on implementing them.

At this juncture, there was no sign of the political will to take the lead among the foreign powers in pursuing a policy of strategic negotiations with "Young China" aimed at revising the unequal treaties with China and addressing the issue of Japan's interests and concessions there. As a result of factors such as the meddling of the Soviet Communist Party, the direction of the nationalist movement in China was becoming too complex for such a policy to be implemented, and circumstances were unfavorable to negotiations based upon a long-term vision.

But an even more decisive factor was the deeply rooted general distrust of the Japanese in the Chinese leadership. The murders of Japanese nationals in the Nanjing Incident inflamed domestic public opinion, and as distrust of China rose, even Japanese diplomats saw Chinese efforts to engage Japan in separate talks as merely another manifestation of the stereotypical Chinese strategy of "using barbarians to control barbarians."[18] Japan's parting of the ways with "Young China" was rooted in a hardening of public opinion, the increasing complexity of the internal situation in China, and the Japanese distrust of China engendered by these factors.

2. THE CAUSES OF THE FIRST SINO-JAPANESE WAR

Japan's Korea policy

The First Sino-Japanese War, from August 1894 to March 1895, began on the Korean peninsula and spread to the coast of China as the two nations contended for control of the seas. As this suggests, the seeds of conflict between China and Japan lay in the Korean peninsula.

From the late 1880s into the early 1890s, Japanese policy with regard to the Korean peninsula rested on four main pillars:

1. Deepening Japan's economic penetration of Korea.
2. Preventing any further expansion of Russian influence into the peninsula.
3. Preventing not only Russia, but other Western colonial powers from extending their influence into Korea (especially after the 1885 British occupation of the Geomundo islands).
4. Preventing Qing China from establishing a preponderant influence or suzerainty over Korea.

Advocacy for cooperation with the Qing—and its failure

In pursuit of these policies, or as an extension of them, Japan groped for some form of cooperation with the Qing dynasty.

In the beginning, the idea of cooperation was, if anything, initiated by the Qing. To deal with the issue of Korea in the aftermath of the Gapsin Coup in 1884 (see table 4–1), the two countries met for talks in Tianjin in March 1885. At the talks, the Qing representative, Li Hong-zhang, proposed an agreement between China and Japan to cooperate in sending troops to Korea in the event the latter was attacked by a third power.[19] However, the Japanese representative, Itō Hirobumi, while not fundamentally opposed to the idea, was also not eager to formally commit to military cooperation with the Qing.[20]

Table 4–1. Developments in Korea Leading to the First Sino-Japanese War

Stage 1	Imo Incident or Mutiny (Imo gullan, 1882) and intensification of rivalry between Japan and Qing. The Daewongun, a former regent, allies himself with forces opposing modernization as antigovernment, anti-Japanese rioting breaks out, and is briefly restored to power. Japan signs the Treaty of Chemulpo with Korea, permitting Japan to station troops to protect the Japanese legation and resident community. The Qing seize the Daewongun and expand their military presence in Korea.
Stage 2	With the Gapsin Coup (Gapsin jeongbyeon, 1884) direct military confrontation between Japanese and Qing forces begins. Kim Okgyun and other reformers seize power in a coup d'état, and there are clashes between Japanese and Qing forces.The coup fails as a result of the Qing military intervention. Japan signs the Treaty of Hanseong with Korea and harbors Korean political refugees, in the meantime concluding the Tianjin Convention (Convention of Tientsin) with the Qing, in which it is agreed that both countries would withdraw their forces from Korea and that any future dispatch of troops would require prior notification to the other side.
Stage 3	The Donghak Rebellion (Donghak nongmin undong, 1894) leads to military intervention in Korea by both Japan and Qing China. Japan demands that the Chinese forces be withdrawn first; a military confrontation between the two sides ensues.

This was probably because Itō was by nature cautious about sending Japanese troops overseas and (at least at this stage) there were still differences between Li and Itō in terms of their perception of the threat posed by Russia. More fundamentally, this was likely to have been out of the consideration that military cooperation between Japan and the Qing, even in the form of a secret agreement, might arouse suspicion and wariness among Britain and the other Western nations. In addition, there were probably fears that military cooperation between Japan and the Qing at this stage might in fact contribute to cementing Chinese suzerainty over Korea.

Yet there were also individuals within the Japanese government who argued strongly for cooperation with the Qing. Foremost among them was Enomoto Takeaki, then Japanese minister to the Qing court. Enomoto doubted the capacity of the Korean government to rule the country and proposed a framework for cooperation between Japan and Qing China to protect Korea from Russian meddling in Korea's internal affairs, which he saw as a likely outcome of the nation's political instability.[21]

Following this, in June 1885 the Japanese government made an eight-point proposal to the Qing that contained the following key points:

1. The inner circle of advisors to the Korean king should be separated from him and removed from political power.
2. Paul Georg von Möllendorff, a German advisor to the Korean government with close ties to Russia, should be replaced with an American.
3. The Qing representative to Korea should be replaced with a reliable individual and given sufficient powers to negotiate directly with the Japanese minister to Korea.
4. The aforementioned policies, after confidential discussions between Japanese representative Inoue Kaoru and Qing representative Li Hongzhang, should be implemented by the latter.[22]

This proposal was somewhat different from what Enomoto had originally suggested, and was an attempt to cooperate with the Qing in a reform of Korea's domestic political situation while giving the Qing the leading public role in this process. It is likely that Japan made this proposal, which risked strengthening at least the appearance of Chinese suzerainty over Korea, because Japan took the British occupation of Geomundo very seriously and sensed that behind it lay at least a tacit agreement between China and Britain.[23] In other words, Japan was trying to convince Qing China that preventing third countries (not only Russia, but Britain as well) from extending their influence into the Korean peninsula was in the best interests of both China and Japan.

The Japanese proposal was rejected by the Qing, for at least two significant reasons. The first was that from the perspective of the Qing, any general or formal agreement to prior consultation with Japan on the reform of Korea's domestic administration would serve to limit China's suzerainty over Korea. The second was that the Qing were dealing with both Russian penetration into Manchuria and the British interests and concessions in South China, and were attempting to maintain the prestige of the Chinese Empire by appropriate accommodations with Britain and Russia and skillful manipulation of the balance among the powers. To put this another way, the Qing did not take the British occupation of Geomundo as seriously as the Japanese; instead, they sought ties with Britain adequate to serve as a foil against Russia, while at the same time seeking a level of cooperation with Russia that could be used to fend off the Japanese.[24]

Despite this rebuff by the Qing, the idea of cooperation with China to reform Korea lingered for some time thereafter in Japanese government circles. And in 1894, as the situation in the Korean peninsula began to display signs of increasing instability, Itō Hirobumi and others initially began to work out a plan for joint Sino-Japanese intervention.

The concept was for a coordination of Japanese and Chinese policy centered on a joint project to build a rail line from Seoul to Incheon. This plan for cooperation with the Qing was even embraced (at least officially) by Japan's military leaders, such as Yamagata Aritomo. During his earlier tenure as prime minister, Yamagata had given an important policy speech to the Diet in which he had declared the Korean peninsula to be a crucial element within Japan's sphere of interests and argued that Japan and China should exercise a joint protectorate over it.[25] As rivalry with Qing China grew more pronounced, there was resistance and opposition within the Japanese government toward such proposals for Sino-Japanese cooperation, but a posture of avoiding decisive conflict with the Qing was maintained until the very eve of the First Sino-Japanese War.

For example, when Chinese troops were about to be dispatched to the Korean peninsula in response to the Donghak Rebellion, the communiqué sent by the Qing government to inform Japan of this deployment used language describing Korea as a vassal state of the Qing Empire. Japanese foreign minister Mutsu Munemitsu was outraged and wanted to strongly protest this assertion. He was, however, overruled by other government leaders, and in the end a much milder communication was sent to the Qing, simply stating that Japan did not acknowledge Korea's status as a dependency of China.[26]

Why cooperation with the Qing broke down

Why did the policy of cooperation with the Qing break down, despite the stance of the Meiji government that sought some form of accommodation down to the eleventh hour?

An overview of Qing China's policies, not just toward the Korean peninsula, but in East Asia generally shows us that at base they were aimed at maintaining the rule of the Qing dynasty and the traditional Sinocentric order through a gradual process of modernization, accommodation with Britain and Russia, and skillful manipulation of the foreign powers. Qing policy toward Japan followed a similar pattern: a certain degree of accommodation with Japan as a rising power, but even this geared towards putting the brakes on Japanese expansion and maintaining Chinese suzerainty over the Korean peninsula.

In contrast, Japan sought to extend the logic of its own modernization to the rest of East Asia, and especially to Korea, where it saw the growing influence of Western colonialism as undesirable from the standpoint of its own national security. Thus the policy orientations of China and Japan were based upon fundamentally different ways of thinking about the modernization of Korea and the state of the international order in East Asia. For Japan, modernization signified an alteration of the traditional Sinocentric world order in East Asia, but China was determined to find a way to make modernization coexist with a maintenance of this traditional order.

In addition, the two countries had differing perceptions of what constituted the principal threat to East Asia. For the Qing, cooperation and accommodation with the Western powers seemed necessary in order to minimize the penetration of the Western order into East Asia. Traditionally, they had even been willing to accept the loss of sovereignty implicit in ceding concessions to the foreign powers in order to reach such accommodation. In contrast, Japan was actively working to introduce the Western world order to East Asia and to solidify its own territorial integrity and sovereignty within that context. Because of this, it tended to see Russia as a primary threat, for geopolitical reasons. Another limitation on alliance and cooperation between Japan and Qing China was that both countries had conflicting assessments of each other's national strength. The Qing tended to underestimate the power of Japan, while Japan tended to overestimate the power and prestige of China.

All of the aforementioned factors contributed to the inability of Japan and China to easily ally or cooperate with one another.

The trigger for war

However, this difficulty in achieving accord or cooperation, while it may have underlain the outbreak of war between Japan and China, was not its proximate cause. After all, even rather significant conflicts and differences may be resolved through peaceful negotiations and compromise. Why did Japan come to see a negotiated settlement as impossible? More specifically, despite the fact that the Qing had no objections to a simultaneous withdrawal of Chinese and Japanese forces from Korea, why was it that Japan insisted that the China should withdraw its troops first—and why did this trigger the war?

According to Takahashi Hidenao, author of *Nisshin Sensō e no michi* (The Road to the Sino-Japanese War), this was a result of apprehension over the impact that a simultaneous troop withdrawal might have on the political situation in Korea.[27] In other words, it was felt that to maintain Japanese prestige and influence in Korea, it was necessary for the Japanese military influence there to surpass that of Qing China. Or, to state it even more pointedly, Japan's policy had become, as vice-minister for foreign affairs Hayashi Tadasu aptly put it, "not to discuss how matters might be brought to a peaceful resolution, but rather how best to start a fight and then go on to win it."[28]

What had brought Japanese thinking to this point? The answer is clearly stated in a letter from foreign minister Mutsu Munemitsu to prime minister Itō Hirobumi: "It seems that at present our influence on Korea still does not measure up to the accumulated prestige of China."[29] All that Japan had to counter China's "accumulated prestige"—the fruit of centuries of having exercised political, economic, and cultural influence over Korea and dominating it as a suzerain—was a resort to military force.

3. THE BACKGROUND TO WAR BETWEEN JAPAN AND MING CHINA: HIDEYOSHI'S VISION OF EAST ASIA AND HIS AGGRESSIVE INTENTIONS TOWARD THE MING

Hideyoshi's unification of Japan
To continue with our look backward at the history of Sino-Japanese conflict, in 1585, Toyotomi Hideyoshi forced Chōsokabe Motochika to surrender, and brought the island of Shikoku under his own control. Then, in 1587, Hideyoshi dispatched an expeditionary force to Kyushu and forced the Shimazu house, lords of Satsuma, to swear allegiance to him, thus achieving the subjugation of Kyushu. This was also the year in which daimyo from all over Japan first gathered at Osaka Castle to pay their New Year's respects to Hideyoshi.

As Hideyoshi proceeded with this successful unification of the country, his own conception of the political and economic entity called "Japan" that was being brought under his control also gradually expanded.

Already, in 1586, Hideyoshi sent a fourteen-point memorandum of instructions to his retainer Mōri Terumoto in which he alluded to crossing the seas to Korea,[30] and the same year gave an audience to the Jesuit vice-provincial in Japan, Gaspar Coelho, in which he spoke of the "conquest" (*seibatsu*) of Korea and China.[31] This suggests that he saw the invasion of the Korean peninsula as a logical extension of his unification of Japan.

The process of negotiations between Japan and Korea

However, Hideyoshi did not proceed with immediate military action. In what amounted to compensation for confirming the daimyo of Tsushima in the possession of his domain, Hideyoshi ordered Tsushima to undertake negotiations with Korea. As detailed in table 4–2, with its second mission to Korea, the domain of Tsushima succeeded in securing a Korean agreement to dispatch an embassy to congratulate Hideyoshi on his unification of Japan.

In the eleventh month of Tenshō 18 (1590), Hideyoshi gave an audience to the Korean embassy in his Jurakutei palace in Kyoto, and dispatched envoys of his own to accompany the Korean embassy back to their country, requesting that Korea use its good offices to assist in restoring the Japanese tributary trade with the Ming. At the same time he demanded that the Koreans permit Japanese armies to transit their country and enter Ming China, threatening military action against Korea if it did not comply.

The Koreans refused the Japanese demands, citing their own long history of friendly relations with the Ming, so Hideyoshi constructed a staging encampment in Kyushu from which he invaded Korea in the fourth month of Bunroku 1 (1592). By the fifth month of the year, Seoul had fallen, and in the sixth month negotiations concerning Japanese demands and the withdrawal of Japanese troops were held at the Taedong River outside Pyongyang. No agreement could be reached, and in the seventh month, at the request of the Koreans, Ming armies entered the conflict to fight against the Japanese forces.

Hideyoshi's conception of East Asia

As noted earlier, for Hideyoshi the subjugation of Kyushu virtually completed the unification of Japan; but with this unification, his sense of the periphery of "Japan" gradually expanded, and it appears that he increasingly felt that Korea and the Ryukyus were either dependent territories or vassal states of Japan (or of the Sō family of Tsushima domain and the Shimazu of Satsuma, respectively). As to why Hideyoshi would have extended this logic and attempted to apply it to

Table 4-2. The Process Leading to the War between the Ming Dynasty and Japan: Japan-Korea Negotiations and the Outbreak of the War

Tenshō 15 (1587)	At Hideyoshi's orders, the Sō family of Tsushima sends their retainer Tachibana Yasuhiro to Korea as an official envoy of Japan, requesting the dispatch of a Korean embassy. The Korean response is unenthusiastic.
Tenshō 17 (1589)	The daimyo of Tsushima, Sō Yoshitoshi, personally participates in a mission to Korea (headed by the Buddhist monk Keitetsu Genso) and succeeds in persuading the Koreans to send an embassy to Hideyoshi.
11th month, Tenshō 18 (1590)	Hideyoshi meets with the Korean envoys at his Jurakutei palace.
2nd month, Tenshō 19 (1591)	Hideyoshi dispatches Genso to Korea a second time, accompanying the Korean embassy on its return home, to request that Korea use its good offices to assist in restoring the Japanese tribute trade with the Ming, and also to permit temporary transit of a Japanese invasion force against the Ming. The threat of military force is clear, but the Koreans refuse these demands.
4th month, Bunroku 1 (1592)	Japanese armies invade Korea.
5th month	Fall of Seoul; Korean king flees city.
6th month	Negotiations at Taedong River; Koreans refuse to serve as intermediaries between Japan and Ming China.
7th month	Ming military intervention; fighting between Japanese and Ming forces.

Ming China, this can probably be seen as connected to the incursion of Western colonialism into Asia, as noted in section 5 of chapter 1.

Similarities and differences with the China policies of modern Japan
Thus, one aspect of Hideyoshi's invasion of Korea and his war with Ming China might be seen as response to the Western colonial penetration of Asia and an intention to build a new East Asian international order based on "Asian" values. And if so, there are certain similarities to Japan's incursions into Asia in modern times, which also exhibited an element of resistance to Western colonial domination. Another noteworthy similarity to modern times is that Hideyoshi was not interested merely in the establishment of political and military dominance, but was also conscious of what might be called an Asian value system.

In connection with this, we should note that after the fall of Seoul, Hideyoshi expressed the intention of installing the Japanese emperor in Beijing, while Hideyoshi himself would reside in Ningbo and promote commerce between China and Japan.[32] Here, Hideyoshi was attempting to reinforce the legitimacy and authority of his own rule by overlapping it with the authority of the emperor.

On the other hand, the conspicuous courtesy Hideyoshi displayed toward the official envoys of the Ming[33] as well as his general attitude toward the products of Ming culture suggest that his real motive in wishing to conquer Ming China was to borrow the mantle of its prestige in East Asia, and that actual territorial ambitions were, if anything, secondary. The fact that the Japanese insisted on being ceded territory on the Korean peninsula in their peace negotiations with the Ming might even be taken as a hint that from the beginning the object of Hideyoshi's desire for conquest may not have extended as far as China proper. In other words, Hideyoshi's strategic intentions toward China may have been not so much to subjugate or dominate it, but to clothe himself in borrowed glory.

Moreover, as noted in chapter 1, we should not forget that Hideyoshi's aggressive ambitions in Asia were at least partly motivated by the desire to expel Christianity and defend the traditions of Shintō, Buddhism, and

Confucianism. Hideyoshi's unification of Japan was accompanied by a clarification and expansion of Japanese national consciousness, and this process also included the formation of what we would today call the concept of Asia—both as a geographic entity and as a community of values.

4. WHY JAPAN AND THE YUAN (MONGOL) DYNASTY
WENT TO WAR

The international situation in East Asia and the Mongol invasions
The attempted Mongol invasions of Japan in 1274 and 1281 were part of a Mongol invasion of all of East Asia.

Mongol military action against Japan took place just as Mongol military operations against Vietnam were beginning to wind down and as Song Chinese armies were successively defeated by Yuan forces, presenting the issue of what needed to be done to secure the allegiance to the Yuan that had been pledged by the surrendering Song generals and their troops. We should also note that the Mongol attacks on Japan were carried out after 1270, the year in which the subjugation of the Korean state of Goryeo to Mongol rule was completed. Thus, the Mongol invasions took place in an international context shaped by Mongol domination of Goryeo, the decline of Song China, and Vietnamese resistance to the Mongol armies. On the other hand, despite the consistently threatening demeanor of the Mongols, in their relations with the Song they adopted a posture that offered possibilities of peace as well as war—by demanding of the Song exorbitant quantities of tribute and the provision of artisans and laborers in exchange for the deferral of military action.

In the same manner, before the 1274 invasion of Japan, the Mongols repeatedly sent envoys to Japan, attempting to persuade it to submit to their authority; in this sense, the Mongol invasions came after a series of diplomatic negotiations between Japan and the Mongols had broken down. Examining the background and causes of war between Japan and the Yuan dynasty primarily means looking at what form these diplomatic negotiations took, and why they ended in failure.

The Mongol approach to Japan and the Japanese response

As we see in table 4–3, the first Mongol envoys were sent to Japan in the summer of 1266, which means that the first negotiations between Japan and the Mongols should have taken place by late that year.

Kublai Khan dispatched the military official He De and the diplomatic official Yin Hong to Goryeo, demanding that they be conveyed to Japan as his official emissaries, sent to inform the Japanese that they must pledge fealty to the Mongols and render tribute to them. But Goryeo was wary of being drawn into a military confrontation between the Mongols and Japan, and chief minister Yi Jangyong and other Goryeo officials managed to dissuade the Mongol emissaries from making the dangerous ocean voyage to Japan, convincing them that Japan was too insignificant a country to bother themselves with, given the misfortunes that might befall them in the course of their voyage or after their arrival there.[34]

The Mongols did not give up the idea of attacking Japan. In the eighth month of Bun'ei 4 (1267), they once again dispatched Yin Hong and He De to Goryeo with a demand that a mission be sent from Goryeo to Japan bearing an official letter from the Khan. Goryeo dispatched an envoy named Pan Bu, who delivered this document to Japan in the first month of Bun'ei 5 (1268), after traveling to the port of Hakata in northern Kyūshū by way of Tsushima.[35]

The Mongol letter was delivered to the shogunate in Kamakura and thence to the imperial court in Kyoto, but as it was dated the eighth month of Bun'ei 3 (1266), it appears to have been the letter brought by the two emissaries on their first aborted mission. What this means is that the Mongols were deliberately choosing to ignore the stance Goryeo had taken in frustrating the first mission. Moreover, Pan Bu, the Goryeo envoy to Japan, had been exiled to Saiun-tō along with Yi Jangyong, the Goryeo chief minister who had prevented the first mission, and it seems likely that his dispatch to Japan was in part intended by the Mongols as a punitive measure against Goryeo.

The Mongol letter mentions that Goryeo has already become a vassal state and suggests that Japan enter into friendly relations with the Mongols—threatening military action (but "who would want that?") if

Table 4–3. The Process Leading to the War between the Yuan Dynasty and Japan: The Mongol (Yuan) Approach to Japan and the Japanese Response

1. 8th month, Bun'ei 3 (1266)	Mongol emissaries to Japan: He De, Yin Hong Goryeo attendants: Song Gunbi, Kim Chan The mission reached Tsushima but then turned back, reporting to the Yuan court on what had happened. Goryeo chief minister Yi Jangyong resists the Mongols and succeeds in preventing the mission from crossing the seas to Japan.
2. 1st month, Bun'ei 5 (1268)	He De and Yin Hong arrive in Goryeo. Pan Bu, Goryeo envoy, lands in Hakata bearing the state letter (translated in Note 35). Japan offers no response, but strengthens its defenses and offers prayers for defeat of the foreign threat.
3. 3rd month, Bun'ei 6 (1269)	A grand embassy of some 70 members led by He De, Yin Hong, and Pan Bu arrives at Tsushima. The Japanese refuse permission to land. The mission departs, seizing two residents of Tsushima as hostages and returns with them to the Yuan by way of Goryeo. The Yuan demand a reply to the previous state letter. The Japanese imperial court drafts a response to the Mongols but this is opposed by the Kamakura shogunate and no reply is sent.
4. 9th month, Bun'ei 6 (1269)	The Mongol envoy Yu Louda visits Goryeo. Accompanied by Goryeo envoys Kim Yuseong and Ko Yu, he arrives in Japan, bringing two hostages from Tsushima and an official letter from a Mongol minister of state. The Japanese consider sending a response from the Dajōkan (Grand Council of State), but in the end send no response.
5. 9th month, Bun'ei 8 (1271)	Mongol envoy Zhao Liangbi arrives in Japan, where he spends approximately a year. He brings another letter of state (translated in Note 37). Again, the Japanese send no response. Meanwhile, the Kamakura shogunate makes preparations for war and the imperial court expands its involvement in prayers for victory over the foreign threat.
6. 10th month, Bun'ei 11 (1274)	First Mongol Invasion (Bun'ei no Eki)
7. 7th month, Kōan 4 (1281)	Second Mongol Invasion (Kōan no Eki)

the Japanese chose not to comply. After much deliberation, the Japanese imperial court decided not to reply to this communication.

Seeing this response (or lack thereof) from the Japanese, in the third month of Bun'ei 6 (1269) the Mongols dispatched to Tsushima a grand embassy of some seventy individuals representing both the Mongols and Goryeo, headed by envoys that included He De and Yin Hong of the Yuan, and Pan Bu of Goryeo. Their intent was no doubt to impress upon the Japanese the strength of the alliance between the Mongols and Goryeo, and demonstrate the power of the Mongol regime. This embassy is believed to have demanded to know why there had been no response to the previous Mongol diplomatic correspondence, and when no answer was forthcoming from the Japanese side, they seized two Tsushima men (Tōjirō and Yajirō) as hostages and departed.

Then, in the ninth month, a Mongol envoy named Yu Louda (Ulodai) arrived in Japan, accompanied by two emissaries from Goryeo (Kim Yuseong and Ko Yu) and bringing with him the two Japanese hostages and a letter from a high-ranking Mongol official. In response, the Dajōkan (Grand Council of State) had Sugawara Naganari draft a reply that stuck mainly to formalities, arguing that Japan's diplomatic relations with China had been broken off long ago, but in the end even this communication was never sent to the Mongols. The gist of Sugawara's draft is believed to have read something like this:

> We have never heard before of the Mongols. Our diplomatic relations with China have been broken off, and we have never had relations with the Mongols. Japan is a peaceful nation which upholds the Buddhist teachings, a divine land ruled by our emperors since the time of the great goddess Amaterasu, and you should think well before attacking us, as neither your wit nor your power can possibly prevail.[36]

This implies that the Japanese imperial court (largely in ignorance of the contemporary international situation) was stressing the idea of Japan as a "divine land" in the hope that this would serve to enhance the authority of the emperor and establish the diplomatic credentials of the court (in this case the fact that the letter came from a Mongol minister of state, not the Khan, and the reply was to be sent from the

Dajōkan and not the emperor himself, made it easier to contemplate drafting a response). Even so, the Kamakura shogunate decided that the Mongol letter was insolent and undeserving of any response, and prevented the court's reply from being sent.

This did not, however, dissuade the Mongols. In the ninth month of Bun'ei 8 (1271) they sent a Jurchen retainer, Zhao Liangbi, accompanied by a small group of military men, to Imazu in Kyushu. The state letter Zhao bore with him took a soft approach, acknowledging that there must be a variety of reasons why a Japanese response to earlier communications had been delayed—but also openly touching upon the possibility of a resort to arms.[37]

After his arrival in Japan, Zhao Liangbi returned briefly to Goryeo, from whence he sent an individual named Zhang Duo to report to the Mongols while Zhao himself returned to Japan, where he spent about a year—making one suspect his primary mission was reconnaissance of the situation in Japan and preparations in Goryeo for impending military action. Meanwhile, the Japanese court sent an imperial decree to major shrines and temples in the land, ordering them to prepare prayers for the defeat of the nation's enemies, and the shogunate ordered all vassals resident in Kyushu or with fiefs or allotments on the island to exert themselves in strengthening the national defenses.

The imperial court wished to send a reply to the latest Mongol communication based on a revision of Sugawara's earlier draft, but in the end none was sent. It is possible that the imperial court itself gave up on the idea in light of the shogunate's intransigent attitude—yet it is just as likely that, as before, the shogunate actively intervened to prevent the delivery of such a message.

What was behind Japan's refusal to respond

As we have seen, the Japanese refused to respond to repeated overtures from the Mongols (except for a rather half-hearted and formalistic attempt by the imperial court to send a reply). Why did they adopt such a hard-line attitude, never sending any kind of written response?

The first reason may have been incapacity—ignorant as they were of the Mongols and the general situation on the Asian continent. For

179

many of the people involved the sudden appearance of the Mongol envoys and their state letters must have been a bolt out of the blue, stunning them into inaction. Konoe Motohira, who held the important court office of regent (*kampaku*) at the time, famously commented in his diary (*Jinshin'in kanpaku ki*, written 1255–68), "This is a completely unprecedented crisis for our nation. Everyone is dumbfounded."

This was connected to the second factor underlying the Japanese response—a policy that amounted to putting Japan's defense in the hands of the gods, attempting to spiritually unite the country so that the foreign invasion might be driven away by prayer and supplication to the deities. The Kamakura shogunate, a warrior regime, naturally called on the military governors (*shugo*) of the provinces to be on the alert and make efforts to strengthen the country's defenses. But at the same time, the shogunate, like the imperial court, offered prayers at the nations's shrines and temples for the defeat of the foreign enemy. These supplications were supported psychologically by a view of the enemy as both fearsome and defiled—and that the purity of the prayers would be most effectively maintained by refusing any form of contact with the enemy.

In other words, the Japanese refusal to make any type of reply to the Mongols was influenced by religious sentiments that sought to overcome the crisis by spiritually distancing Japan from its enemies while uniting it internally. This spiritual approach was in turn connected to a third factor—the political.

The arrival of diplomatic communications from the Mongols happened to coincide with the spread of Nichiren's *Risshō ankoku ron* (On Establishing the Correct Teaching for the Peace of the Country), which predicted that if the *nenbutsu* teachings of Hōnen were not prohibited, disaster would befall the country in the form of invasion by foreign enemies. With this type of sentiment rising, the shogunate had no choice but to take a resolute stance toward the Mongols. Since the Mongols appeared to fulfill Nichiren's warnings of the threat of enemy invasion, the shogunate could afford to show no weakness, lest it be criticized from various quarters for failing to defend the nation. With such political considerations operating so strongly within the country, the shogunate had no choice but to adopt a hard-line stance.

But the shogunate's hard line was even more deeply enmeshed in another domestic power struggle. In 1272, the shogunate experienced what later became known as the Nigatsu Sōdō (Second-month Rebellion),[38] and at this juncture the stability of Hōjō Tokimune's regime was uncertain. And since the arrival of the Mongol emissaries more or less coincided with this period of domestic political conflict and unrest, the response to these emissaries naturally enough became enmeshed with these struggles.

In addition, there was jostling between the imperial court and the shogunate over who held the authority to conduct foreign policy, making it a natural outcome that advocates for maintenance of a firm stand should gain the upper hand. When a regime is infected with internal discord—overt or nascent—unifying national opinion behind a hardline stance can be an essential means for keeping a lid on the conflict.

The strengthening of the hard line

Thus, in 1274, the first Mongol invasion of Japan (Bun'ei no Eki) was attempted, resulting in a direct military confrontation between Japan and the Yuan dynasty. But the Yuan also attempted to pursue a peaceful resolution to the matter, dispatching in the fourth month of Kenji 1 (1275) an official embassy with Du Shizhong as chief envoy and He Wenzhu as his deputy to the port of Murotsu in the province of Nagato (now Toyoura in Yamaguchi Prefecture) with an official state letter.[39]

Nagato was closer to the capital of Kyoto than Hakata, and the Yuan were probably attempting to establish direct negotiations with the imperial court, unmediated by the Dazaifu, the imperial office governing Kyushu. (It is also likely that the envoys had a subsidiary intention of gathering intelligence on Nagato, which was an important transport route between Kyushu and the heartland of Japan, especially the capital.)

The shogunate had the Yuan emissaries escorted to the shogunal capital at Kamakura, where, in the ninth month of the same year, all five members of the mission were beheaded. Then, in the sixth month of Kōan 2 (1279), the Yuan ordered the defeated Song general Fan Wenhu to invade Japan, and Fan sent two of his subordinates, Zhou

Fu and Luan Zhong, to Hakata in northern Kyushu with a letter urging the Japanese to surrender.[40]

It would seem that the Yuan were attempting to find some means to persuade the Japanese to submit peacefully, by making it clear that the Song dynasty with which the Japanese had centuries of contact had fallen to the Mongols, and that former Song officials were now working for the Yuan—a second motivation at work here was probably a desire to eliminate the potential for domestic conflict by involving former Song military leaders and their troops in overseas expeditions.

However, this diplomatic strategy on the part of the Yuan seems to have backfired. The Japanese regarded the dispatch of the letter from a former Song retainer to be an insult, and made an issue of it. The shogunate then ordered the Yuan emissaries beheaded in Hakata.

Thus, in the wake of the first Mongol invasion attempt, the Japanese response to the Yuan took an even harder line. This can be seen as an effort to stiffen domestic resolve in the face of what was clearly developing into a second attempt to invade Japan. And it is important to note that as the Japanese took an increasingly hard line against the Yuan, the ideology representing Japan as a "divine land" (*shinkoku*) intensified. Behind the rise of this ideology during the period surrounding the Mongol invasions of Japan, along with the doctrines of Nichiren, was clearly an effort to unify the nation ideologically and maintain domestic solidarity—though other internal political factors were also involved, such as efforts by the shogunate to strengthen its control over shrines and temples, as well as the increasing politicization of sectarian conflict.

What should be noted here is that the shogunate, as it engaged in the defense of Japan, was able to clothe itself in the divine land ideology, and thereby effect a transformation of itself from merely a locus of power to an agent fully vested with governing authority. The divine land ideology thus became a means for a military regime to add a more legitimate authority to the armed might it already possessed. When warfare actually commences, a military regime will quickly move to amass greater authority—and the more it does so, the harder the line it will take in foreign policy in order to manifest its prestige and determination.

What prevented greater flexibility in negotiations with China

Why, despite the repeated overtures of the Yuan to Japan, was the end result a plunge into warfare? Clearly, the aggressive intentions of the Yuan toward Japan and its desire to strengthen control over Goryeo were operative from the beginning. But from the perspective of diplomacy some explanation is still required for why Japan adopted such a hard-line attitude in the process leading toward war, completely refusing to participate in any negotiations or even reply to the official correspondence of the Mongols—even if one grants that the Mongols were a complete unknown to the Japanese and considers the fear they must have felt at the prospect of being subjected to a form of domination similar to that which befell Goryeo.

One major reason for such inflexibility was the existence of internal power struggles within the Kamakura shogunate, and the nature of the response to the foreign threat being unavoidably intertwined with these conflicts. In addition, the shogun and the imperial court had a delicate relationship with one another regarding the authority to make foreign policy, and there was political conflict between them as well. In the context of these internal political struggles, foreign policy inclined towards a harder line. Later, too, the *sonnō jōi* ("revere the emperor, expel the barbarians") ideology in the run-up to the Meiji Restoration of 1868 was clearly connected to the power struggle between the Tokugawa shogunate and the powerful provincial lords who eventually overthrew it; and it exerted a similarly large constraint upon the foreign policy options available to the shogunate. And we should also recall that in the process leading to Japan's war with China in the 1930s, the political power of the Japanese military and the power struggle it waged with the civilian government and political parties was a major factor in making a more flexible China policy impossible.

Second, as awareness grew of the national crisis posed by the threat of invasion by the Yuan, it was only natural that there would be increased movement towards a spiritual unification of the country. And we should note that this had more than mere strategic significance; it was connected to a certain type of ideological and philosophical movement. It would appear that a kind of vicious cycle was created in which this spiritual movement took on a life of its own; as an increasingly hard line was taken in foreign policy the Japanese "spirit" was increasingly stressed and utilized politically—and the result was an even harder foreign policy stance. That the Kamakura shogunate responded to the Mongol overtures from beginning to end with a display of uncompromising determination, displaying no interest whatsoever in using Goryeo as an intermediary, suggests that this vicious cycle—in which a hardline stance took on a certain spiritual cachet that invited the adoption of an even more uncompromising position—had indeed taken hold, regardless of internal power struggles. Conversely, we might say that this also speaks volumes regarding the lack of any coherent strategy in Japan's policies toward China, as well as an underlying inadequacy of awareness of the situation on the Asian continent and a failure to conceive of politics in international terms.

5. THE BACKGROUND TO MILITARY CONFRONTATION BETWEEN JAPAN AND TANG CHINA

We tend to imagine the Tang dynasty as an era of peaceful relations between Japan and China, conjuring up images of Japan's embassies to the Tang court and the culture of the Heian period (794–1185). But in fact, Japan and Tang China had a major military confrontation in the southern part of the Korean peninsula in 663, and the Japanese embassies dispatched before and after this (as noted earlier) appear to have been strategic, for the purpose of diplomatic negotiations. The Korean peninsula at the time was divided among the three states of Goguryeo, Baekje, and Silla. The clash between Japan and Tang China drew Silla and Baekje into the conflict, and was part of a larger struggle between China and Japan for control over the peninsula.

In 642, Yeon Gaesomun led a coup d'état in the Korean state of Goguryeo, making the strengthening of sovereign authority a pressing concern. There are records indicative of a major revolt in the state of Baekje the same year,[41] suggesting that here, too, the instability of sovereign power tended to be closely enmeshed with external warfare (in this case conflict with Silla). The result of the political situation in the states of the Korean peninsula and their foreign policy strategies was an intensification of the struggle between Baekje and Silla and a deepening of the conflict between Goguryeo and Tang China—leading eventually to a strategic alliance between Silla and the Chinese.

How was Japanese diplomacy towards Korea and China deployed under these circumstances? Japan's policy with regard to the Korean peninsula might be summed up by saying that it did not have a dependable partner among the Korean states. Goguryeo, which controlled the northern part of the Korean peninsula, did have cordial relations with Japan—prompting a Japanese emperor to remark, "Our envoys to Goguryeo, and the envoys of the Son of Heaven of Goguryeo to us, have a short history but promise a longer future"— but Japan and Goguryeo essentially remained remote from one another.

Baekje had sent a special envoy to Japan in the year that Emperor Kōtoku passed away (654), but during his reign there had only been one previous embassy from Baekje, in 645, the year he had ascended the throne. This would appear to be connected to the fact that Baekje had ceased paying the tribute formerly rendered to Japan by a state known as Mimana (Imna in Korean), the existence of which was symbolic of Japanese control of a portion of the Korean peninsula.[42] In any event, in the context of the intensification of conflict between Baekje and Silla, this can probably be seen as evidence of a cooling of relations between Baekje and Japan, especially in contrast to Silla, which was sending frequent embassies to Japan that took a form similar to that of tribute missions.

Silla, on the other hand, displayed significant interest in its relations with Japan in the form of these frequent missions, while simultaneously using them to keep an eye on Japan. But, the Japanese were troubled by Silla's relations with China, and resisted Silla's attempts to borrow the power and prestige of the Tang in its diplomatic approaches to Japan. (For example, in 651, when envoys from Silla arrived in Kyushu attired in Tang court dress, they were driven away.[43]) In 646, Japan dispatched Takamuko no Kuromaro to Silla, where he conveyed Japan's stance that it did not recognize Silla's territorial claims over

Mimana, and demanded that Silla provide hostages to Japan—suggesting increasing tension in Japan's relations with Silla.

Developments in Japan's relations with Tang China

Meanwhile, how were Japan's relations with Tang-dynasty China faring? In 648, using Silla as an intermediary, Japan dispatched a letter to the Tang court "informing of our affairs" (reporting on the state of the nation).[44] This may be interpreted as a friendly gesture toward the Tang, probably undertaken with encouragement from Silla. Following up on this (and probably with the additional motive of gaining intelligence on the internal situation in China), the Japanese sent an official embassy to the Tang in 653. The Tang took this occasion to instruct Japan to assist them against the Goguryeo-Baekje alliance.[45]

Despite the fact that the Japanese did not heed this instruction, they sent further missions to the Tang in 658 and 659 in an attempt to adjust their diplomatic relations with China, but by this time the Tang were already embroiled in warfare with Goguryeo. The Japanese envoys of 659 were told that the Tang were determined to subjugate the Korean peninsula the following year, and for the time being the envoys could not be permitted to return home; the Japanese mission was thus temporarily interned in the Tang capital of Luoyang.[46] This was tantamount to a severing of diplomatic relations between the two countries.

Japan's diplomacy with China was thus stalemated and it refrained from military action on the Korean peninsula. So in July 660, Baekje fell to the combined armies of Tang China and Silla. The king of Baekje was captured and taken to Luoyang, and Tang officials were appointed to rule Baekje. But they were unable to fully pacify the countryside, and a restoration movement arose, led by the Baekje general Boksin. This movement took as its sovereign Prince Buyeo Jang (Buyeo Pungjang), a member of the Baekje royal family who had escaped to Japan, and called upon the Japanese for assistance. A Japanese army of more than 20,000 men was dispatched to the Korean peninsula, resulting in the famous Battle of Hakusukinoe (known in Korea as the Battle of Baekgang), pitting the forces of Japan and the Baekje loyalists against the combined armies of Tang China and Silla.

The motivation for Japan's military assistance to Baekje

What were Japan's motives in making this decisive commitment to the support of Baekje?

The first was the restoration of the Baekje royal house. As noted above, prior to the Battle of Hakusukinoe, relations between Japan and Baekje had cooled somewhat. But precisely because of this, it seems plausible that Japan hoped that by lending its support to the establishment of a new king in Baekje, the awkwardness in relations between the two states would be overcome and Japanese influence over the royal house of Baekje reestablished.

The second motivation was a desire to punish Silla. In the *Nihon shoki* it is recorded that as early as 649, one of the principal Japanese ministers of state, Kose no Tokuda, had argued that if Japan did not immediately strike against Silla, the opportunity would be lost. In the section of the chronicle treating the Battle of Hakusukinoe it is described in a manner that indicates the intention of mounting a punitive expedition against Silla.

A third motive was related to efforts to bring the northern part of the Japanese archipelago under the control of the imperial court. In 658 the Japanese general Abe no Hirafu conquered the Mishihase (Suksin), and in the following year led a large-scale and victorious expedition against the Emishi. (The Mishihase and the Emishi were indigenous peoples of northern Japan.)

Other entries in the *Nihon shoki* relate that some members of the Mishihase accompanied a Silla embassy to Japan and that two Emishi (a man and woman) were taken by one of the Japanese missions to Tang China and presented to Emperor Gaozong. Thus it would seem that Japan's pacification of the northern tribes had become a factor increasing tension in relations with similar peoples in the Korean peninsula and northeastern China and, by extension, in Japan's relations with Silla and with the Chinese. In other words, the expansion of the sphere of control of the Japanese "empire" northwards might be said to reflect the shift in Japan's stance toward a hard-line position regarding China and Silla.

And finally, there was the problem of Japan's relations with the Tang. That the Japanese envoy to the Tang was given instructions to come to the aid of Silla was a clear indication that Japan was in danger of moving from a relationship with the Tang that (formalities aside) was essentially independent, to one in which the de facto relationship would be one of fealty or vassalage. In this context, Japan's possession of its own sphere of influence on the Korean peninsula became an even more important way of asserting its independence, both tacitly and explicitly. In short, Japan's (or Yamato's) position as a "great power" now "stood in danger of being gravely damaged by the denial of Yamato's position and the effort to reduce it to a dependency" of Tang China.[47] And this was almost certainly a major motive in Japan's decision to fight the Battle of Hakusukinoe.

6. THREE LESSONS FROM HISTORY FOR THE PRESENT

As we have seen, over nearly two millennia of history, Japan and China have gone to war on five occasions: the Battle of Hakusukinoe (or the Battle of Baekgang; seventh century) between Japan and Tang China; the attempted Mongol invasions of Japan during the Yuan dynasty (thirteenth century); combat with Ming-dynasty Chinese armies intervening against Hideyoshi's invasions of Korea (sixteenth century); the First Sino-Japanese War of 1894–95; and the Second Sino-Japanese War of 1937–45.

Analysis of these conflicts reveals at least three lessons that present generations should learn from the past. The first is that all of these wars began with struggles for influence over the Korean peninsula. The fuse that lit the Second Sino-Japanese War may appear to have been the issue of rights over Manchuria (or China's Northeast), but underlying this was the historical current of Japan's efforts to stabilize its control over the Korean peninsula (and to suppress both the Korean independence movement and the rise of progressive forces in Japan). This speaks eloquently of the crucial importance—at present and in the future—of dialogue between Japan and China concerning Korean issues. Thus it would seem that Japan and China (not necessarily at the governmental level, but along the so-called "third track") should deepen and expand their conversation regarding how each country envisions the future of the Korean peninsula.

The second lesson that emerges from our historical investigation concerns the relationship between foreign and domestic politics. The Battle of Hakusukinoe was clearly connected to the domestic political motivation of establishing the authority of the emperor. The attempted Mongol invasions of Japan were deeply intertwined with the domestic political issue facing the Yuan dynasty of how to deal with the defeated Song Chinese (and especially with their surrendered armies). Hideyoshi's invasions of Korea were intimately related to his efforts to establish control over the daimyo and consolidate his unification of Japan. The First Sino-Japanese War was greatly affected by the reactionary character of the Qing court and its determination—above all else— to preserve its monarchical prerogatives in the domestic sphere. And in the case of the Second Sino-Japanese War, Japanese politics were swayed towards militarism by nationalist sentiment over control of Manchuria and protection of Japanese nationals on the continent, while China's internal political conflicts and civil war made it almost impossible to engage in calm and deliberate negotiations with Japan.

In light of this past history, both Japan and China must make efforts to ensure that their mutual relationship is not used—and abused—for domestic political purposes. There are those who would argue that in a democratic society, and in a networked society, it is impossible to contain popular discontent and sentiment. But this is an attitude that encourages tendencies towards populism or even mobocracy in politics. Political leaders must not pander to the masses, but rather appeal to the people with a vision of what the future of the country should be in fifty or a hundred years. And it is for this reason also that it is essential to look at Sino-Japanese relations in the context of their two-thousand-year history.

Third, Sino-Japanese relations have been deeply affected by both nations' relations with Europe, Russia, and the United States. While the clash between Hideyoshi's armies and those of Ming China might appear to have been one over hegemony over the Korean peninsula, it was also an aspect of Japan's response to the Western colonial penetration of East Asia. And in modern times Sino-Japanese relations have frequently been less connected with bilateral strategic considerations than they have been with diplomacy and attempts at policy accommodation with third parties such as Britain or Russia.

The fact that Sino-Japanese relations have developed in ways that have eluded their bilateral intentions suggests that imbedding Sino-Japanese relations within a framework of international cooperation can minimize friction between the two countries, but also, conversely, alienate them from one another. The extent to which Sino-Japanese relations can be effectively dealt with in terms of bilateral strategy alone is something that both countries must continually keep in mind.

Chronology
238–1995

238	Himiko sends embassy headed by Nashonmi to the kingdom of Wei.
478	"King Bu of Wa" (Emperor Yūryaku) sends embassy to Liu Song dynasty (embassies by the so-called Five Kings of Wa to the Liu Song began in 421).
607	Prince Shōtoku sends embassy headed by Ono no Imoko to the Sui court.
630	First embassy to Tang China headed by Inugami no Mitasuki.
646	Takamuko no Kuromaro sent to Silla to convey Japan's stance that it did not recognize Silla's territorial claims over Mimana.
654	Takamuko no Kuromaro arrives in Tang China; later dies there.
660	Battle of Hakusukinoe (clash of allied armies of Tang China and Silla vs. Japanese and Baekje loyalist forces).
702	Japanese envoy Awata no Mahito praised by the Tang court.
759	Fujiwara no Nakamaro lays plans for expedition against Silla (–761).

804	Saichō, Kūkai, and other Buddhist monastics accompany embassy to the Tang.
894	Sugawara no Michizane's memorial to the throne terminates nearly two centuries of embassies to Tang China.
983	The monk Chōnen arrives in Song China and has an audience with Emperor Taizong, informing the latter of the longevity of the Japanese imperial house.
1078	The monk Chūkai arrives in Song China, delivering a response to the official letter and gifts bestowed by Emperor Shenzong on an earlier Japanese visitor, the monk Jōjin, in 1073.
1260	Nichiren writes *Risshō ankoku ron* (On Establishing the Correct Teaching for the Peace of the Country).
1266	Yuan dynasty sends first emissary to Japan.
1274	Bun'ei no Eki (First Mongol Invasion of Japan).
1281	Kōan no Eki (Second Mongol Invasion of Japan).
1401	Ashikaga Yoshimitsu sends embassy to Ming China (the first in a series of embassies until around 1408).
1583	Jesuit missionary Matteo Ricci begins mission work in Guangdong.
1587	Toyotomi Hideyoshi issues edict expelling Christian missionaries.
1592	Toyotomi Hideyoshi invades Korean peninsula (Bunroku/Keichō no Eki, –1598).
1607	First Korean embassy (*Chōsen tsūshinshi*) to Tokugawa Japan, headed by Yeo Ugil.
1616	Shipping from anywhere other than Ming China limited to the Japanese ports of Nagasaki and Hirado.
1635	Ming shipping limited to Nagasaki.
1644	Ming dynasty falls to Qing (Manchu) forces; requests military assistance from Japan but is refused by the Tokugawa shogunate.

1715	The "Shōtoku Shinrei" regulations, authored by Arai Hakuseki, limit trade with Qing China to half its previous level.
1861	Yamada Yasugorō, a Confucian scholar from Matsuyama domain, advocates an invasion of China's Shandong region and the Korean peninsula.
1882	Imo Mutiny (the reactionary regent Daewongun seizes power in Korea, leading to deeper involvement by Qing China in Korean affairs).
1884	Gapsin Coup (failed coup attempt by Kim Okgyun and associates leads to confrontation between Qing China and Japan).
1885	Osaka Incident. Britain occupies Korea's Geomundo islands. Tianjin Convention signed between Japan and Qing China.
1893	Eulmi Incident; assassination of Queen Min.
1894	First Sino-Japanese War (–1895); Donghak Rebellion.
1895	Treaty of Shimonoseki between Japan and Qing China.
1896	Li-Lobanov treaty between Qing China and Russia (intended as a type of offensive-defensive alliance vs. Japan).
1900	Boxer Rebellion.
1901	Katsura cabinet forms; transformation of Korea into a Japanese protectorate is stated as policy goal.
1902	First Anglo-Japanese Alliance.
1904	Russo-Japanese War (–1905); First Korean-Japanese Convention.
1905	Second Anglo-Japanese Alliance; Second Korean-Japanese Convention.
1907	Third Korean-Japanese Convention.
1908	Tatsumaru Incident; anti-Japanese agitation in China.
1909	Ahn Junggeun assassinates Itō Hirobumi in Harbin.
1910	Japan-Korea Annexation treaty signed.

1911	Third Anglo-Japanese Alliance; Xinhai Revolution (Revolution of 1911 by Sun Yat-sen and his associates against rule of China by the Qing dynasty).
1915	R. B. Bose enters Japan under an assumed name, intent on establishing international cooperation among Asian anticolonialist movements.
1919	Japanese delegation to the Paris Peace Conference (Versailles Treaty Conference) proposes inclusion of a racial equality clause in the League of Nations Charter; it is rejected.
1925	Japan issues the Twenty-One Demands to China.
1927	Nanjing Incident; Shandong Expedition (–1928).
1928	Assassination of Zhang Zuolin.
1931	Manchurian Incident.
1941	Pacific War begins with attack on Pearl Harbor; Indian National Army formed under command of Captain Mohan Singh raises the flag of revolt against British forces.
1943	Indian independence movement leader Subhas Chandra Bose visits Japan to attend the Greater East Asia Conference and emphasizes the common cause with Japanese forces.
1944	Imphal Campaign.
1945	Japan surrenders.
1965	Normalization of Japan's relations with South Korea.
1972	Normalization of Japan's relations with the People's Republic of China; Kim Daejung kidnapping.
1979	Assassination of Park Jeonghui; Cheon Duhwan takes power.
1989	Tiananmen Incident in Beijing.
1995	Statement by Prime Minister Murayama Tomiichi on the 50th anniversary of the end of World War II.

Notes

CHAPTER ONE

The Ethos of Japan's Asian Diplomacy

1. Hōnen (1133–1212) taught that simply by reciting Amida Buddha's name (*nenbutsu*) people would achieve rebirth in Amida's Pure Land (*Jōdo*).

2. A copy of this document, dated the eighth month of the third year of the Zhiyuan era (1266), has been preserved in the archives of the temple Tōdaiji in Nara. The English translation that follows is from Kenneth W. Chase, "Mongol Intentions towards Japan in 1266: Evidence from a Mongol Letter to the Sung," *Sino-Japanese Studies*, 9:2 (1990), 13–22.

> Favored by the decree of Highest Heaven, the emperor of the Great Mongol Nation sends this letter to the King of Japan.
>
> Since ancient times the sovereigns of small countries whose territories adjoined each other have taken it as their duty to cement peaceful relations by upholding good faith. How much more so [should this apply in this case], since Our ancestors received a clear mandate from Heaven and controlled all of China, and those from distant places and other regions who fear Our awesomeness and embrace our virtue have been countless.
>
> When We first ascended the throne, as the innocent people of Korea had long suffered from spearheads and arrowheads, We immediately disbanded the soldiers and returned their frontier fortresses and

sent their old and young back [to their homes]. The Korean sovereign and subjects came to Our court to express their thanks. Although in righteousness we were sovereign and subject, we were as happy as father and son. We believe that your subjects already know this.

Korea is Our eastern frontier. Japan is close to Korea. From the founding of your country you have also occasionally had contact with China, but to us you have not sent even 'an envoy with a single cart' to communicate friendly [intentions].

Fearing your kingdom knows this but has not considered it [carefully], We have specially dispatched an envoy with a letter to proclaim Our intention. We hope that hereafter we will exchange greetings and establish friendly [relations] in order to have mutual affection and friendship. The sage treats all within the four seas as family; could it be the principle of a family not to mutually exchange friendly [greetings]?

As for using soldiers and weapons, who would want that?

King, consider this.

[This] does not fully express [Our meaning].

3. Satō Kazuhiko and Higuchi Kunio, *Hōjō Tokimune no subete* (Jinbutsu Ōraisha, 2000), 159.

4. The following English translation of Hideyoshi's letter is taken from Wm. Theodore de Bary, Donald Keene, and George Tanabe, eds., *Sources of the Japanese Tradition*, second edition, *Volume 1: From the Earliest Times to 1600* (New York: Columbia University Press, 2001), 466–67.

Hideyoshi, the Imperial Regent of Japan, sends this letter to His Excellency, the King of Korea.

I read your epistle from afar with pleasure, opening and closing the scroll again and again to savor the aroma of your distinguished presence.

Now, then: This empire is composed of more than sixty provinces, but for years the country was divided, the polity disturbed, civility abandoned, and the realm unresponsive to imperial rule. Unable to stifle my indignation at this, I subjugated the rebels and struck down the bandits within the span of three or four years. As far away as foreign regions and distant islands, all is now in my grasp.

As I privately consider the facts of my background, I recognize it to be that of a rustic and unrefined minor retainer. Nevertheless: As I was about to be conceived, my dear mother dreamt that the wheel of the sun had entered her womb. The diviner declared, 'As far as the sun shines, so will the brilliance of his rule extend. When he reaches his prime, the Eight Directions will be enlightened through his benevolence and the Four Seas replete with the glory of his name. How could anyone doubt this?' As a result of this miracle, anyone who turned against me was automatically crushed. Whomever I fought, I never failed to win; wherever I attacked, I never failed to conquer. Now that the realm has been thoroughly pacified, I caress and nourish the people, solacing the orphaned and the desolate. Hence my subjects live in plenty and the revenue produced by the land has increased ten-thousand-fold over the past. Since this empire originated, never has the imperial court seen such prosperity or the capital city such grandeur as now.

Man born on this earth, though he live to a ripe old age, will as a rule not reach a hundred years. Why should I rest, then, grumbling in frustration, where I am? Disregarding the distance of the sea and mountain reaches that lie in between, I shall in one fell swoop invade the Great Ming. I have in mind to introduce Japanese customs and values to the four hundred and more provinces of the country and bestow upon it the benefits of imperial rule and culture for the coming hundred million years.

Your esteemed country has done well to make haste in attending on our court. Where there is farsightedness, grief does not come near. Those who lag behind [in offering homage], however, will not be granted pardon, even if this is a distant land of little islands lying in the sea. When the day comes for my invasion of Great Ming and I lead my troops to the staging area, that will be the time to make our neighborly relations flourish all the more. I have no other desire but to spread my fame throughout the Three Countries, this and no more.

I have received your regional products as itemized. Stay healthy and take care.

Tenshō 18. XI.
Hideyoshi
Imperial Regent of Japan

5. Translation from Wm. Theodore de Bary, Donald Keene, and George Tanabe, eds., *Sources of the Japanese Tradition*, second edition, *Volume 1: From the Earliest Times to 1600* (New York: Columbia University Press, 2001), 6–7.
6. Takemitsu Makoto and Yamagishi Ryōji, *Yamatai-koku o shiru jiten* (Tōkyōdō Shuppan, 1999), 129 ff.

7. The *Wei zhi* provides the following account of Himiko as a ruler (de Bary, et. al, *Sources of the Japanese Tradition*, 7):

> The country formerly had a man as a ruler. For some seventy or eighty years after that there were disturbances and warfare. Thereupon the people agreed upon a woman for their ruler. Her name was Pimiko [Himiko]. She occupied herself with magic and sorcery, bewitching the people. Though mature in age, she remained unmarried. She had a younger brother who assisted her in ruling the country. After she became ruler there were few who saw her. She had one thousand women as attendants but only one man. He served her food and drink and acted as a medium of communication. She resided in a palace surrounded by towers and stockades, with armed guards in a state of constant vigilance....

8. Takemitsu and Yamagishi, 69 ff.

9. Shiraishi Masaya, *Betonamu minzoku undō to Nihon · Ajia* (Gannandō Shoten, 1993), 412 ff.

10. See, for example, the article "France et Japon" in *Le Matin*, 16 January 1905, and "Le Peril Jaune" in *Le Journal de Rouen*, 19 January 1905.

11. Ogura Kazuo, "Kindai Nihon no Ajia gaikō no kiseki" 8, in *Kan* (Winter 2010), 237–38.

12. Ibid., 328.

13. Kuzuu Yoshihisa, *Tō-A senkaku shishi den*, vol 1 (Taikōsha, 1997), 629 ff; Miyazaki Tōten, *Miyazaki Tōten: Sanjūsan-nen no yume* (Nihon Tosho Center, 1998), 211 ff.

14. Fujii Shōzō, *Son Bun no kenkyū* (Keisō Shobō, 1996), 21.

15. Kuzuu, *Tō-A senkaku shishi den*, vol 1, 630. For the request from the US ambassador to Japan in connection with this incident, see "Nunobi-ki-maru Incident" in *Nihon gaikō bunsho* 32.

16. According to notes made by the author, who was present at the meeting.

17. The fact that after his appointment as president Kim made a point of having official meetings with Doi Takako and Den Hideo, Japanese socialist politicians who had been his friends during his years in opposition, also suggests his appreciation for such past associations.

18. For further details on this matter, see Ogura Kazuo, "Son Bun to Nihon gaikō," in *Kan* (Summer 2010).

19. *Nihon gaikō bunsho* 37:1, document 383. English version in James Brown Scott, *Korea: Treaties and Agreements* (Washington: Carnegie Endowment for International Peace, 1921), 36.

20. *Nihon gaikō bunsho* 37:1, document 302. English version in James Brown Scott, *Korea: Treaties and Agreements* (Washington: Carnegie Endowment for International Peace, 1921), 33.

21. *Nihon gaikō bunsho* 38:1, document 60. English version in James Brown Scott, *Korea: Treaties and Agreements* (Washington: Carnegie Endowment for International Peace, 1921), 41.

22. *Nihon gaikō bunsho* 34, document 22.

23. Naraoka Sōchi, "Igirisu kara mita Itō Hirobumi tōkan to Kankoku tōchi," in Itō Yukio and Lee Sung-hwan, eds., *Itō Hirobumi to Kankoku Tōchi* (Minerva Shobō, 2009), 64.

24. *Nihon gaikō bunsho* 14, document 3, appendix 2.

25. *Nihon gaikō bunsho*, Taishō 3, vol. 3, document 570; Taishō 4, vol. 3, document 137.

26. *Nihon gaikō bunsho*, Taishō 3, vol. 3, documents 170, 174.

27. Ibid., document 208.

28. Ibid., document 314.

29. Ōkuma-kō Hachijūnen-shi Hensankai, eds., *Ōkuma-kō hachijūgonen-shi*, vol. 3 (Hara Shobō, 1970), 169.

30. On the relationship between the Asian Monroe Doctrine and Japan's China policy, see Kobayashi Michihiko, "Sekai taisen to tairiku seisaku no hen'yō—1914–16 nen," in *Rekishi kenkyū*, no. 656 (1994).

31. Aoki Shūzō, Japanese minister to Germany during this period, wrote of German thinking on this subject in the following manner:

> The main point of the political strategy the nations of Europe should adopt toward Qing China should be a conservative defense of the status quo. If at some point before the European powers are capable of partitioning and occupying all of China, the Japanese should pre-empt them by occupying strategic points in south and north China and establishing their influence there, then the Chinese will be over-whelmingly indoctrinated by the Japanese, having no choice but to abandon their backward and outdated customs and attain a European level of civilization, eventually refusing to accept the tutelage of the Westerners and, in the economic realm, cease imports of European agricultural products. Not only that: if the Japanese and Chinese reach a common understanding along the lines of "Asia for the Asians," and conclude an alliance offering each other mutual assistance, both offensive and defensive, the power of the yellow races shall grow ever more vigorous, to the inevitable detriment of white society. Thus,

at present we must on the one hand restrain the Japanese and the development of their power, while at the same time seeking to prevent Chinese from progressing toward the realm of civilization. . . .

From *Aoki Shūzō jiden*, edited and annotated by Sakane Yoshihisa (Heibonsha, 1970), 286.

32. Tachi Sakutarō, "Meiji 27–28 nen no sen'eki to Doitsu gaikō," in *Kokusaihō gaikō zasshi*, nos. 1–3, vol. 26, 1927.

33. *Nihon gaikō bunsho* 14, document 3, appendix 2. The English text is from the original letter sent from Wilhelm II to Nicholas II on 16 April 1895, reproduced in Isaac Don Levine, ed., *Letters from the Kaiser to the Czar* (New York: Frederick A. Stokes Company, 1920), 10.

34. Letter from Wilhelm II to Nicholas II, 26 September 1895, in Ibid., 16–17.

35. Henry Norman, *The Peoples and Politics of the Far East* (New York: Charles Scribner's Sons, 1895).

36. Ibid., 318–19; 396.

37. Kajima Heiwa Kenkyūjo, eds., *Nihon gaikōshi 8: Dainikai Nichi-Ei dōmei to sono jidai* (Kajima Kenkyūjo Shuppankai, 1970), 40.

38. *Nihon gaikō bunsho* 38, vol. 1, document 77, appendix, p. 77.

39. In this regard, the cabinet resolution of 24 May 1905, which set Japan's basic foreign policy orientation following the Russo-Japanese War, contained the following noteworthy passage:

> While the present war has made the powers acknowledge the true worth of our nation and has received their acclaim, we must also accept that behind this lurk feelings of alarm and suspicion. Because these feelings are likely to continue to grow as our national power develops in the postwar period, we cannot but be concerned that our nation might be made to stand in isolation. Yet if we conclude an offensive-defensive alliance with Great Britain, we should be able to forestall this misfortune, and avoid being pushed aside by others.
>
> *Nihon gaikō bunsho* 38:1, document 18.

40. In this regard, see the following passage from *Nihon gaikō bunsho* 36: 1, document 50:

> Preventing a resurgence of Yellow Peril hysteria
> We have heard considerably less of white fear of the "yellow race" running rampant—in other words, the so-called Yellow Peril hysteria—in recent times, but such sentiments still lie dormant in the hearts of Europeans, ready to be aroused at the slightest provocation,

and there is concern that these unfounded beliefs will unite them [against us]. Because of this, if Japan and China should join in a war against Russia, this could become the impetus for a resurgence of the Yellow Peril hysteria, creating considerable concern that this might result in other nations such as Germany and France involving themselves in the conflict.

41. Anatole France, *The White Stone*, tr. Charles E. Roche (London: Lone Lane, 1910), 159–60.

42. For the racial equality proposal and the developments surrounding it, see *Nihon gaikō bunsho*, Taishō 8 (1929), "Kōwa kaigi keika chōsho," *sono* 3–6.

43. Kajima Morinosuke, *Nihon gaikōshi* 12: *Pari kōwa kaigi* (Kajima Kenkyūjo Shuppankai, 1971), 188.

44. *Nihon gaikō bunsho*, Taishō 8 (1929), "Kōwa kaigi keika chōsho," *sono* 6.

45. Ibid., *sono* 7. Original English quotation from Shizuka Imamoto, "Racial Equality Bill: Japanese Proposal at Paris Peace Conference: Diplomatic Manouevres; and Reasons for Rejection" (M.A. thesis, Macquarie University, 2006), 95.

46. Ikeuchi Hiroshi, *Bunroku Keichō no eki*, Seihen (Yoshikawa Kōbunkan, 1914), 15–16.

47. Matsuda Kiichi, *Toyotomi Hideyoshi to Nambanjin* (Chōbunsha, 2001), 31.

48. As early as 1582, Hideyoshi had already promised Kamei Korenori, castellan of Shikano Castle in Inaba Province, that he would in future be granted the Ryukyus as a fiefdom, and in later years, when he was forced to acknowledge Shimazu Yoshihisa's hegemony over the islands, Hideyoshi promised Kamei he would be given the Ming province of Zhejiang in recompense. See Akamine Mamoru, *Ryūkyū Ōkoku* (Kōdansha, 2004), 85–86.

49. It is worth noting that in Hideyoshi's official correspondance (the so-called "vermilion seal letters") and elsewhere, references to the "land of the southern barbarians" (*Nanban-koku*) appear almost as frequently as to Korea (*Kōrai*) and China (*Kara*), even though it is possible this did not necessarily signify the European countries of Spain and Portugal but territories such as the present-day Philippines.

50. Matsuda Kiichi, *Toyotomi Hideyoshi to Nambanjin* (Chōbunsha, 2001), 111–13

51. In this regard, some commentators have read *waka* poems written by Hideyoshi as close in spirit to the later concept of the Greater East Asian Co-Prosperity Sphere. See, for example, Ishihara Michihiro, *Bunroku-Keichō no eki* (Hanawa Shobō, 1963), 42. For another view of the relationship between

Hideyoshi's national consciousness and his foreign policy, see Asami Shōzō, "Hideyoshi gaikō ni okeru kokka ishiki," *Rekishi kyōiku*, 8:6 (1933).

52. Ogura Kazuo, "Kankoku hogokoku-ka to Nihon gaikō (*sono* 1)," *Kan* (Winter 2011).

53. Cabinet document of 30 December 1903 (Meiji 36). *Nihon gaikō bunsho* 36:1, document 50.

54. *Nihon gaikō bunsho* 36:1, document 50.

55. *Nihon gaikō bunsho* 37:2:5, "Rokoku kankei hensan," no. 1153. A similar perception was expressed by a delegation of Poles who called at the Japanese embassy in Austria in July 1904 and praised Japan for "taking up arms for the cause of civilization." Ibid., no. 1094.

CHAPTER TWO

The Interaction of Domestic and Foreign Policy

1. "Zuisho wakoku den," in Ishihara Michihiro, ed. and trans., *Shintei Gishi wajin den hoka sanpen* (Iwanami Shoten, 1951), 32, 67, 129.

2. Ishihara Michihiro, ed. and trans., *Kutōjo Wakoku Nihon den* (new edition) (Iwanami Shoten, 1982).

3. For a discussion of this see Ogura Kazuo, "Kentōshi o meguru gaikō senryaku," *Tō-A* (July 2008).

4. This diplomatic correspondence is described in Kamiya Nobuyuki, *Taikun gaikō to Higashi Ajia* (Yoshikawa Kōbunkan, 1997), 10 ff. The Ming dynasty permitted ships of "tributary" countries to trade by issuing official certificates or tallies called *kanhe* (J. *kangō*).

5. *Ikoku nikki* 2, ed. and annotated by Tsuji Zennosuke, *Shien*, no. 1–2 (1928).

6. Tanaka Takeo, *Chūsei taigai kankei shi* (Tokyo Daigaku Shuppankai, 1975), 65; Usui Nobuyoshi, *Ashikaga Yoshimitsu* (Yoshikawa Kōbunkan, 1989), 179.

7. According to the *Zenrin kokuhō ki*. For a translation into modern Japanese of the complete texts of the state letters between Yoshimitsu and the Ming, see Sakuma, *Nichi-Min kankei shi no kenkyū*.

8. Tamura Eitarō, *Shiryō kara mita Hideyoshi no shōtai*, vol. 2 (Yūzankaku, 1965), 280 ff; 285.

9. Yi Chin-hui, *Richō no Chōsen tsūshinshi* (Kōdansha, 1976).

10. The embassy sent to congratulate Tsunayoshi on his accession to the office of shogun might be cited as a similar example. See Ogura Kazuo, "Tokugawa jidai no tai-Chū gaikō to anteiki no tai-Chōsen gaikō," *Tō-A* (March 2009).

11. Park Jaeyang, *Tōsa manroku* (*Dongsa: A Rambling Essay*), 23 January 1885, quoted in Song Min, "Meiji shoki ni okeru Chōsen tsūshinshi no Nihon kenbun," http://www.nichibun.ac.jp/graphicversion/dbase/forum/text/fn121.html

12. Suzuki Yasutami, *Kodai taigai kankeishi no kenkyū* (Yoshikawa Kōbunkan, 1985), 197.

13. One embassy is said to have been dispatched for the purpose of securing the position of a crown prince by seeking a Chinese elixir that could cure him of a "disease of the chest." Ibid., 124.

14. Examples suggesting conflict among members of the missions include personnel changes among the vice-envoys of the embassy of 777 and the refusal of chief envoy Saeki no Imaemishi to make the voyage to China on account of illness, as well as a similar refusal on grounds of illness by chief envoy Ono no Takamura in 838. See Tōno Haruyuki, *Kentōshi sen* (Asahi Shimbunsha, 1999), 12–13.

15. The text of Michizane's memorial is as follows (original text in Sugawara Michizane, "Sho kugyō o shite kentōshi no shinshi o gitei seshimen koto o kou no jō," in *Kanke bunsō*, vol. 9 [n.p., n.d., 1667]; in *Nihon Koten Bungaku Taikei*, vol 72 [Iwanami Shoten, 1966]):

> A Memorial Requesting Deliberation by the Imperial Court Concerning the Continuation or Suspension of the Embassies to Tang China
>
> My lords, I respectfully report that in the third month of last year I have received communications from the monk Chūkan, presently in China, sent via the merchant Wang Ne and others, concerning the current state of affairs in China. I have appended copies of his letter to this memorial. It contains a detailed account that the Tang dynasty, once a great power, has now fallen into ruin. Therefore we should tell the Tang that we have no desire to render tribute, and we shall stop sending envoys. Chūkan may be no more than a traveling monk, but he is deeply loyal to our sacred realm. As the saying goes, even the horses and birds do not forget their homes; is this not even more true of human custom? In my examination of the ancient records I find many examples of former envoys who perished in their attempts to cross the sea, while others lost their lives to attacks by pirates. There has been no recovery and the Tang court pretends not to see the suffering and deprivation that prevail there. Even though Chūkan's reported on this to the Tang court, there is no knowing how the report was handled. So I your loyal subject respectfully implore you to make the details of Chūkan's report widely known to the

nobles and wise men of this land, so that they may reach a decision on this issue [of terminating the missions to Tang China]. This is not merely for my own sake; it is a matter of gravest importance for our nation. I therefore bow before you in humble sincerity and await your disposition of this matter. With greatest respect, I remain,

Your imperial servant, Sugawara

14th day, 6th month of Kanpei 6 [894]

16. See, for example, Sakamoto Tarō, *Sugawara no Michizane* (Yoshikawa Kōbunkan, 1997), 88–89. Regarding this point, some are of the opinion that the timing of the abdication of Emperor Uda influenced the decision to cancel Michizane's embassy, since Uda would no longer have been on the throne to hear the report of the envoy he appointed, and this would be an obstacle to the proper exchange of letters of state with the Tang (see Suzuki, *Kodai taigai kankeishi no kenkyū*).

17. For details see Sakamoto, *Sugawara no Michizane*, 49 ff.

18. From the diary of Fujiwara no Kanezane, *Gyokuyō* (book 5), in *Shiryō ni yoru Nihon no ayumi: Chūsei hen* (Yoshikawa Kōbunkan, 1996), 61.

19. Fujiwara Reinosuke, *Nitchū kōryū nisennen* (Tokyo Daigaku Shuppankai, 1988), 130.

20. Compiled by the author from information in Ishihara Michihiro, ed. and tr., *Chūgoku seishi Nihon den*, vol. 2 (Iwanami Shoten, 1986) and Fujiwara, *Nitchū kōryū nisennen*.

21. For a more detailed discussion, see Ogura Kazuo, "Kiyomori no 'keizai gaikō'," *Tō-A* (August 2008).

22. In the eleventh century we begin to see officials punished for conducting private trade, notable examples being Kiyohara no Moritake (1047) and Fujiwara no Korefusa (1094).

23. In 1227, as Dōgen was about to return to Japan after completing three years of study in China, his teacher Rujing is said to have given him parting instructions "not to draw close to sovereigns and ministers of state and to make your abode deep in the mountain fastnesses" (Nakamura Shintarō, *Nihon to Chūgoku no nisennen*, vol. 2 [Tōhō Shuppansha, 1978], 324). This suggests, conversely, that among the Buddhist clergy there were many who did draw close to secular power. And in fact, Eisai, the first patriarch of the Rinzai sect in Japan, is reputed to have had close relations with Taira no Kiyomori and his stepbrother Yorimori, as well as with Minamoto no Yoritomo and his wife Masako, indicative of the connections between the clergy and the powerful political figures of the era. It is also worth noting that the voyages of Japanese monks to China were seen by both sides as a medium for the collection of intelligence.

24. *Honchō tsugan*, vol. 17 (Kokusho Kankōkai, 1919), 796.

25. Miyazaki Michio, *Arai Hakuseki* (Yoshikawa Kōbunkan, 1989), 212–23.

26. For a detailed look at these developments, see Ronald P. Toby, *State and Diplomacy in Early Modern Japan: Asia in the Development of the Tokugawa Bakufu* (Princeton: Princeton University Press, 1984).

27. *Hayashi Razan bunshū* (Kōbunsha, 1930), 126.

28. From *Nisshin kōsaishi teiyō*, part 1, "Hottan" in *Nihon gaikō monjo*, Meiji era supplement, vol. 1 (Nihon Kokusai Rengō Kyōkai, 1962).

29. The text of the expulsion order read as follows (translation from Wm. Theodore de Bary, et al., *Sources of the Japanese Tradition*, vol. 2 [New York: Columbia University Press, 2005], 168.):

    1. Japan is the Land of the Gods. That a pernicious doctrine should be diffused here from the Kirishitan Country is most undesirable.

    2. To approach the people of our provinces and districts, turn them into [Kirishitan] sectarians, and destroy the shrines of the gods and temples of the Buddhas is something unheard of in previous generations. Whereas provinces, districts, localities, and fiefs are granted to their recipients temporarily, contingent upon the incumbent's observance of the laws of the realm and attention to their intent in all matters, to embroil the common people is miscreant.

    3. In the judgement of His Highness, it is because the Bateren [priests] amass parishioners as they please by means of their clever doctrine that the Law of the Buddhas is being destroyed like this in the Precincts of the Sun. That being miscreant, the Bateren can scarcely be permitted to remain on Japanese soil. Within twenty days from today they shall make their preparations and go back to their country. During this time, should anyone among the common people make unwarranted accusations against the Bateren, it shall be considered miscreant.

    4. The purpose of the Black Ships is trade, and that is a different matter. As years and months pass, trade may be carried on in all sorts of articles.

    5. From now on hereafter, all those who do not disturb the Law of the Buddhas (merchants, needless to say, and whoever) are free to come here from the Kirishitan Country and return. Be heedful of this.

    That is all.

    Tenshō 15. VI. 19

30. Iwao Seiichi, *Sakoku* (Chūō Kōronsha, 1984), 87.

31. Kōda Shigetomo, *Nichi-Ō tsūkōshi* (Iwanami Shoten, 1942), 312–13.

32. Watsuji Tetsurō, *Sakoku* (Chikuma Shobō, 1964), 392.

33. Murai Shōsuke, *Hōjō Tokimune to Mōko shūrai* (NHK Shuppan, 2001), 97 ff.

34. See Hayashi Yūsuke, "Isshinkai no zenpanki ni kansuru kisoteki kenkyū: 1906-nen 8-gatsu made," in Takeda Yukio, ed., *Chōsen shakai no shiteki tenkai to Higashi Ajia* (Yamakawa Shuppansha, 1997).

35. See cabled instructions from the Japanese foreign minister to the Japanese minister to Korea, dated 30 December 1904, in *Nihon gaikō monjo*, vol. 37, 1485 ff.

36. For an analysis of the Japanese cabinet resolution of 6 July 1900 and its significance, see Ogura Kazuo, "Kindai Nihon no Ajia gaikō no kiseki 6" in *Kan* (Summer 2009).

37. For developments in Taiwan, see Nagai Kazumi, "Gosō hogo yakushō to Amoi jiken," *Shinshū Daigaku Bunri Gakubu kiyō*, no. 10 (1961).

38. Confidential communication, dated 12 November 1884, from Japanese minister to Korea Takezoe Shin'ichirō to councillors (*sangi*) Itō Hirobumi and Inoue Kaoru in *Nikkan gaikō shiryō shūsei*, vol. 3.

39. Cable dated 12 November 1884 from acting foreign office representative to minister Takezoe, ibid.

40. *Nihon gaikō monjo*, vol. 18, document 198, appendix 1.

41. Tabohashi Kiyoshi, *Kindai Nissen kankei no kenkyū*, vol. 1 (Bunka Shiryō Chōsakai, 1940), 1042.

 Moreover, with regard to the boarding of the *Chitose Maru* by Kim Okgyun and his associates, Korean sources, including Kim's biography, say that Japanese government officials were not involved, and that it was arranged by Japanese acquaintances and the ship's captain. This is acknowledged by Japanese scholars writing on the incident (for example, Ōhata Tokushirō "Kim Okgyun no seiji bōmei to Nihon," *Waseda hōgaku*, vol. 15 [March 1976], 140), but given the events surrounding Kim's flight to Japan, it is difficult to believe that Japanese officials were completely uninvolved.

42. Geum Byeongdong, *Kim Okgyun to Nihon* (Ryokuin Shobō, 1991), 163–65.

43. *Nihon gaikō monjo*, vol. 18, documents 67, 68.

44. Geum, *Kim Okgyun to Nihon*, 227; Tabohashi, *Kindai Nissen kankei no kenkyū*, 143.

45. Geum believes this assassination to have been a collaborative effort of the Japanese, Qing, and Korean governments. See Geum, *Kim Okgyun to Nihon*, 316 ff.

46. Sōma Kokkō and Sōma Yasuo, *Ajia no mezame: Indo shishi Behari Bose to Nihon* (Tō-A Bunmeisha, 1953), 180–81.

47. Diplomatic Archives of Japan, *Teikoku naisei kankei zassan: Eiryō Indo no bu; Kakumeitō kankei (1)*, document 1540.

48. Ibid., document 1656.

49. Ibid., document 1670

50. Nakajima Takeshi, *Nakamura-ya no Bose* (Hakusuisha, 2005), 82.

51. Sōma Kokkō, "Ras Behari Bose oboegaki," in Takeuchi Yoshimi, ed., *Gendai Nihon shisō taikei 9, Ajia shugi* (Chikuma Shobō, 1963)

52. Mohan Singh, *Soldiers' Contribution to Indian Independence: The Epic of the Indian National Army* (New Delhi: Army Educational Stores, 1974), 85–87.

53. The idea of bringing Bose to Japan was the subject of a discussion among Japanese Army colonel Iwakuro Hideo; Iwata Reitetsu, the second secretary of the Japanese embassy in Thailand; and Dr. Ernst Wendler, German Ambassador to Thailand, according to a cable sent from the Japanese ambassador in Bangkok to the Japanese foreign minister (Cable No. 1157, dated 10 June 1942).

54. "Sensō-chū ni okeru tai-Indo shisaku keii" in Editorial Committee of the Diplomatic Archives of Japan, eds., *Dai Tō-A Sensō kankei ikken, Indo mondai.*

55. In this regard, see "Dai niji taisen chū ni okeru waga tai-Indo shisaku keii gaiyō," in *Nihon gaikō monjo: Taiheiyō sensō 2.*

56. "Indo shisaku keii shōnin ni kansuru ken," an Imperial General Headquarters and Government Liaison Conference resolution dated 9 October 1943, and accompanying documents.

57. Sisir K. Bose, ed., *A Beacon Across Asia: A Biography of Subhas Chandra Bose* (New Delhi: Orient Longman, 1973), 143. However, I have been unable to locate the Japanese document referred to in this book.

58. "Sensō-chū ni okeru tai-Indo shisaku keii" in Editorial Committee of the Diplomatic Archives of Japan, eds., *Dai Tō-A Sensō kankei ikken, Indo mondai.*

59. The Amoy Incident was a plot by the Japanese army to utilize the confusion caused by the Boxer Rebellion to extend Japan's sphere of influence in South China from Taiwan into nearby Fujian province, staging an incident of arson at a Japanese temple in Amoy (Xiamen) to provide a pretext for dispatching Japanese troops to the area. Kodama Gentarō, the Japanese governor-general of Taiwan, is also thought to have been involved.

60. Sympathizers of Sun Yat-sen commenced an armed uprising in October 1900 in the city of Huizhou, not far from Hong Kong, and for a time controlled an area as far south as Shenzhen, but the revolt ultimately failed.

61. It is said that Sun Yat-sen's friend Uchida Ryōhei made a clandestine appeal to Sun, then living in Singapore, to use his influence to help suppress the boycott. Sun's response was apparently that the anti-Japanese movement was receiving financial backing from local representatives of the Qing court, and that to counter this he would need funds from Japan. The Japanese government was fully aware of these developments, and Uchida was in written communication with Ishii Kikujirō, then head of the Commercial Affairs Bureau of the Foreign Ministry, discussing the use of the good offices of the Chinese revolutionaries in order to terminate the boycott.

62. Chen Deren and Yasui Sankichi, *Son Bun to Kōbe* (Kōbe: Kōbe Shinbun Sōgō Shuppan Sentā, 2002), 83.

63. Ibid., 84.

64. Yu Xintun, *Shingai Kakumei-ki no Chū-Nichi gaikōshi kenkyū* (Tōhō Shoten, 2002), 4.

65. For a discussion of the concrete response of the Japanese government to these issues, see Ogura Kazuo, "Shingai Kakumei e no gaikōteki taiō," *Kan* (Autumn 2010).

66. For example, see Suzue Gen'ichi, *Son Bun den* (Iwanami Shoten, 1950), 153–54, on the subtle differences between the stances of the British and French concerning Sun's presence in Singapore.

67. Ibid.

68. Kobayashi Yasuko, *Hakusukinoe-no-tatakai to Jinshin-no-ran* (Gendai Shichōsha, 1987), 45.

69. The text of this poem, in classical Chinese, is believed to have first appeared in the late-fourteenth century chronicle *Teiō hen'nenki*.

> I [Kuromaro] was a Japanese traveler in the Tang capital
> You are one who once shared a home with me
> For it was determined in a previous life that we be father and son
> But meetings and partings are the way of this world
> For many years I wept alone in a tumbledown hut
> The passing days only made thoughts of home ever more keen
> Now, in the Tang capital, I have been transformed into a human torch
> And all I wish for is to return to my homeland and put my soul to rest

70. Sakamoto Tarō, *Sugawara no Michizane* (Yoshikawa Kōbunkan, 1997), 49 ff.

71. Wada Sei, et al., eds., *Kutōjo Wakoku Nihon den* (Iwanami Shoten, 1979), 35.

72. For a detailed account of the negotiations, see Ogura Kazuo, *Nitchū jitsumu kyōtei kōshō* (Iwanami Shoten, 2010).

73. For the Seirankai, *Seirankai* (Roman, 1973), edited by its leader, Nakagawa Ichirō.

74. Nakao Eiichi, "Seirankai wa kaku tatakau," in Nakagawa, *Seirankai*.

75. For details of these developments, see Ogura, *Nitchū jitsumu kyōtei kōshō*.

76. For the overtures made by the Tokugawa family and the Tokugawa shogunate toward restoring relations of amity with Korea, see Nakamura Hidetaka, *Nitchū kankeishi no kenkyū*, vol. 3 (Yoshikawa Kōbunkan, 1969), Chapter 3; and Miyake Hidetoshi, *Kinsei Ajia no Nihon to Chōsen hantō* (Asahi Shinbunsha, 1993), 24–29.

77. The veracity of this story of the forged letter has been the subject of debate. See, for example, Takahashi Kimiaki, "Keichō 12-nen no kaitō ken sakkanshi no rai-Nichi ni tsuite no ichi kōsatsu," *Nagoya Daigaku Bungakubu kenkyū ronshū* (March 1985) and Min Dokki, *Zenkindai Higashi Ajia no naka no Kan-Nichi kankei* (Waseda Daigaku Shuppanbu, 1994).

78. Cable No. 2242, dated 12 September 1981, from the Japanese embassy in Seoul to the Japanese Foreign Minister.

79. According to notes taken during the drafting of this letter by the author and its submission for approval while serving in the Ministry of Foreign Affairs.

80. *Nihon gaikō monjo*, vol. 37 (1), document 368.

81. *Nihon gaikō monjo*, vol. 37 (1), document 370.

82. Arai Hakuseki, *Oritaku shiba no ki*, ed. and annotated by Matsumura Akira (Iwanami Bunko, 1999), 200–201.

83. Ishihara, *Shintei "Gishi wajin den" hoka sanpen*, 67.

84. Ibid. See also the relevant section of *Nihon shoki*.

85. By 1884, the functioning of the Tsongli Yamen, created to serve as a central foreign office, had greatly weakened, and there was a reversion to earlier precedents of dealing with foreign affairs at the periphery—a development which might be seen as a manifestation of the desire of the Qing court to maintain its prestige.

86. In 1884 the status of the Silla region of Korea within the Qing administrative system was redefined from that of a *fan* (vassal state or feudatory; implying greater autonomy) to that of a *sheng* (province; implying tighter integration into the system of centralized rule). Similarly, in 1885 Taiwan was separated from Fujian Province and elevated to the status of a province in its own right. Both of these developments might be said to be a part of this phenomenon.

87. In this regard, see Fujimura Michio, *Nisshin Sensō zengo no Ajia seisaku* (Iwanami Shoten, 1995), 219.

88. Kobata Atsushi, *Chūsei Nisshi tsūkō bōeki shi no kenkyū* (Tōkō Shoin, 1942), 5 ff.

89. Ogura Kazuo, "*Min no tai-Nichi gaikō to Nihon no tai-Min gaikō*," *Tō-A* (October 2008), note 21.

90. Sakuma Shigeo, *Nichi-Min kankeishi no kenkyū*, vol. 2 (Yoshikawa Kōbunkan, 1969), 110.

91. For a translation of this letter into modern Japanese, see Ogura, "Min no tai-Nichi gaikō to Nihon no tai-Min gaikō," note 26.

92. The assumptions made in this section regarding the volume and forms of Yoshimitsu's economic expenditure are based on Usui Nobuyoshi, *Ashikaga Yoshimitsu* (Yoshikawa Kōbunkan, 1989), 187; Tanaka Takeo, *Chūsei taigai kankei shi* (Tokyo Daigaku Shuppankai, 1975), 80; and Kobata Atsushi, "Kang bōeki to wakō," in *Iwanami kōza Nihon rekishi* 7 (1963).

93. Satō Susumu, "Muromachi bakufu ron," in *Iwanami kōza Nihon rekishi* 7 (1963).

94. On this point, see the sources listed in Ogura, "Min no tai-Nichi gaikō to Nihon no tai-Min gaikō," note 32.

95. Murai Shōsuke, *Ajia no naka no chūsei Nihon* (Azekura Shobō, 1988), 90.

PART II

FOREIGN RELATIONS OF JAPAN, CHINA, AND KOREA IN

HISTORICAL PERSPECTIVE

CHAPTER THREE

The History of *Seikanron* Thought

1. For opinions, pro and con, regarding the idea that Prince Kume's death itself was the work of Korean spies, see Naoki Kōjirō, *Kodai Nihon to Chōsen Chūgoku* (Kodansha, 1988), 134 ff.

2. Regarding this, see, for example, Hon'iden Kikushi, "Taishi no gaikō seisaku," in Takemitsu Makoto and Maenosono Ryōichi, eds., *Shōtoku Taishi no subete* (Shinjinbutsu Ōrai Sha, 1988).

3. Ibid.

4. For this incident, see Ishii Masatoshi, "Ōtomo no Komaro sōgen ni tsuite: Kyokō-setsu no shōkai to sono mondaiten," *Hōsei shigaku*, no. 35.

5. *Shoku Nihongi*, volume 12.

6. For an interpretation of this, see Satō Makoto, "Kodai no 'Ōomi gaikō' ni tsuite no ichi kōsatsu," in Murai Shūsuke, et al., eds. *Kyōkai no Nihonshi* (Yamakawa Shuppansha, 1997) .

7. On this point, see Kishi Toshio, *Fujiwara no Nakamaro* (Yoshikawa Kōbunkan, 1987), 292.

8. Ishii Masatoshi, *Nihon Bokkai kankeishi no kenkyū* (Yoshikawa Kōbunkan, 2001), pp. 429–451.

9. Hotate Michihisa, *Ōgon kokka* (Aoki Shoten, 2004), 71.

10. Aida Nirō, *Mōko shūrai no kenkyū* (Yoshikawa Kōbunkan, 1971), 142.

11. Ibid., 145.

12. Wei Jung-chi, *Gen-Nichi kankeishi no kenkyū* (*Kyōiku Shuppan Sentā*, 1993), 121.

13. Murai Shōsuke, *Hōjō Tokimune to Mōko shūrai* (NHK Shuppan, 2001), 114.

14. In chapter 3.3.

15. In this regard, there may have been an additional factor directly connecting Hideyoshi's conquest of Kyūshū with his invasions of Korea, and that was the pro-Ming tendencies on the part of Kyūshū daimyo, particularly the Shimazu family of Satsuma. One piece of evidence supporting this is that a Chinese doctor in Satsuma, Xu Yijun, entrusted a compatriot, Zhu Gyunwang, with a letter secretly informing the Ming of Hideyoshi's intentions to conquer China. In this letter, Xu wrote that the daimyo of Satsuma "honored the Great Ming" and "had always held the Great Ming in highest respect," and for this reason intended to "secretly withdraw his troops to places such as Luzon and Damsu and there stand by to await the outcome of the fighting." (Ishihara Michihiro, *Bunroku Keichō no eki* [Hanawa Shobō, 1963], 49–50).

In this book Ishihara also touches on the relationship between Hideyoshi's China invasion plans and the *wakō* pirates, but further research is probably needed to determine if one of Hideyoshi's aims was to control the trade relations that had developed between these so-called "Japanese pirates" and China during the course of the Muromachi period (1333–1568), and by extension the ties to China that daimyo of western Japan had developed by overtly or covertly utilizing the *wakō*.

16. Takeda Katsuzō, "Hakushaku Sō-ke shozō Hō-kō monjo to Chōsen-jin," *Shigaku* 4:3 (August 1925), 441–454, published by Mita Historical Association of Keio University.

17. Ikeuchi Hiroshi, *Bunroku Keichō no eki, seihen* (Yoshikawa Kōbunkan, 1914), 158–59.

18. Nakamura Hidetaka, *Nichi-Min kankeishi no kenkyū*, vol. 2 (Yoshikawa Kōbunkan, 1969), 87.

19. The Koreans had been concerned for some time about connections between domestic "rebels" and the *wakō* pirates. In this regard, see Ikeuchi, op. cit., 165.

20. According to an official annal of the Joseon dynasty, *Joseon wangjo sillok*. A Japanese translation of the relevant portion appears in Kitajima, op. cit., 23.

21. Han Uheun, tr. into Japanese by Hiraki Minoru, *Kankoku tsūshi* (Gakusei-sha, 1976), 299–301.

22. Tabohashi Kiyoshi, *Kindai Nikkan kankei no kenkyū*, vol. 1 (Bunka Shiryō Chōsakai, 1963), 299 ff.

23. Ibid., 121 ff.

24. *Nihon gaikō monjo* 1:2, document no. 706.

25. *Nihon gaikō monjo* 3, document no. 88, appendix 1.

26. *Nihon gaikō monjo* 6, document no. 119.

27. Tabohashi, op. cit., 304.

28. Ibid., 306.

29. Ibid., 309.

30. Ibid., 322.

31. See, for example, Unno Fukuju, *Kankoku heigō-shi no kenkyū* (Iwanami Shoten, 2000), 87.

32. For the Hwalbindang, see Takeda Yukio, ed., *Chōsenshi* (Yamakawa Shuppansha, 1993), 232. For the Yeonghakdang, see Han Yeonguu, tr. Yoshida Mitsuo, *Kankoku shakai no rekishi* (Akashi Shoten, 2003), 488.

33. *Nihon gaikō monjo* 37:1, document no. 326.

34. The full text of the protocol in English translation is as follows:

> Protocol.—February 23, 1904
>
> M. Gonsuke Hayashi, Envoy Extraordinary and Minister Plenipotentiary of His Majesty the Emperor of Japan, and Major General Yi Jiyong, Minister of State for Foreign Affairs *ad interim* of His Majesty the Emperor of Korea, being respectively duly empowered for the purpose, have agreed upon the following Articles:
>
> Article I. For the purpose of maintaining a permanent and solid friendship between Japan and Korea and firmly establishing peace in the Far East, the Imperial Government of Korea shall place full confidence in the Imperial Government of Japan, and adopt the advice of the latter in regard to improvements in administration.

Article II. The Imperial Government of Japan shall in a spirit of firm friendship ensure the safety and repose of the Imperial House of Korea.

Article III. The Imperial Government of Japan definitively guarantee the independence and territorial integrity of the Korean Empire.

Article IV. In case the welfare of the Imperial House of Korea or the territorial integrity of Korea is endangered by the aggression of a third power or internal disturbances, the Imperial Government of Japan shall immediately take such necessary measures as circumstances require, and in such case the Imperial Government of Korea shall give full facilities to promote the action of the Imperial Japanese Government. The Imperial Government of Japan may for the attainment of the above mentioned objective occupy when the circumstances require such places as may be necessary from strategic points of view.

Article V. The Governments of the two countries shall not in future without mutual consent conclude with a third power such an arrangement as may be contrary to the principles of the present protocol.

Article VI. Details in connection with the present Protocol shall be arranged as the circumstances may require between the representative of Japan and the Minister of State for Foreign Affairs of Korea.

Hayashi
Yi Jiyong

As cited in *Korea: Treaties and Agreements* (Washington, D.C.: Carnegie Endowment for International Peace, 1921), 36–37. The Japanese text may be found in *Nihon gaikō monjo* 37:1, document no. 383.

35. The thinking at the root of such opinion is expressed in the following passage from *Nihon gaikō monjo* 37:1, document no. 390, "Teikoku no tai-Kan hōshin."

The fate of Korea is linked to the security of our Empire, and we absolutely cannot leave it to be swallowed up by another power. This is precisely why our Empire has always exerted itself to the utmost to maintain the independence and territorial integrity of Korea. In fact, this is one of the fundamental reasons we have staked the fate of our nation on crossing swords with our powerful neighbor [Russia]. With the earlier signing of the Japan-Korea Protocol our two countries have defined a new relationship, and now, with the successive victories of our Imperial armies over the Russians, there are signs that Koreans, high and low, are placing increasing trust in Japan. Even so, it is clear that the decadence of the Korean government and corruption of the popular mentality make it virtually impossible for the country to permanently maintain its independence. Given these circumstances, it has been appropriate for our country to gradually establish political, military, and economic footholds there, and take all necessary steps to ensure the self-defense of our Empire and eliminate the fear that similar disorders might be engendered in the future. Even though our Empire has been able to secure a certain degree of protectorship through the Japan-Korea Protocol, it is the most urgent task facing us at present to press ahead to establish an even more reliable and appropriate treaty and attendant arrangements regarding national defense, diplomacy, finance, etc., thereby establishing our full rights of protectorship with regard to that country and allowing us to at the same time acquire all necessary rights and privileges in economic relations, so that this administration may be implemented as smoothly as possible.

36. Itō Hirobumi (1841–1909), was the first prime minister of Japan's modern state; founder of the influential political party, the Seiyūkai; and resident-general in Korea, 1905–1909.

37. *Nihon gaikō monjo* 37:1, document no. 313, "Itō tokuha taishi naietsu shimatsu."

38. However, at this stage, in order to avoid giving the impression that Japan had unilaterally engineered a de facto usurpation of Korea's diplomatic rights, it was decided that the diplomatic adviser to be designated by Japan was to be a foreigner rather than a Japanese.

39. The text of the Second Korean-Japanese Convention, signed November 17, 1905, is as follows:

> "The Governments of Japan and Korea, desiring to strengthen the principle of solidarity which unites the two Empires, have with that object in view agreed upon and concluded the following stipulations to serve until the moment arrives when it is recognised that Korea has attained national strength:
>
> Article I. The Government of Japan, through the Department of Foreign Affairs at Tokio, will hereafter have control and direction of the external relations and affairs of Korea, and the diplomatic and consular representatives of Japan will have the charge of the subjects and interests of Korea in foreign countries.

Article II. The Government of Japan undertake to see to the execution of treaties actually existing between Korea and the other Powers, and the Government of Korea engage not to conclude hereafter any act or engagement having an international character, except through the medium of the Government of Japan.

Article III. The Government of Japan shall be represented at the Court of His Majesty the Emperor of Korea by a Resident General, who shall reside at Seoul, primarily for the purpose of taking charge of and directing matters relating to diplomatic affairs. He shall have the right of private and personal audience of His Majesty the Emperor of Korea. The Japanese Government shall also have the right to station Residents at the several open ports and such other places in Korea as they may deem necessary. Such Residents shall, under the direction of the Resident General, exercise the powers and functions hitherto appertaining to Japanese Consuls in Korea and shall perform such duties as may be necessary in order to carry into full effect the provisions of this agreement.

Article IV. The stipulations of all treaties and agreements existing between Japan and Korea not inconsistent with the provisions of this Agreement shall continue in force.

Article V. The Government of Japan undertake to maintain the welfare and dignity of the Imperial House of Korea.

In faith whereof, the Undersigned duly authorized by their Governments have signed this Agreement and affixed their seals."

Official English text as cited in *Korea: Treaties and Agreements* (Washington, D.C.: Carnegie Endowment for International Peace, 1921), 55–56.

40. *Nihon gaikō monjo* 34, document nos. 20, 22.

41. Ibid., document no. 21.

42. Ibid., document no. 23.

43. For details of the negotiation process, see Ogura Kazuo, "Kankoku hogokoku-ka to Nihon gaikō (sono 2)," in *Kan* (Spring 2011).

44. G. P. Gooch and H. W. V. Temperley, eds. *British Documents on the Origins of the War, 1898–1914* (London: H. M. Stationery Office, 1929), vol 4, no. 118. Japanese text in *Nihon gaikō monjo* 38:1, document no. 19.

45. Gooch and Temperley, vol. 4, no. 155. *Nihon gaikō monjo* 38:1, document no. 32.

46. Article III of the revised treaty reads:

Japan possessing paramount political, military and economic interests in Korea, Great Britain recognizes the right of Japan to take such measures of guidance, control and protection in Korea as she may deem proper and necessary to safeguard and advance those interests, provided always that such measures are not contrary to the principle of equal opportunities for the commerce and industry of all nations.

47. In this regard, see Ogura Kazuo, "Kankoku hogokoku-ka to Nihon gaikō (sono 2)," in *Kan* (Spring 2011), note 30.

48. Britain's recognition of Japan's paramount position in Korea came only after the United States had also assented to this, and only after Britain had confirmed (with Japan) that in the event of a dispute between the United States and Japan, Britain could not take Japan's side, despite the bond of the Anglo-Japanese Alliance.

49. Gaimushō, eds., *Nihon gaikō nempyō narabi shuyō monjo* (Hara Shobō, 1965), 232.

50. Tokutomi Iichirō, ed., *Kōshaku Katsura Tarō den, konkan* (Ko Katsura Kōshaku Kinen Jigyōkai, 1917), 316–17.

51. On this point see Gim Giseok, "Kōbu-tei no shuken shugo gaikō, 1905–1907: Isshi jōyaku no mukō sengen o chūshin ni," in Unno Fukuju, ed., *Nikkan kyōyaku to Kankoku heigō* (Akashi Shoten, 1995).

52. The text of the Third Korean-Japanese Convention, as cited in *Korea: Treaties and Agreements* (Washington, D.C.: Carnegie Endowment for International Peace, 1921), 58–59, is as follows:

The Governments of Japan and Korea, desiring to speedily promote the wealth and strength of Korea and with the object of promoting the prosperity of the Korean nation, have agreed to the following terms:

1. In all matters relating to the reform of the Korean Administration the Korean Government shall receive instruction and guidance from the Resident-General.

2. In all matters related to the enactment of laws and ordinances and in all important matters of administration, the Korean Government must obtain the preliminary approval of the Resident-General.

3. There shall be clear differentiation of the Korean Executive and the Korean Judiciary.

4. In all appointments and removals of high officials the Korean Government must obtain the consent of the Resident-General.

5. The Korean Government shall appoint to be officials of Korea any Japanese subjects recommended by the Resident-General.

6. The Korean Government shall not appoint any foreigners to be officials of Korea without consulting the Resident-General.

7. The First Article of the Agreement signed on August 22, 1904, shall be rescinded.

In witness of the above the undersigned Plenipotentiaries, duly accredited by their respective Governments, have signed the present Convention:

Done at Seoul, the 25th day of the 7th month of the 40th year of Meiji, corresponding to the 24th day of the 7th month of the 11th year of Kwangmu.

> (signed) Itō Hirobumi, Marquis;
> *Resident-General*
>
> Yi Wanyong,
> *Prime Minister of Korea*

A secret memorandum appended to this convention called for the appointment of Japanese subjects as district court judges, prison superintendents, and undersecretaries in all government departments, speaking eloquently of the fact that Korean domestic administration had been placed under de facto Japanese control.

53. *Nihon gaikō monjo* 37:1, document no. 369.

54. *Nihon gaikō monjo* 37:1, document no. 340.

55. This raises the question as to why, having come this far with the conversion of Korea into a protectorate, Japan did not simply move to annex the country at the time of the Third Korean-Japanese Convention (1907). The answers are probably to be found in the international situation and in the lack of unity of Japanese opinion at that time. Moreover, the prospect of annexation raised a number of practical issues that needed to be resolved, beginning with the question of the extent to which Japan's domestic legal system should apply to an annexed Korea—issues for which even the most basic preparation had yet to be undertaken.

In this regard, for discussion of external factors, see Moriyama Shigenori, *Kindai Nikkan kankeishi kenkyū: Chōsen shokuminchi-ka to kokusai kankei* (Tokyo Daigaku Shuppankai, 1987), 213. For internal factors, see Itō Yukio, "Itō Hirobumi no Kankoku tōchi to Kankoku heigō: Hague misshi jiken ikō," *Hōgaku ronsō*, vol. 164 (Kyoto Daigaku Hōgakukai, 2009).

Or we might also ask why, having achieved a protectorate, Japan decided to embark on the annexation of Korea—and particularly whether one reason for this was the desire to eliminate the existing foreign concessions to the same extent as in Japan itself. Another question is how to evaluate the fact that the protectorate had dissolved the Korean armed forces, but that these former soldiers were becoming a problem for public order as dissident elements. But these are questions that lie beyond the scope of this book, which is chiefly concerned with examining the developments leading to the protectorate.

Even so, another issue to touch on here is how to assess the existence of forces in Korea that at least publicly welcomed alliance with and even annexation by Japan, such as the Iljinhoe. The Iljinhoe was organized by Song Byeongjun, later minister of commerce and industry in the cabinet of Yi Wanyong, and Yi Yonggu, a former leader of the Donghak movement, and by 1910 had developed into a major political organization with a membership of more than 90,000.

The Iljinhoe has traditionally been seen as a pro-Japanese group organized by Japan to promote the annexation of Korea (for example, see Han, *Kankoku tsūshi*, 341). But even if it is true that Japan skillfully manipulated this organization, the number of its members and the fact that as of 1908 the Iljinhoe plotted to force Itō's resignation as resident-general in an attempt to promote a Korea-Japan annexation against his intentions are indications that it cannot be seen purely as a pro-Japanese organization. If we look at the responses of Japanese diplomats and the military to the Iljinhoe at the time, it is also difficult to think of it as completely a puppet organization of the Japanese authorities. If this is the case, then what were the participants in the Iljinhoe—and particularly its leaders—thinking?

In his book *Nikkan heigō shōshi* (Iwanami Shoten, 1966), Yamabe Kentarō quotes *Chōsen heigō shi* by Tokio Shunjō, who was a resident in Korea at the height of the Iljinhoe's activities, to the effect that Song Byeongjun had drawn closer to Japan out of self-protection, as he was suspected by the Korean imperial house and highly placed government officials of being guilty of harboring Kim Okgyun after the latter's failed coup attempt in concert with the Japanese.

While it is easily imaginable that such personal motives were in fact present, it is difficult to believe that most of the nearly 100,000 members of the Iljinhoe approved of the movement toward Korea's annexation by Japan purely out of a desire for self-protection. It should be noted that members of the Iljinhoe complied with the government edict regarding the cutting of the traditional topknot, which aroused the wrath of conservative Confucians. Taking all of this into consideration, it seems reasonable to assume that the Iljinhoe was opposed to the old order in Korea (or the maintenance of the status quo) and desired to see new forms of stability and development in Korea's domestic administration and economy, seeing alliance with or even annexation by Japan as a means to achieving these ends. In any case, a thorough reassessment of those known in Korea as the *chinilpa* (Japanese collaborators) is an issue that remains for future scholarship. There has been considerable research on the Iljinhoe, but for a valuable objective analysis of its relationship to Japanese diplomatic officials and the Japanese military, see Hayashi Yūsuke, "Iljinhoe no zenpanki ni kansuru kisoteki kenkyū—1906-nen 8-gatsu made," in Takeda Yukio, ed., *Chōsen shakai no shiteki tenkai to Higashi Ajia* (Yamakawa Shuppansha, 1997) and "Iljinhoe no kōhanki ni kansuru kisoteki kenkyū—1906-nen 8-gatsu kara kaisan made," in *Tōyō bunka kenkyū* (March 1999).

CHAPTER FOUR

Two Millennia of Sino-Japanese History: Five Wars and Their Antecedents

1. Ogura Kazuo, "Santō shuppei to tai-Chūgoku gaikō no hatan," *Kan* (Summer 2012), 409 ff.
2. Ibid., 412.
3. Banno Junji, *Kindai Nihon seijishi* (Iwanami Shoten 2006), 133–35.
4. On this point, see *Nihon gaikō monjo: Shōwa-ki*, part 1, vol. 2, Second Shandong Expedition, document 305; Satō Motoei, *Kindai Nihon no gaikō to gunji* (Yoshikawa Kōbunkan, 2000); Ogura, "Santō shuppei," 419, note 29.
5. Uemura Shin'ichi, *Nihon gaikōshi 17: Chūgoku nashonarizumu to Nikka kankei no tenkai* (Kajima Kenkyūjo Shuppankai, 1971), 252.
6. For details see "Nankin jiken no shinsō ni kansuru hōkoku," a report by Consul Morioka Shōhei of the Japanese consulate general in Nanjing, in *Nihon gaikō monjo* (hereafter, *Gaikō*), Appendix No. 437.
7. *Gaikō*, No. 423. See also No. 418.
8. *Gaikō*, No. 437.
9. "Sekinin jisatsu o kuwadateta Araki Tai'i wa jūtai," Yomiuri shimbun, March 30, 1927.
10. "Moshi tatakattara Nikō jiken no ninomai," Yomiuri shimbun, March 30, 1927.
11. *Gaikō*, Nos. 416 and 420.
12. For details on this aspect of matters, see Ogura Kazuo, "Shanhai-Nankin jiken e no Nihon no taiō," in *Kan*, no. 49 (Spring 2012).
13. *Gaikō*, Nos. 423 and 426.

14. *Gaikō*, No. 430.
15. *Gaikō*, No. 456.
16. For details of this proposal, see the supplementary cable attached as an appendix to the previously cited document.
17. *Gaikō*, No. 461.
18. Ogura, "Shanhai-Nankin jiken."
19. Ichikawa Masaaki, ed. *Nikkan gaikō shiryō*, vol. 3 (Hara Shobō, 1979), 365.
20. Ibid., 429.
21. Ibid., 446–47.
22. *Gaikō*, Meiji era supplementary vol. 1, 359, 360, 380, 381.
23. For a detailed analysis of this point, see Takahashi Hidenao, *Nisshin Sensō e no michi* (Tōkyō Sōgensha, 1995), 192 and note on 198.
24. For negotiations between the British and the Qing, see ibid., 199, note 35.
25. Ōyama Azusa, ed., *Yamagata Aritomo ikensho* (Hara Shobō, 1968), 196–98.
26. Mutsu Munemitsu, *Kenkenroku* (Iwanami Shoten, 1983), 129–30.
27. Takahashi, *Nisshin Sensō e no michi*, 387.
28. Masumi Junnosuke, *Nihon seijishi 2* (Tōkyō Daigaku Shuppankai, 1988), 39.
29. For the correspondence between Mutsu and Itō, see Takahashi, *Nisshin Sensō e no michi*, 382.
30. Ikeuchi Hiroshi, *Bunroku Keichō no eki, seihen* (Yoshikawa Kōbunkan, 1914), 15–16.
31. Hideyoshi's comments to Coelho on the subject of Korea and China were as follows:

> After I settle matters in Japan and pacify the country, I am determined to leave Japan in the hands of my younger [half-]brother Mino no kami [Hashiba Hidenaga] and personally lead an expedition to cross the seas and conquer Korea and China. For this purpose I will have enough wood harvested to build two thousand ships to carry the expeditionary force. I would like the *bataren* [Jesuit priests] to provide me with two well-equipped [Western-style] sailing ships.
> Quoted in Matsuda Kiichi, *Toyotomi Hideyoshi to Nambanjin* (Chōbunsha, 2001), 31.

32. Ikeuchi, *Bunroku Keichō no eki*, 15–16.
33. Ibid., 177–84.
34. According to Goryeosa. For details, see Ogura Kazuo, "Mōko no tai-Nichi gaikō apurōchi to Nihon no taiō," *Tō-A* (September 2008), note 1.

35. A copy of this document, dated the eighth month of the third year of the Zhiyuan era (1266), has been preserved in the archives of the temple Tōdaiji in Nara. The English translation that follows is from Kenneth W. Chase, "Mongol Intentions towards Japan in 1266: Evidence from a Mongol Letter to the Sung," *Sino-Japanese Studies* 9:2 (1990), 13–22.

> Favored by the decree of Highest Heaven, the emperor of the Great Mongol Nation sends this letter to the King of Japan.
>
> Since ancient times the sovereigns of small countries whose territories adjoined each other have taken it as their duty to cement peaceful relations by upholding good faith. How much more so [should this apply in this case], since Our ancestors received a clear mandate from Heaven and controlled all of China, and those from distant places and other regions who fear Our awesomeness and embrace our virtue have been countless.
>
> When We first ascended the throne, as the innocent people of Korea had long suffered from spearheads and arrowheads, We immediately disbanded the soldiers and returned their frontier fortresses and sent their old and young back [to their homes]. The Korean sovereign and subjects came to Our court to express their thanks. Although in righteousness we were sovereign and subject, we were as happy as father and son. We believe that your subjects already know this.
>
> Korea is Our eastern frontier. Japan is close to Korea. From the founding of your country you have also occasionally had contact with China, but to us you have not sent even "an envoy with a single cart" to communicate friendly [intentions].
>
> Fearing your kingdom knows this but has not considered it [carefully], We have specially dispatched an envoy with a letter to proclaim Our intention. We hope that hereafter we will exchange greetings and establish friendly [relations] in order to have mutual affection and friendship. The sage treats all within the four seas as family; could it be the principle of a family not to mutually exchange friendly [greetings]?
>
> As for using soldiers and weapons, who would want that?
>
> King, consider this.
>
> [This] does not fully express [Our meaning].

Stephen Turnbull, *The Mongol Invasions of Japan, 1274 and 1281* (Oxford: Osprey Publishing, 2010), 14–15, translates the same letter as follows:

> The Emperor of the Great Mongols, being commissioned by Heaven, hereby respectfully presents a letter to the King of Japan. From time

immemorial rulers of small states, the borders of which closely adjoin, have always endeavoured to maintain friendly relations with each other and have manifested mutual respect and trust. On our part, we, from the time of our forefathers, have received the Mandate of Heaven and have ruled the universe. Innumerable people in far-off lands have learned to fear our power and have longed for our virtuous rule. When we first ascended the throne, the innocent and helpless people of Korea had suffered for long from military struggles. We therefore ordered a cessation of hostilities, restored their land, and returned the captive Koreans, young and old.

In gratitude both ruler and people of Korea now present themselves at our court. Although the legal relation between ourselves and the Koreans is that of sovereign and subjects, yet in feeling we are as father and children. We assume that Your Highness and your subjects have known this. Korea is our eastern tributary state. Japan is located near to Korea and since her founding has time and again established relations with the Middle Kingdom. However, since our accession you have not yet sent an envoy to our court; nor have you indicated a desire to establish friendly relations with us. We are afraid this is because Your Kingdom has not yet been well informed of this. Therefore we now send a special envoy bearing our state papers to inform you of our desire. We hope that henceforth you will enter into friendly relations with us, and that both our people and yours will enjoy peace and harmony. Moreover, the sages consider the entire universe one family. Therefore, if we should not establish friendly relations with each other, how could it be in accordance with the doctrine of one family? Who would care to appeal to arms?

I hereby leave the matter to Your Highness's careful consideration.

36. Ogura, "Mōko no tai-Nichi gaikō apurōchi," note 15.

37. The Mongol state letter of 1271 read as follows. The text used for this translation is a Japanese rendering of the Chinese original, cited in Yamaguchi Osamu, *Mōko shūrai* (Tōgensha, 1979).

Perhaps you have heard the expression, "Nothing is alien to the sovereign." The state of Goryeo and I have already become as one family. Your kingdom is our neighbor. Because of this I have sent emissaries to you in an effort to establish friendly relations, but they have been refused passage by your border officials. We have ordered the relevant officials to take good care of the two individuals we seized [the two

Tsushima residents abducted by the earlier mission] and return them to their country, bearing with them a message from us, but still there is only silence from you. Even had you wished to exchange greetings with us, the recent revolt by the Goryeo official Im Yeon would have made this difficult to accomplish. So it is impossible to know, O King, if you had decided for this reason not to send an envoy, or if an envoy was sent but prevented along the way from completing his voyage. In any case, Japan has always called itself a nation which observes the rules of proper behavior; how could the sovereign's ministers fail to do so? We have recently destroyed Im Yeon, restored the monarch [of Goryeo], and pacified the people. And I have specially dispatched an important official, Zhao Liangbi, as an envoy of our nation, bearing this and other documents to you. If you should immediately dispatch an envoy of your own to return with him, we shall live harmoniously and peacefully as neighbors, a splendid thing for your country. For who would be gladdened at having to resort to arms? O King, consider this most thoroughly.

38. A political power struggle pitting the shogunal regent (*shikken*) Hōjō Tokimune against his elder half-brother Tokisuke, and involving a number of other powerful regional warlord families such as the Nagoshi.

39. The text of this letter has not been preserved, but from what occurred before and after, it is reasonable to assume that it admonished Japan for not entering into friendly relations with the Yuan, and threatened military action if Japan refused to submit.

40. This letter has also been lost.

41. Korean and Japanese sources are said to disagree in this regard, but see Kitō Kiyoaki, *Yamato chōtei to Higashi Ajia* (Yoshikawa Kōbunkan, 1994), 109–30.

42. *Nihon shoki*, Chapter 25, chronicling the reign of Ameyorozu Toyohi no Sumeramikoto (Emperor Kōtoku).

43. Ibid.

44. Wada Sei, et al., eds. *Kutōjo Wakoku Nihon den* (Iwanami Shoten, 1956), 36.

45. *Xin Tang shu*, book 220, "Dong yi chuan." See reference materials listed in note 4.

46. For details, see Kobayashi Yasuko, *Hakusukinoe no Tatakai to Jinshin no Ran* (Gendai Shichōsha, 1987), 59–60.

47. *Kōza Nihon rekishi 2: Kodaishi* (Tōkyō Daigaku Shuppankai, 1984), 266.

Index